THE METAPHYSICS OF THEISM

D0087461

THE METAPHYSICS OF THEISM

Aquinas's Natural Theology
in Summa contra gentiles *I*

NORMAN KRETZMANN

BX
1749
T7K74
1997
VAN

CLARENDON PRESS · OXFORD
1997

CONCORDIA UNIVERSITY LIBRARIES

SH

Oxford University Press, Great Clarendon Street, Oxford OX2 6DP

Oxford New York
Athens Auckland Bangkok Bogota Bombay
Buenos Aires Calcutta Cape Town Dar es Salaam
Delhi Florence Hong Kong Istanbul Karachi
Kuala Lumpur Madras Madrid Melbourne
Mexico City Nairobi Paris Singapore
Taipei Tokyo Toronto
and associated companies in
Berlin Ibadan

Oxford is a trade mark of Oxford University Press

Published in the United States
by Oxford University Press Inc., New York

© Norman Kretzmann 1997

All rights reserved. No part of this publication may be reproduced,
stored in a retrieval system, or transmitted, in any form or by any means,
without the prior permission in writing of Oxford University Press.
Within the UK, exceptions are allowed in respect of any fair dealing for the
purpose of research or private study, or criticism or review, as permitted
under the Copyright, Designs and Patents Act, 1988, or in the case of
reprographic reproduction in accordance with the terms of the licences
issued by the Copyright Licensing Agency. Enquiries concerning
reproduction outside these terms and in other countries should be
sent to the Rights Department, Oxford University Press,
at the address above

British Library Cataloguing in Publication Data
Data available

Library of Congress Cataloging in Publication Data
Kretzmann, Norman.
The metaphysics of theism: Aquinas's natural theology in Summa
contra gentiles I / by Norman Kretzmann.
Includes bibliographical references and index.
1. Thomas, Aquinas, Saint, 1225?–1274. Summa contra gentiles.
2. Metaphysics. 3. Theism. 4. Natural theology. I. Title.
BX1749.T7K74 1996 210'.92—dc20 96-26276
ISBN 0-19-823660-3

1 3 5 7 9 10 8 6 4 2

Typeset by Best-set Typesetter Ltd., Hong Kong
Printed in Great Britain
on acid-free paper by
Biddles Ltd., Guildford and King's Lynn

For Eleonore

PREFACE

The chapters of this book are revisions of the Wilde Lectures in Comparative and Natural Religion, which I delivered at the University of Oxford in the spring of 1994 under the general title 'Philosophy from the Top Down'. I'm grateful to the Wilde Lecture Committee for inviting me, to Professor Richard Swinburne and Sir Anthony and Lady Nancy Kenny for hosting me and my wife, Barbara Ensign Kretzmann, during our stay in Oxford, and to Balliol College for providing me with a study in college.

Most of the research for, and the writing of, the lectures that became Chapters One–Five were done during the academic year 1992–3, while I was a Senior Fellow of the National Humanities Center in North Carolina. I'm grateful for their support. The Center's staff, its facilities and services, and the stimulating company of the other Fellows provided an ideal setting for the work. And since I was lucky enough to have my office next to Scott MacDonald's and to drive to and from the Center with him every day, the poor man could hardly avoid talking to me about every problem I ran into—which may have helped prepare him to write his helpful comments on every chapter, for which I thank him.

The lectures that became Chapters Six–Eight I wrote in the summer and the fall of 1993, when I returned to teaching at Cornell. (A version of Chapter Eight appeared in a special issue of the *Modern Schoolman*, 72 (1995), 125–48.) In the spring semester of 1994 I was the mostly grateful recipient of almost more critical comments than I could use, generously provided by the members of my graduate seminar on Aquinas's natural theology: Professor John Boler (of the University of Washington), Dr Blake Dutton, Hannes Jarka-Sellers, Lucy Bell Jarka-Sellers, Claudia Eisen Murphy, Sean Eisen Murphy, Nadia Small, and Katherine Welch. In 1994–5 I conducted a tutorial on the same topic for Mark Case and Christina Van Dyke, who provided me with further help as I was turning the lectures into chapters. I am grateful to them, and to my terrific research assistant, Nancy Davenport, who is responsible for the book's *index locorum*.

William Alston, Christopher Hughes, Anthony Kenny, William

Rowe, and Richard Sorabji all read the whole manuscript, at their own request. If they hadn't volunteered, they would have been recruited. I found their detailed written comments invaluable. And I will never forget Hughes's brilliant, hours-long, critical talk with me about one of the lectures just before I delivered it.

As soon as I had a rough draft of any part of this book, I sent it first to Eleonore Stump, as I've done with everything I've written for two decades and more. With this book, as with all those many other things, she helped me more than I can say. Beginning in the years when she was my student at Cornell, I've learned more from her than from anyone else I know. The first impetus toward everything I'm trying to do in this book and its proposed sequels stems from her. And so I'm very pleased to be able to dedicate it to her, my co-worker and my friend.

NORMAN KRETZMANN

January 1996

CONTENTS

ABBREVIATIONS

CT	*Compendium theologiae*
In BDT	*Expositio super librum Boethii De trinitate*
In DA	*Sententia super De anima*
In DDN	*Expositio super librum Dionysii De divinis nominibus*
In EN	*Sententia libri Ethicorum*
In Met.	*Sententia super Metaphysicam*
In PA	*Sententia super Posteriora analytica*
In PH	*Sententia super Peri hermenias*
In Phys.	*Sententia super Physicam*
In Sent.	*Scriptum super libros Sententiarum*
QDP	*Quaestiones disputatae de potentia*
QDV	*Quaestiones disputatae de veritate*
SCG	*Summa contra gentiles*
ST	*Summa theologiae*

INTRODUCTION

1. Aims of this book

The book's subtitle—'Aquinas's Natural Theology in *Summa contra gentiles* I'—may suggest that I'm undertaking a project in philosophical scholarship, developing my critical exposition of a thirteenth-century enterprise. It's certainly true that one reason I had for undertaking this study was my conviction that Aquinas's systematic natural theology is a philosophically interesting subject that has been neglected or misunderstood. And so in the eight chapters below I do try to present, explain, and evaluate the first part of that enterprise of his. I hope the book does, in that way, make a contribution to medieval philosophical scholarship. If that were the only aim I had in view, I could turn at once to the material I begin to deal with in Chapter One. But other considerations also motivated me, considerations that make Aquinas's natural theology important, I think, as well as interesting. They have led me to approach it not merely as the monumental achievement it already is, but also as a continuously active enterprise for which Aquinas's work has provided rich material developed in promising patterns. So in this book I mean also to engage co-operatively in that ongoing enterprise and to enlist the critical co-operation of others in pursuing the development of a metaphysics of theism along the lines Aquinas drew.

In my view a great deal—not all—of theology's traditional subject-matter is really continuous with philosophy's subject-matter, and ought to be integrated with it in practice. Most philosophers who lived before the twentieth century would share that view, and no substantive developments in the last hundred years should have obscured it. In the first three-quarters of this century it surely was obscured, but we may be witnessing a development in which that view is no longer so hard to find among philosophers: as late twentieth-century theologians have been moving away from their traditional subject-matter, philosophers have been moving in.[1] And natural theology, a branch of philosophy, interests me especially, because it provides the traditional and still central means of integrating philosophy with (some of) theology.[2]

Integrating them by means of natural theology amounts to developing within philosophy some of the subject-matter specifically associated with theology. Developing it within philosophy amounts to forgoing appeals to any putative revelation or religious experience as evidence for the truth of propositions, and accepting as data only those few naturally evident considerations that traditionally constitute data acceptable for philosophy generally. That's what makes it *natural* theology. What makes this part of philosophy natural *theology* is, of course, its agenda: investigating, by means of analysis and argument, at least the existence and nature of God and, in a fuller development, the relation of everything else— especially human nature and behaviour—to God considered as reality's first principle.[3]

And Aquinas's ambitious project in *Summa contra gentiles* Books I–III is the most fully accomplished and most promising natural theology I know of. So, I mean not merely to be offering a critical exposition of Aquinas's natural theology but also to be advocating it, or at least my version of some aspects of it, and perhaps even to be helping it along a little, here and there.[4]

---

[1] Perhaps the fullest, clearest evidence of this development can be found most conveniently in the thriving journal *Faith and Philosophy*, founded in 1984 and associated with the Society of Christian Philosophers.

[2] Details of my conception of natural theology emerge in Ch. One below. For an authoritative general account of its nature and status I couldn't do better than present this passage from Alston 1991: 289: '*Natural theology* is the enterprise of providing support for religious beliefs by starting from premises that neither are nor presuppose any religious beliefs. We begin from the mere existence of the world, or the teleological order of the world, or the concept of God, and we try to show that when we think through the implications of our starting point we are led to recognize the existence of a being that possesses attributes sufficient to identify Him as God. Once we get that foothold we may seek to show that a being could not have the initial attributes without also possessing certain others; in this manner we try to go as far as we can in building up a picture of God without relying on any supposed experience of God or communication from God, or on any religious authority. The credentials of this enterprise have often been challenged in the modern era. Hume and Kant are prominent among the challengers. Its death has repeatedly been reported, but like the phoenix it keeps rising from its ashes in ever new guises.'

[3] In Ch. One I discuss kinds of theology and the links and rifts between theology and philosophy.

[4] In the eight chapters below I deal only with the topics of Book I: 'matters associated with God considered in himself' (I.9.57). I hope to be able to go on in two

In an earlier form, this book's chapters were the Wilde Lectures in Comparative and Natural Religion, which I delivered in Oxford in the spring of 1994. Because of that general designation for the lecture series, I didn't need to explain, then and there, why I was focusing on natural theology, or how natural theology is viewed by our contemporaries. However, I'm now outside those special, fostering circumstances, and I'm undertaking to expound, occasionally to criticize, but mostly to defend and promote, a system of natural theology. And so, before I begin to work at it directly, I want to point out some features of the current philosophical climate that strike me as pertinent to this project.

2. Attitudes toward natural theology

The single most accomplished contemporary practitioner and advocate of natural theology is Richard Swinburne, whose series of books constitutes a monumental achievement in this field.[5] I learn from his work and admire it, especially his intelligent use of twentieth-century science, and I share his sanguine view of natural theology's capacities. But the more familiar philosophical attitude toward natural theology is not so favourable.

Natural theology is as old as the rest of philosophy,[6] and the most familiar sort of criticism of it must be almost equally ancient, because it's just the sort that any philosophical undertaking is bound to generate within philosophy itself. The methods of natural theology are analysis and argument, the methods of the rest of philosophy; and, like any other branch of philosophy, natural theology submits its results to rational assessment. The people who constitute the primary audience for natural theology, in this as in any period of the history of philosophy, are philosophers who are willing to assess its results on philosophical grounds. Anyone who in that way develops particular objections to particular arguments of natural theology is simply giving natural theology what it asks for. And, of course, it has had plenty of it. But offering a refutation of

further volumes to deal with the topics of Book II, 'the emergence of created things from him', and of Book III, 'the ordering and directing of created things toward him as their goal' (ibid.).

[5] His first trilogy—Swinburne 1977, 1979, 1981—is more strictly devoted to natural theology than are some of his more recent books—e.g. Swinburne 1992 and 1994.

[6] See e.g. Webb 1915; Gerson 1990a.

an argument for, say, the existence of God is a paradigmatically
philosophical objection, which doesn't by itself imply a negative
attitude toward the enterprise of natural theology in which the
rejected argument arose.

There aren't many philosophical atheists whose atheism explicitly drives part of their philosophical agenda, but, naturally, they
can be among the most dedicated challengers of natural theology's
results.[7] And sometimes their criticism has been developed to such
an extent that it could be taken as a basis for repudiating the entire
enterprise on philosophical grounds. In this respect, among others,
natural theology resembles metaphysics, which some philosophers
have sometimes rejected wholesale. The reason why both disci-
plines keep rising from their ashes in ever new guises is that their
fundamental questions are undeniably and irresistibly *there*, in the
substructure of rational inquiry, demanding yet another attempt
at a systematic answer. And so a general philosophical repudiation
of either inquiry is likely to be based, too narrowly, on the
unsatisfactoriness of a particular set of answers with their supporting arguments, or, less effectively, on the impossibility of pursuing
either inquiry by some favoured method or other—for example,
those of the natural sciences.

Atheists haven't been the only philosophers to adopt negative
attitudes toward natural theology. Philosophers who are theists
are, of course, more likely to take an active interest in natural
theology, and no doubt they're the only ones who ever engage in it
constructively. Those who do so will, naturally, sometimes raise
philosophical objections against particular arguments in natural
theology, as Aquinas famously does against Anselm's (see Ch.
Two, sect. 2). Religious philosophers may, however, generate or
adopt not only philosophical objections to particular arguments;
they may also raise religious objections to the whole enterprise of
natural theology. There are many kinds of religious objections, a
few of which we'll have to sample below, but their general nature
and the spirit in which they're often offered can be nicely summed
up in Alvin Plantinga's characterization of them: negative religious
attitudes toward natural theology look 'a little like the attitude
some Christians adopt toward faith healing: it can't be done, but
even if it could it shouldn't be' (1983: 63). Philosophers who repu-

---

[7] For paradigms see Flew 1976; Mackie 1982.

diate natural theology on religious grounds alone do so otherwise than as philosophers, however, and non-philosophical attitudes toward it won't directly concern me in this book except as part of the intellectual climate I'm sampling in this introduction.

I am more concerned with positions recently taken by some philosophical theists who do recognize important connections between theism and philosophy, especially in theory of knowledge, where, naturally, the focus is on the epistemology of religious belief. Among the most interesting positions developed by such philosophers are the ones associated with Alvin Plantinga and William Alston. Their positions differ generally, and so do their expressed attitudes toward natural theology. Putting the issues baldly to begin with, I might say that natural theology takes propositions such as 'God exists' or 'God loves his creatures' to have the same epistemic status as most other propositions seriously considered in philosophy—that is, to stand in need of clarification by analysis and support by argumentation. It's hard to imagine any philosopher denying their need for clarification. As for support by argumentation, however, Plantinga has maintained that such propositions are rationally acceptable without support of any kind—a claim I'll return to below. Alston thinks that they do ordinarily need support, but that natural theology is only one source of it—and not the most interesting one.

3. Alston on natural theology

Alston's attitude toward natural theology has at least three essential components. First, he favours it, in a sensibly cautious way: 'As for myself, though I have no tendency to suppose that the existence of God can be *demonstratively proved* from extrareligious premises, I find certain of the arguments to be not wholly lacking in cogency. In particular, I think that there is much to be said for the ontological, cosmological, and moral arguments, in certain of their forms' (Alston 1991: 289; emphasis added).

But, second, he boldly assigns it as broad a scope as it could possibly have. Commenting on the remarks I just quoted, he says, 'This characterization of natural theology sticks closely to the classically recognized "arguments for the existence of God", but it need not be construed that narrowly. It also includes attempts to show that we can attain the best understanding of this or that area of our experience or sphere of concern—morality, human life, society, human wickedness, science, art, mathematics, *or whatever*—if we look at it from the standpoint of a theistic . . . metaphysics' (ibid.; emphasis added). The idea of a natural theology that goes far beyond existence arguments is one Alston shares with Aquinas, though, as we'll see, Aquinas's idea is perhaps less broad than Alston's. At any rate, Aquinas explicitly sets the concerns of natural science outside the scope of the project he's engaging in, and he shows no signs of having thought about including art or mathematics. But Alston's implied characterization of natural theology as 'theistic metaphysics' is very like what Aquinas seems to have had in mind, as the title of my book is meant to suggest, and as I think the following chapters will show.[8]

These first two components of Alston's attitude look as if they might have been intended to form part of the basis for the third— his assigning an important supporting role to natural theology in his epistemology of religious belief, in which a form of religious experience takes the lead: 'The central thesis of this book [Alston 1991] is that experiential awareness of God . . . makes an important contribution to the grounds of religious belief. More specifically, a person can become justified in holding certain kinds of beliefs about God by virtue of perceiving God as being or doing so-and-so. The kinds of beliefs that can be so justified I shall call "M-beliefs" ("M" for *manifestation*). . . . [T]he support given to M-beliefs by mystical experience is only one part of the total basis of religious belief. . . . What are these other possible grounds, and how does mystical experience interact with them in the larger picture? . . . I distinguish between various kinds of experiential grounds, various sorts of 'revelation', and natural theology. . . . [T]he different grounds interact not only by adding up to a total that is greater than any of its components, but also in more intimate ways—for example, by one source contributing to the background system presupposed by another source, or by one source helping to remove doubts about another' (pp. 1 and 7–8).[9] It's not hard to see how

[8] I favour 'the metaphysics of theism' over 'theistic metaphysics' mainly because the latter characterization of natural theology suggests metaphysics done within the context of an established theism rather than metaphysics developed in a way that leads to establishing and exploring theism.

[9] I've examined this epistemological position of Alston's generally, without taking special account of his attitude toward natural theology, in Kretzmann 1994. (A

natural theology might contribute to 'the background system' pre-supposed by either of the other two sources, or how it might help to remove doubts about their results. But since, as Alston himself points out, natural theology engages 'in building up a picture of God *without* relying on any supposed experience of God or com-munication from God, or on any religious authority',[10] it's not easy to see how putative religious experience or divine revelation could perform those services for natural theology.[11]

Religious experience plays no role at all in Aquinas's natural theology, but he does make a special, restricted use of revelation. Often at the end of a chapter, after having argued for some propo-sition in several different ways, each of which scrupulously omits any reference to revelation, he will cite Scripture by way of showing that what has just been achieved by unaided reason agrees with what he takes to be revealed truth. On those occasions he's cer-tainly not using revelation to remove doubts about natural theol-ogy's results; but could this use count as revelation's contributing to the background system presupposed by natural theology? Maybe, but only if such a contribution is construed as not much more than an aid to navigation. Reason could, of course, validly derive infi-nitely many further propositions from any one of the propositions previously argued for. But Aquinas's systematic natural theology is designed to show that reason unsupported by revelation could have come up with many—not all—of just those propositions that consti-tute the established subject-matter of revealed theology. So he needs Scripture in these circumstances as providing both a chart to guide his choice of propositions to argue for, and a list of specifica-tions that can be consulted to see that reason's results in Book I of *Summa contra gentiles* are in fact building up a picture of 'God considered in himself'.

When Alston comes to examine the possibility of natural theol-ogy's supplying the most important kind of support for the practice of forming M-beliefs, the practice he labels 'MP', he unexpectedly ignores his broad conception of natural theology, just when it

very slightly different version of the same article appears as Kretzmann 1995.) See also e.g. Pasnau 1993.

[10] Emphasis added, see n. 2 above.

[11] Although the discipline itself is formally incapable of receiving such support, the system of beliefs of any *practitioner* of natural theology might well be enhanced in such ways.

seems that its breadth might have been particularly relevant: 'The most obvious candidates for a noncircular support for the reliability of MP come from natural theology and revelation. . . . [But] even if we can establish the existence and basic nature of God without reliance on MP, how do we get from that conclusion to the informational efficacy of MP? Natural theology operates at too high a level of abstraction to enable us to do this job. The standard arguments for the existence of God give us no reason to think that God is interested in displaying himself to our experience' (Alston 1991: 144). That's obviously true about the standard existence arguments. But a wide-ranging natural theology of the sort envisaged by Alston elsewhere in the same book and actively developed by Aquinas in *Summa contra gentiles* does, in fact, get around to giving us some 'reason to think that God is interested in displaying himself to our experience' (see Ch. Eight).

Every thoughtful religious person recognizes the difficulty of explaining objectively what it is about his or her religion that makes it preferable to all the others. Alston's backing MP as the main source of justification for religious belief exacerbates the difficulty, since his position looks especially awkward when confronted with the fact that 'the general enterprise of forming perceptual religious beliefs is carried on in different religions in such a way as to yield incompatible results' (Alston 1991: 255). He devotes a whole chapter to 'The Problem of Religious Diversity', 'the most difficult problem for my position' (ibid.), a position in which the '*Christian* mystical perceptual practice' (ibid. 193; emphasis added) is ranked ahead of all others. Without examining the problem or Alston's solution to it, I want just to observe that his view of the modest contribution natural theology can make toward a solution strongly resembles what I take to be Aquinas's view of the efficacy of natural theology from the standpoint of Christianity. Alston puts it this way: 'The Christian may have recourse to natural theology *to provide metaphysical reasons for the truth of theism as a general world-view.* . . . I believe that much can be done to support a theistic metaphysics' (ibid. 270; emphasis added). And I believe that in *Summa contra gentiles* I–III Aquinas has in fact done much in just that line. Distinctively Christian theism he deals with only in the fourth and last book, where he resumes his consideration of the nature of God and works his way down through human beings, addressing in particular just those specifically Christian proposi-

tions—for example, the doctrines of the Trinity and the Incarnation—to which reason would have no initial access without the
revelation he accepts. And he does this, he says, with the aim of
showing that even those propositions, which cannot be *arrived at* by
reason alone, 'are *not opposed* to natural reason' (IV.1.3348).

Alston's attitudes toward natural theology, then, are often like
Aquinas's, and some of the developments and applications he en-
visages for it are, broadly speaking, like those Aquinas actually
carries out. However, in Alston's view, natural theology's most
important function is to contribute toward the epistemic justification of certain religious beliefs, and that, as I'll suggest below, is not
the way Aquinas sees it.[12]

4. 'The Reformed Objection to Natural Theology'

Atheism aside, the most *apparent* contemporary opposition to taking natural theology seriously is associated with Alvin Plantinga.
His own appraisal of natural theology considered in itself may well
have been obscured in work he's done recently, but that work
seems to have been interpreted by many readers as bypassing,
discounting, or even repudiating natural theology. In several well-
known articles,[13] he has tried to establish the rationality of believing without any evidence or argument that God exists. One of those
articles—'Reason and Belief in God' (Plantinga 1983)—has
emerged as the *locus classicus* of the position he and others have
called 'Reformed epistemology'. The following passage can serve
as a statement of the thesis of Reformed epistemology: '[I]t is
entirely right, rational, reasonable, and proper to believe in God
without any evidence or argument at all' (ibid. 17). In the context of
foundationalism, which informs much of the discussion in Plantinga
1983, beliefs maintained without ulterior propositional evidence
(evidence presented in propositions other than the one believed)
are interpretable as *basic* beliefs. S's belief that *p* is a belief that is
basic for S just in case S believes that *p* but not on the basis of any

[12] This aspect of Alston's view of natural theology is the one that naturally gets
emphasized in the special context of his project in Alston 1991. I have it on unimpeachable authority that his view of natural theology outside that special context is
even more like Aquinas's.

[13] Besides the one I draw on just below, see e.g. Plantinga 1986*a*, 1986*b*, and 1987.

other belief(s) of S's. In that context the question of the *rationality* of believing without ulterior propositional evidence becomes the question whether a given basic belief is *properly* basic, whether the belief is justified simply by the nature of the believed proposition itself or the circumstances of the formation of the belief. So the thesis of Reformed epistemology appears to be interpretable as the claim that, for any S, S's belief that God exists is, or could be, properly basic.

I've argued elsewhere that Plantinga's position isn't really so radical or so opposed to evidentialism as that thesis and his development of the thesis make it seem, and I won't review those arguments now.[14] Taken at face value, as Plantinga does take it in his 1983 article, the thesis does at least devalue, and might well be read as repudiating, natural theology, which traditionally begins with (and has sometimes been confined to) arguments for the existence of God. Reformed epistemology's opposition to natural theology needn't be inferred from some reading of its thesis, however, since it appears to be developed explicitly in Part III, 'The Reformed Objection to Natural Theology' (ibid. 63–73).[15] The objection has its historical roots in the Protestant Reformation, as does the thesis itself, according to Plantinga. In his view, the thesis expresses '[w]hat the Reformers [especially Calvin and Calvinists] meant to hold', but '[w]hat they say . . . has been for the most part unclear, ill-focused, and unduly inexplicit'; and he sets out to 'try to remedy these ills' because, he thinks, the Reformers' 'fundamental insights here are correct' (ibid. 16–17). Among those insights he includes 'the Reformed rejection of natural theology', '*understood as* an implicit rejection of *classical* foundationalism in favor of the view that belief in God is properly basic' (ibid. 17; emphasis added).[16]

---

[14] See Kretzmann 1992; also e.g. Maitzen 1995.

[15] An earlier version of this appears as Plantinga 1982. Part III of Plantinga 1983 has been excerpted and reprinted separately (along with most of Part IV D, 'Fideism') in Plantinga 1992.

[16] The fact that Plantinga argues that the belief that God exists is 'properly basic' shows that his constructive project in his 1983 article isn't operating entirely independently of foundationalism. His opposition to it is directed exclusively (or at least primarily) against what he calls 'classical' foundationalism, just because of its restrictions on proper basicality: 'Ancient and medieval foundationalists tended to hold that a proposition is properly basic for a person only if it is either self-evident or evident to the senses: modern foundationalists—Descartes, Locke, Leibniz, and the like—tended to hold that a proposition is properly basic for S only if either self-evident or incorrigible for S. . . . [A] *classical foundationalist* is any one who is either an ancient and medieval or a modern foundationalist' (Plantinga 1983: 58–9).

So, as Plantinga sees it, it is precisely *in* their explicit, religious rejection of natural theology that the Reformers are supposed to have implicitly endorsed the philosophical thesis of Reformed epistemology. I'm interested primarily in the use Plantinga makes of the various objections that contribute to what he describes as the Reformed rejection of natural theology. And I'm indirectly interested in those objections themselves, despite the fact that they're not philosophical, because the way he presents them is designed to translate those religious objections to natural theology into a philosophical position: Reformed epistemology. That position itself might, conceivably, not be intended to imply any philosophical objection to natural theology. But it's hard to be certain about what, if any, philosophical attitude toward natural theology is implicit in Reformed epistemology as Plantinga develops it here.

His presentation begins by limiting the notion of natural theology to 'the attempt to prove or demonstrate the existence of God' (ibid. 63). This narrowing of the notion is drastic, and not only as regards its scope. But I suppose it can be allowed here, since every systematic natural theology includes, at or near its beginning, an attempt at least to argue for God's existence (if not to prove or demonstrate it). He mentions 'among its adherents many of the truly great thinkers of the Western world. One thinks, for example, of Anselm, Aquinas, Scotus, and Ockham, of Descartes, Spinoza, and Leibniz. . . . [B]ut for the most part the Reformed attitude [toward natural theology] has ranged from tepid endorsement, through indifference, to suspicion, hostility, and outright accusations of blasphemy. . . . What exactly, or even approximately, do these sons and daughters of the Reformation have against proving the existence of God? What *could* they have against it?' (ibid.).

Plantinga develops his answer to those questions by examining attacks on natural theology by three 'representative Reformed thinkers' (ibid. 64): Bavinck, Calvin, and Barth.

Bavinck

He sums up the first of them in these words: 'According to Bavinck, then, belief in the existence of God is not based upon proofs or arguments. . . . Christians do not *need* such arguments. Do not need them for what?' (ibid.). Plantinga's answer to that question consists in these two claims, derived from Bavinck: (1) 'arguments or proofs are not, in general, the source of the believer's confidence in God';

(2) 'argument is not needed for *rational justification* ... The believer does not need natural theology in order to achieve rationality
or epistemic propriety in believing' (ibid. 64–5).[17]

In claim 1, 'the source' might mean not merely what *causes* the
believer's confidence, but also what serves as its *epistemic ground*.
But, in juxtaposition with claim 2, claim 1 is more reasonably
interpreted as being about just the cause. On that interpretation,
claim 1 is surely beyond dispute as regards theistic believers *generally*, even if 'confidence in God' is taken to mean merely belief that
God exists (which is how I take it here). Of course, an argument for
the existence of God might well be used in an attempt to convert
someone from atheism or agnosticism to theism, and if it succeeded, then, of course, an argument would have been the cause
(and, at least to begin with, also the ground) of that believer's
belief.[18] But such cases—probably rare—are compatible with claim
1, the denial in which is only 'in general'.

What's interesting about claim 1 here is that it offers at most a
basis for objecting to claims for a particular practical *application* of
natural theology, and no basis at all for objecting to natural theology considered as what it is—a branch of philosophy. The fact that
a lay person's beliefs about the existence and nature of atoms do
not, in general, have their *source* in arguments or proofs has no
tendency to denigrate, much less to undercut, atomic physics. Just
as obviously, in *acquiring* one's religious beliefs, one typically does
not, and certainly need not, engage in philosophical analysis and
argumentation of any sort. And this is just what the great natural
theologians, such as Augustine, Anselm, and Aquinas, have always
claimed. But, of course, they go on to insist, one way or another,
that this faith acquired on the basis of an initially unquestioning

---

[17] I'm focusing here on Plantinga's presentation of Bavinck rather than on the
material he quotes from him; but the opening sentence of the quotation is worth
repeating here as an indication of the universality of Bavinck's categorical rejection:
'A distinct natural theology, obtained apart from any revelation, merely through
observation and study of the universe in which man lives, does not exist' (quoted
ibid. 64).

[18] In summing up 'The Reformed Objection to Natural Theology', Plantinga
acknowledges as much, though not very encouragingly: 'One who holds this view
need not suppose that natural theology is of no use. ... [N]atural theology could be
useful in helping someone move from unbelief to belief. ... [T]here may be (in fact
there are) people who accept propositions and argument forms out of which a
theistic argument can be constructed' (ibid. 73). As far as I can tell, Plantinga
himself is one of those people; see below.

acceptance of, say, parental or priestly authority *should seek* understanding, at various levels, by various means. What we call natural theology is the theoretical inquiry they recognized as occupying the highest level and providing the most reliable means available to reason independent of revelation.[19]

The second of the claims into which Plantinga analyses Bavinck's position is just as surely *not* beyond dispute, especially as illustrated by Plantinga: 'the believer is entirely within his epistemic right in believing, for example, that God has created the world, even if he has no argument at all for that conclusion' (ibid. 65). But even if one accepted this particular instance of the thesis of Reformed epistemology, it seems clear that it could, at best, offer rational justification only in an epistemic vacuum, which human nature abhors. Even the non-philosophical believer is likely to acknowledge her need for supportive evidence and argument in case her belief is shaken or disappointed by her own experience—a sort of thing that happens often enough to believers. And if her belief is expressly challenged by other people, none of them are going to consider her belief (or her) to be rationally justified if her response is 'I just believe it; that's all'. But an educated, intelligent person living, as we do, in a society in which many educated, intelligent people disbelieve, 'for example, that God has created the world' lives in circumstances replete with challenges of that sort.

None the less, even if claim 2 were granted, it wouldn't provide a basis for rejecting natural theology except in response to someone who had foolishly claimed that natural theology is practically and universally indispensable to theists. In expounding Bavinck, Plantinga says that the believer's 'belief in God can be perfectly rational even if he knows of no cogent argument, deductive or inductive, for the existence of God' (ibid. 65). That's undoubtedly true regarding some believers, in some circumstances. And such a believer, considered simply as such, really does have no more need for natural theology than he has for philosophy of mathematics when balancing his cheque book—which is no objection to philosophy of mathematics.

Plantinga extracts three more claims from Bavinck's attack, the first of which is this: (3) 'we cannot come to knowledge of God on the basis of argument; the arguments of natural theology just do

---

[19] See Kretzmann 1990.

not work' (ibid.). Here, in the second clause of claim 3, there certainly is a straightforward objection to natural theology itself; but it's just the extra-large size of the sort of objection any philosopher practising natural theology should expect and know how to deal with. And many of them—Aquinas, for instance—might even welcome such objections: 'if any people want to write back against what I have said, I will be very gratified, because there is no better way of uncovering the truth and keeping falsity in check than by arguing with people who disagree with you' (*De perfectione* 26).[20] But even if it were true that none of the available arguments worked, that wouldn't support the strong claim in the first clause (even when 'knowledge of God' is interpreted only as knowledge that God exists). The failure of every known argument for the existence of God might mean no more than that natural theology hadn't yet succeeded in doing what it set out to do. So, while the second clause of claim 3 contains what is unmistakably a general philosophical objection to natural theology itself, it would take a lot of careful work to back up that inductive generalization. And the strong claim in the first clause, which is really independent of the one in the second clause, is no more an objection to natural theology than is claim 1, which it markedly resembles.

In connection with claim 3, unlike the others, Plantinga distances himself from Bavinck, who, he says, 'follows this passage [the one Plantinga is drawing on] with a more or less traditional attempt to refute the theistic proofs, including an endorsement of some of Kant's fashionable confusions about the ontological argument' (1983: 65). The way Plantinga expresses himself here suggests that he thinks Bavinck's rejection of the existence arguments is unsophisticated, and perhaps even excessive. None the less, in concluding his discussion of the Reformed objection to natural theology, Plantinga *appears* to imply his own rejection of 'the theistic proofs' when, by way of showing that even the Reformed objector 'need not suppose that natural theology is of no use', he says that 'if there *were* good arguments for the existence of God, that would be a fact worth knowing in itself' (ibid. 73; Plantinga's emphasis).[21]

---

[20] Although this passage does not appear in Aquinas's presentation of his natural theology, it expresses his view, shared with truth-seekers in all times and places, of the best way of making intellectual progress in general—a way codified and institutionalized in the disputational 'scholastic method' that characterizes much of medieval philosophy and theology, including Aquinas's.

[21] The passage continues in this way: '—just as it would be worth knowing (if true) that the analogical argument for other minds is successful, or that there are good

In an earlier book of his, however, he himself developed an important version of the ontological argument. In appraising the stages of his argument there, he says, 'Clearly they are valid; and hence they show that if it is even possible that God, so thought of, exists, then it is true and necessarily true that he does. The only question of interest, it seems to me, is whether its main premiss— that indeed unsurpassable greatness is possibly exemplified, that there is an essence entailing unsurpassable greatness—is *true*. I think this premiss is indeed true. Accordingly, I think this version of the Ontological Argument is sound' (Plantinga 1974: 216–17). And he seems not to have changed his mind on that point at the time he wrote his 1983 article.[22] This is one of the reasons why I find Plantinga's attitude toward natural theology in general hard to read. But I think there's no doubt about his particularized opposition to it in connection with the development of Reformed epistemology in Plantinga 1983, and in examining that opposition, I've so far not found any formidable objection, philosophical or religious, to natural theology itself.

The fourth claim Plantinga extracts from Bavinck is this: (4) 'Scripture "proceeds from God as the starting point," and so should the believer. There is nothing by way of proofs or arguments for God's existence in the Bible; that is simply presupposed. The same should be true of the Christian believer then; he should *start* from belief in God rather than from the premises of some argument whose conclusion is that God exists. What is it that makes those premises a better starting point anyway?' (Plantinga 1983: 65). Unlike the other claims Plantinga finds in Bavinck, 4 is religious and parochial, stated in a way that expressly pertains only to Christians. As an objection to natural theology, then, claim 4 could on its strongest interpretation provide no more than a specific religious scruple against engaging in the enterprise or taking its results seriously. But in fact there is nothing in the first three sentences of claim 4 that even Christian practitioners of natural theology would hesitate to endorse. By way of showing that this endorsement gives them no religious qualms about their enterprise, however, they might very well cite some familiar scriptural passages—for example, Psalm 19: 1: 'The heavens declare the glory of God; and the

arguments from self-evident and incorrigible propositions to the existence of other minds'. On his view of arguments for other minds, see below.

[22] See e.g. his remarks on the ontological argument in Plantinga 1985: 70–1.

firmament showeth his handiwork'; Romans 1: 20: 'For the invisible things of him from the creation of the world are clearly seen, being understood by the things that are made, even his eternal power and Godhead'; 1 Peter 3: 15: '[B]e ready always to give an answer to every man that asketh you a reason of the hope that is in you.' And as for the rhetorical question with which claim 4 ends, most Christian practitioners of natural theology would have an answer for it: those premises are starting-points that are better only for the purpose of argumentation, and what makes them better for that purpose is that the truth of those premises is typically established by more widely shared kinds of human experience than those on the basis of which the authority of Scripture is accepted.[23] And so they have higher initial plausibility—a desirable quality in a premiss.

Claim 5: '[B]elief in God relevantly resembles belief in the existence of the self and of the external world—and, we might add, belief in other minds and the past. In none of these areas do we typically *have* proof or arguments, or *need* proof or arguments' (Plantinga 1983: 65).[24] Belief in the existence of the self seems clearly *not* to resemble belief in God in relevant respects. If any belief does count as properly basic in virtue of the circumstances of the formation of the belief, rather than the nature of the believed proposition itself, it's the belief each of us has in 'I exist'. Belief in God, even if formed in circumstances of overwhelming mystical experience, can't claim proper basicality of that same highest degree, just because it's technically vulnerable to sceptical doubts as belief in one's own existence is not. And as for our beliefs in the external world, in other minds, and in the past, philosophers do have arguments supporting them—not proofs, of course, but dialectical, probable arguments of the sort that figure most prominently everywhere in philosophy. Belief in the external world, for instance, can be systematically contrasted with competing hypotheses, and grounds can be produced for rationally, pragmatically preferring realism to idealism, say. Something of that sort might

---

[23] But cf. Calvin's notion of a universally shared *sensus divinitatis*, discussed below.

[24] See n. 21 above. See further this remark in Plantinga 1983: 67–8: 'From Calvin's point of view, believing in the existence of God on the basis of rational argument is like believing in the existence of your spouse on the basis of the analogical argument for other minds—whimsical at best and unlikely to delight the person concerned.'

well be constructed in support of theism, too. Outside philosophy we certainly don't need arguments supporting our belief in the external world, but that's because formidable sceptical arguments challenging that belief arise only within philosophy. Obviously the same can't be said regarding arguments that challenge theism.

As Plantinga interprets Bavinck's general religious objections, then, regardless of whether or not they can indeed be construed in the terms of Reformed epistemology's thesis, as he supposes they can, they do not constitute grounds for formidable philosophical objections to natural theology. And, in Plantinga's presentations of the three Reformers here, it is Bavinck's objections that provide the most promising material of that sort.

Calvin

Plantinga's quotations from Calvin, the second in his list of three Reformers, include this religious objection to one sort of use of natural theology: 'The prophets and apostles do not . . . dwell upon rational proofs. . . . If we desire to provide in the best way for our consciences . . . we ought to seek our conviction in a higher place than human reasons, judgments, or conjectures, that is, in the secret testimony of the Spirit' (quoted in Plantinga 1983: 67). Interpreting the religious objection philosophically, Plantinga says: 'If my belief in God is based on argument, then if I am to be properly rational, epistemically responsible, I shall have to keep checking the philosophical journals to see whether, say, Anthony Flew has finally come up with a good objection to my favorite argument. . . . [A]nd what do I do if someone does find a flaw in my argument? Stop going to church?' (ibid.). But it would be unlikely to turn out that way, even for someone who does take natural theology to provide epistemic justification for her belief in God. More probably, it would be like the circumstances of a philosopher who founds her epistemology on what she takes to be her rational conviction that there is an external world, and who is consequently interested in new formulations of scepticism because they might reveal flaws in the formation or presentation of her conviction. In such circumstances it *would* be irrational for her to ignore or disdain scepticism's objections. But her reaction to a cogent objection would normally be a refurbishing of her formulation of realism, not a conversion to solipsism.

The firmest basis available for any objection to natural theology that Calvin might raise can be seen in his very strong declarations regarding a natural, universal human awareness of God—the *sensus divinitatis*. This characteristic doctrine of his may seem to insulate his position, by fiat, from any serious interest in, let alone use for, natural theology's existence arguments: ' "There is within the human mind, and indeed by natural instinct, an awareness of divinity." This we take to be *beyond controversy*. . . . [M]en one and all perceive that there is a God and that he is their Maker . . . From this we conclude *that it is not a doctrine that must first be learned in school*, but one of which each of us is master from his mother's womb and which nature itself permits no one to forget' (quoted ibid. 65–6; first emphasis added). In glossing this declaration, Plantinga weakens it significantly, in a way that makes it less implausible: 'Calvin's claim, then, is that God has created us in such a way that we have a strong tendency or inclination toward belief in him. . . . The fact is, Calvin thinks, one who does not believe in God is in an epistemically substandard position' (ibid. 66). Judging only on the basis of the bit of Calvin that Plantinga quotes here, I think Calvin would have to describe the unbeliever as in an epistemically *impossible* position, and I find that consequence and the doctrine on which it apparently depends unbelievable.

Although this doctrine of the universally innate, unforgettable, unignorable *sensus divinitatis* would seem to render existence arguments pointless, Plantinga's Calvin, a little surprisingly, also makes use of the idea that is central to arguments from design, attributing to it more efficacy than even proponents of such arguments are likely to claim for it: God 'daily discloses himself in the whole workmanship of the universe. As a consequence, men cannot open their eyes without being compelled to see him' (quoted ibid. 66). Plantinga seems not to want to deny that 'some version of the teleological argument' might be discerned here. Instead, he again denies that the believer *needs* such support: 'It is not that such a person [beholding the starry heavens, for instance] is justified or rational in so believing by virtue of having an implicit argument . . . No; he does not need any argument for justification or rationality. His belief need not be based on any other propositions at all' (ibid. 67). Well, if such people are, as Calvin says we all are, made in such a way that they 'cannot open their eyes without being compelled to see him', then what Plantinga says here is plainly true. But if that plain truth is to have any philosophical efficacy, many of us would, embarrassingly enough, need some evidence that we are, indeed, made in that way, endowed with the *sensus divinitatis*.

Barth

As presented by Plantinga, Barth is the most belligerent of these Reformed objectors to natural theology, but certainly no more genuinely threatening than the other two. For one thing, Barth's objection could have force only against Christian practitioners of natural theology. He accuses them of being in 'the standpoint of unbelief', which is 'to hold that belief in God is rationally accept-able *only if it is more likely than not with respect to the deliverances of reason*. . . . [Such a person's] ultimate commitment is to the de-liverances of reason rather than to God. Such a person "makes reason a judge over Christ," or at any rate over the Christian faith. And to do so, says Barth, is utterly improper for a Christian' (Plantinga 1983: 70–1).

For another thing, Barth's accusation is manifestly unfair, as Plantinga recognizes. He presents a reasonable defence against it, one that seems also to count as a defence of natural theology itself, even in the light of Reformed epistemology. '[A] natural theologian . . . offers or endorses theistic arguments, but why suppose that her own belief in God must be based upon such argument? . . . Perhaps her aim is to point out to the unbeliever that belief in God follows from other things he already believes, so that he can continue in unbelief (and continue to accept these other beliefs) only on pain of inconsistency' (ibid. 71). What he says here about his imagined Christian natural theologian is also perfectly suited to such real ones as Augustine, Anselm, and Aquinas, as long as we recognize that the aim spelled out in his example isn't the only one they had.

What interests Plantinga about Barth's objection to natural the-ology is not the objection itself: 'here he is probably wrong, or at any rate not clearly right. More interesting is his view that belief in God need not be based on argument' (ibid. 71). In fact, considered in themselves, probably none of these Reformed objections to natural theology interest Plantinga much or strike him as providing grounds for a philosophical repudiation, or even devaluation, of the enterprise itself, despite some of the things he says in introducing them. He comes close to showing this, I think, in his summary interpretation of the Reformed rejection: 'In rejecting natural theology, therefore, these Reformed thinkers mean to say first of all that the propriety or rightness of belief in God in no way depends upon the success or availability of the sort of theistic arguments that form the natural theologian's stock in trade. I think this is their central claim here, and their central insight. . . . The correct or proper way to believe in God, they thought, was not on the basis of arguments from natural theology or anywhere else; the correct way is to take belief in God as basic' (ibid. 72).

As we've been seeing, and as that passage itself indicates, these Reformed thinkers are not really 'rejecting natural theology', but only one possible application of it. And since they are raising *religious* objections against that application, what *they* would mean by 'the propriety or rightness of belief in God' or '[t]he correct or proper way to believe in God' would constitute a *religious*, not an epistemological, approbation of shunning evidence or argument as a basis for believing in God. But in finally paraphrasing these Reformers as having thought that 'the correct way is to take belief in God as basic', Plantinga seems again to be suggesting that the high spiritual value they place on believing without evidence constitutes an epistemological appraisal, the one he expresses in the thesis of Reformed epistemology. I think he's overinterpreting them.

As far as I can see, then, 'the Reformed objection to natural theology' is a religious objection directed not against natural theology but against only one possible application of it, a religious objection that does not support any formidable philosophical objections, a religious objection that therefore provides a dubious basis for Reformed epistemology.[25]

5. Conclusion

Alston, we've seen, is friendly to natural theology considered as one source of epistemic justification for religious belief. And what-

---

[25] On Plantinga and natural theology, see also Kenny 1992*a* and esp. 1992*b*.

ever opposition to natural theology Plantinga does clearly manifest is specifically directed against using it as a source of epistemic justification for religious belief. Aquinas, however, doesn't expressly view his natural theology as having that role. As I said above, his is designed to show that reason without revelation's support could have arrived at many—not all—of the propositions that constitute revelation. In that way, and to that extent, he is showing the unity of reason and faith. I think, though, that he would cheerfully admit that of course his natural theology could in certain circumstances also supply epistemic justification for religious belief.

I can't in this Introduction show in detail how Aquinas views natural theology: that's one of my aims in the rest of the book. But the following passage from Nicholas Wolterstorff, himself a prominent contributor to Reformed epistemology, provides a helpful preliminary sketch of what I think will turn out to be apparent in our investigation of Aquinas's project.

[T]he evidentialist challenge and objection to theistic conviction, along with the attempt to cope with that challenge by practicing evidentialist apologetics, are peculiar to modernity. Some will question this claim by pointing to the practice of natural theology among the medievals. The reply is that natural theology was a different project from evidentialist apologetics—even though the same arguments may occur in both. . . . Taking Anselm and Aquinas as typical, it becomes clear, then, that the medievals were doing something quite different in their project of natural theology from meeting the evidentialist challenge. They were engaged in the transmutation project of altering belief (faith) into knowledge.[26] No one in their milieu was claiming that it was permissible to believe that God existed only if one did so on the basis of adequate evidence, and with a firmness not exceeding the strength of the evidence. (Nonetheless Aquinas

---

[26] As my preliminary characterizations have been indicating, I don't think this is exactly right as a description of Aquinas's project in *natural* theology. It comes closer to characterizing his *philosophical* theology, which does take revealed propositions as part of its subject-matter (see Ch. One). Like natural theology, which is subordinate to metaphysics, philosophical theology is a subordinate science. Aquinas identifies the 'science' (*scientia*) to which it is subordinate as God's knowledge (*scientia*) of himself and everything else, available to human beings directly and completely only in the afterlife (*Summa theologiae* Ia.1.2c). As he says in an earlier work, 'For us, the goal of faith is to arrive at an understanding of what we believe—[which is] as if a practitioner of a subordinate science were to acquire in addition the knowledge possessed by a practitioner of the [corresponding] higher science. In that case the things that were only believed before would come to be known, or understood' (Commentary on Boethius's *De trinitate* 2.2, ad 7).

did, in chapter 6 of his *Summa Contra Gentiles*, defend the thesis 'that to give assent to the truths of faith is not foolishness even though they are above reason.') (Wolterstorff 1983: 140–1)[27]

I'm convinced that natural theology still offers the best route by which philosophers can, as philosophers, approach theological propositions, and that the one presented in this book is, all things considered, the best available natural theology.

[27] The passage he quotes from *Summa contra gentiles* is the title of chapter 6 of Book I, which Aquinas himself is not responsible for, and it may not express just what Wolterstorff is looking for. By 'the truths of faith . . . [that] are above reason', Aquinas means only those doctrinal propositions to which reason has no access without revelation, the 'mysteries'. Because of their initial inaccessibility to unaided reason, these are the propositions he deals with not in his natural theology at all, but in Book IV of *Summa contra gentiles*, where he's practising philosophical theology. And in this same chapter 6 of Book I he goes on to offer evidence supporting the claim expressed in its title: 'For divine wisdom itself, which knows all things most fully, has deigned to reveal to human beings those secrets of divine wisdom. By appropriate indications (*argumentis*) it reveals its own presence and the truth both of its teaching and of its inspiration, while to establish things that lie beyond natural cognition it displays, visibly, works that surpass the capacity of all of nature'—i.e. miracles, some of which he goes on to cite (I.6.36).

ONE

THEOLOGY FROM THE BOTTOM UP

1. Theology and philosophy

I'm a philosopher, not a theologian. Even if theologians were inclined to pay any attention to a layman's notions about their field,
what I have to say about theology's nature and subject-matter
wouldn't contribute anything to the wide-ranging arguments
they've been having over those basic issues. My approach in this
book is uninfluenced by any consideration of that debate, and is
guided simply by the very idea of theology—I mean the idea embedded in the etymology of the word and instantiated more or less
fully in the work of just about all dead theologians and most dead
philosophers, too, from the pre-Socratics through the seventeenth
century at least. Living theologians are of course familiar with the
idea, and almost all of them would repudiate it as utterly obsolete.[1]

Broadly speaking, the idea of theology is the idea of a rational
investigation of the first principles and most fundamental aspects of
reality in general and of human nature and behaviour in particular.
That broad characterization could obviously accommodate theology's more readily recognizable, traditional topics: God's existence, God's nature, and the relations to God of all other things,
especially human beings. Still, it's likely to seem *too* broad, leaving
theology indistinguishable from philosophy, to which the description seems better suited, even if old-fashioned. But theology
and philosophy really are traditionally indistinguishable, broadly
speaking. Traditionally, either theology is part of philosophy, or
theology and philosophy are two species of the same genus, the

---

[1] See e.g. Kaufman 1989; Stump and Kretzmann 1990 (a reply to Kaufman 1989)
(p. 329a, omitted from the second of these articles, appears in the immediately
following issue of the journal, vol. 7, no. 4); also Griffiths 1993; Stump and
Kretzmann 1994 (a reply to Griffiths 1993).

very one picked out in that description. I don't know of an established name for that genus, but 'Grandest Unified Theory' strikes me as appropriate.

Obviously, the two-species conception of theology and philosophy must involve a sharper distinction between them than the part–whole conception does. But what essentially differentiates those two species traditionally is really only the starting-points of their investigations, not their goals or their methods or even their subject-matters.[2] Theology, on this view of it as specifically different from philosophy, finds data for its version of the Grandest Unified Theory in what it takes to be divinely revealed truths. Starting with what one takes to be divinely revealed truths about the first principles and most fundamental aspects of reality in general and of human nature and behaviour in particular is starting with the conviction that God exists and with some conception of God's nature. This non-philosophical 'revealed' theology, then, can be thought of as theology from the top down. Though theology from the top down is specifically different from philosophy, it does share philosophy's goals, generically considered. But the putatively revealed truths it accepts appear to give this theology a head start toward those common goals. It's a decidedly unphilosophical head start because, of course, philosophy's data—which traditionally consist of nothing more than what seems boringly obvious to everybody, and only a little even of that—are accepted under constraints that rigorously rule out revelations. So philosophy from the bottom up might reasonably be thought to be the only kind of philosophy there could be.

On the other hand, there has never been general agreement that theology is exclusively from the top down in this sense of having been handed its data by the central subject of its investigation. Still, theology from the top down, revealed theology, is theology as most people think of it. It's not the theology I'll be focusing on. But I should note in passing that, traditionally, not even revealed theology is unphilosophical in all its developments. It begins, naturally, with 'dogmatic' theology, which extracts religious doctrine from revelation and codifies doctrine into articles of faith. Dogmatic theology is definitely not philosophical—except in the discountable

---

[2] No theory that leaves God entirely out of consideration could count as theology, and of course plenty of philosophical theories have nothing to do with God. But philosophical theories, too, have often included God as an essential component.

sense that it sometimes uses techniques and standards of analysis and argument that philosophers discovered and developed. But dogmatic theology's processing of the raw data of revelation gives rise, traditionally, to 'philosophical' theology, the analytical and argumentative clarification, extension, and defence of the articles of faith. Philosophical theology is what was produced by most medieval theologians, whether or not they would have been happy with that designation, and what is being produced now by many philosophers of religion.[3] Technically and traditionally, philosophical theology is part of revealed theology rather than of philosophy. And it's only philosophical theology, never philosophy herself, that can and should be recognized under philosophy's old job description of *ancilla theologiae*, theology's maid-servant.[4]

2. *Theology in philosophy*

As for the theology that is not specifically different from, but part of, philosophy—the 'natural' theology that is at the centre of my interests here—the first thing that should be clear about it is that, as a part of philosophy, it must be theology from the bottom up, in the sense that it must forgo the unphilosophical head start apparently provided by putative revelation and accept as its data only those few naturally evident considerations that traditionally constitute data acceptable for philosophy as a whole. So it seems clear that natural theology's agenda for rational investigation will have the existence of God as its first distinctive item—the first item that marks it off as the theological part of philosophy. If God's existence can be plausibly argued for, its second large-scale topic will be what can be inferred about God's nature; its third, the relation of everything else to God considered as the first principle of reality in general; its fourth, the particular relations of human nature and behaviour to God considered as their first principle.

Because of the difficulties in the first undertaking that distinguishes natural theology from other parts of philosophy, its development as an independent inquiry has typically been stunted,

---

[3] Perhaps especially by those associated with the Society of Christian Philosophers.

[4] For an excellent account of philosophical theology, see MacDonald, forthcoming.

giving it the look of an investigative dead end. It has that look about it largely because most philosophers have held natural theology to standards of argumentation more stringent than those applied in other branches of philosophy, conceiving of it as a narrowly focused enterprise of attempting to develop airtight proofs of the existence, or non-existence, of God. That conception dominated Anglo-American philosophy of religion through at least the first three-quarters of the twentieth century. On the other hand, when natural theology has been fully integrated into the rest of philosophy, it has usually appeared as the culmination of metaphysics, when metaphysics was developed in such a way that the rational investigation of the first principles and most fundamental aspects of reality in general resulted finally in arguments that warranted identifying them, or it, as divine—in, for instance, an argument concluding to the necessity of an ultimate, universal, unmoved mover. When Aristotle calls metaphysics 'theology', he has this sort of culmination of it in view.[5] Purely philosophical metaphysics from the bottom up reaches its traditional top in this integrated natural theology. But even it has been typically, and understandably, limited to sketchy developments of the first three items on natural theology's agenda, the distinctly metaphysical ones.

But suppose we were to take a metaphysically based natural theology—a metaphysics of theism—as the first phase of a systematic presentation of the rest of philosophy. Beginning with the establishment and investigation of what metaphysics has often finally identified as reality's first principle has all the natural appeal of beginning at the real beginning, and it doesn't violate philosophy's strictures against including revealed truths among its data. And suppose we succeed in getting through the first two items on natural theology's agenda, providing philosophically good reasons for thinking that God exists and that God's nature is such that it might be seriously considered as the first principle of reality in general and of human nature and behaviour in particular. Then, in so far as God is the first thing we argue for and we consider all other things in their relations to God, there's a sense in which we're presenting philosophy from the top down by beginning its presentation with theology from the bottom up. And if the metaphysical tradition was on the right track, and the first principles and most

---

[5] *Metaphysics* VI 1, 1026a7–23.

fundamental aspects of reality in general are in some philosophically meaningful sense divine, then from the top down is the most
sensible way for philosophy to go, at least as regards the systematic
presentation of it.

But if such an enterprise could be made to look feasible and its
results illuminating, wouldn't it follow that philosophy from the top
down just *is* natural theology, all the way down? Well, yes—in a
way. Philosophy from the top down does look like the metaphysics
of theism developed far beyond the very familiar first two items on
its agenda. But, after all, if it can be made plausible that the first
principles and most fundamental aspects of reality in general are
divine, then the subject-matter of the Grandest Unified Theory is
God and everything else in relation to God. And in that case the
most illuminating systematic presentation of philosophy will be
theological—certainly not in the philosophically unacceptable
sense of starting from revealed propositions or relying on them to
settle arguments, but only in the sense that the part of philosophy
called natural theology will be treated as foundational rather than
peripheral.

In this book I'm going to engage in, and try to defend, the
metaphysics of theism, focusing on what I take to be its paradigm,
Thomas Aquinas's *Summa contra gentiles*. In the first three books
of that *Summa* Aquinas develops the project fully, right through
the consideration of human nature and behaviour in particular, so
that his metaphysics of theism extends to philosophy of mind and
ethics. I won't be able to go that far in this book, but I do mean to
work through the more familiar, logically prior, more obviously
metaphysical items on natural theology's agenda.[6]

3. Aquinas's work

It is often pointedly said of Aquinas that he was a theologian.[7] No
one-word characterization of him based on his work could be more
clearly right, as long as we recognize that being a theologian is not
always different from being a philosopher; that sometimes, however rarely, the designation 'theologian', like 'epistemologist', can

---

[6] And I hope to be able to work through the rest of Aquinas's natural theology in
two further volumes.
[7] See e.g. Jordan 1993.

simply pick out a philosopher with a particular interest or specialization. But I'll have to say more about this apparently trivial matter of terminology as I go along, because there's a widespread tradition of classifying Aquinas as a theologian primarily in order to deny that he wrote philosophy (except, perhaps, in his commentaries on Aristotle), and because the classification of his work really is complicated.

Aquinas lived an active, demanding academic and ecclesiastical life that ended before he turned 50 (1224/5–74); but he managed, none the less, to produce very many works, varying in length from a few pages to a few volumes, and covering in different ways all the topics in the vast range of subject-matter that was considered to be academic theology's domain in the thirteenth century. His writings are standardly sorted along the following lines. He wrote four theological syntheses, more than a dozen academic disputations (i.e. either 'disputed' questions or 'quodlibetal' questions), expositions of, or commentaries on, several books of the Old and New Testaments, commentaries on twelve of Aristotle's works, and four commentaries on works by other authors, along with many relatively short polemical writings, treatises on special subjects, expert opinions, letters, liturgical pieces, and sermons (see Appendix I).

Material relevant to my purposes in this book can be found almost anywhere in those varied writings of his. In order to explain my choice of Aquinas's *Summa contra gentiles* as the work to focus on, as the paradigm of the metaphysics of theism, I need to say something about its place in his own conceptions of theology and philosophy. Since the *Summa contra gentiles* is one of his four theological syntheses, and since those four systematic works present his attempts at a full-scale development of the Grandest Unified Theory, they are the only ones about which I want to say anything now.

The earliest of them, written during his late twenties, when he was a bachelor of theology at the University of Paris, is the *Scriptum super libros Sententiarum* (1253–6), an extended examination in standard scholastic form of doctrinal issues as they had been presented in Peter Lombard's *Sentences*, a twelfth-century compilation of opinions of Patristic and later authors on the articles of faith. Thirteenth-century bachelors of theology were expected to write (and deliver in lectures) *Scripta*, or commentaries, on the *Sentences*, and the standard organization of those assigned writings followed pretty closely the organization of the *Sentences* themselves. Consequently, Aquinas's *Scriptum*, the most youthful of his systematic works, is also the one that shows us less than any of the others do about his own, distinctive conceptions of how to approach, develop, organize, and present the topics of theology.[8]

In chronological order, the other systematic works are *Summa contra gentiles* (SCG) (1259–65),[9] *Compendium theologiae* (1265–7),[10] and *Summa theologiae* (ST) (1266–73).

Stylistically, the *Compendium* is like SCG, since it's written in ordinary prose divided into chapters, and unlike ST, which follows 'the scholastic method' based on the formal disputations of medieval university classrooms. Moreover, in composing the *Compendium*, Aquinas borrowed from SCG. But in being entirely a work of revealed theology, the *Compendium* is unlike SCG and like ST. Among Aquinas's four systematic works the *Compendium* is unique in the brevity of its discussions and in having been organized around considerations of the theological virtues of faith, hope, and charity. If it had been completed, it might have provided a novel reorientation of the vast subject-matter of medieval theology; but Aquinas wrote only ten short chapters of the second section, under the heading of 'Hope', and none at all of the third section, under 'Charity'. He did complete the first section, under 'Faith'; but since most of its 246 chapters simply provide briefer treatments of almost all the topics of theology that Aquinas had already dealt with in SCG, the *Compendium* as he left it seems important mainly as a précis of material that is developed more fully in SCG (and ST).[11]

4. *ST and* catholica veritas

ST is, of course, Aquinas's single greatest and most characteristic work. Like everyone else who examines Aquinas's thought, I have

---

[8] The *Scriptum* does, however, contain much valuable material that hasn't yet been studied as much as it should be, primarily because it was superseded in most respects by his great *Summa contra gentiles* and *Summa theologiae*.

[9] This most widely accepted dating for SCG has not gone unchallenged. For a concise, well-informed summary of the dispute, see Jordan 1986*b*: 174 n. 7.

[10] The *Compendium* was once thought to have been written much later and to have been left incomplete because of Aquinas's death, but its similarity to SCG in style and in content has lately led scholars to assign it to this earlier period (see e.g. Torrell 1993).

[11] Aquinas's enthusiasm for the new approach he takes in ST may well have been what led him to abandon work on the quite differently organized *Compendium*.

consulted it over and over again in writing this book, and I will often refer to it explicitly. Why, then, am I focusing not on ST but on the earlier SCG? I've already given a short, preliminary answer to this question: I'm interested in a fully developed natural theology, and among Aquinas's systematic works only SCG provides an instance of it—and not merely an instance but, as I've said, the paradigm. The *Scriptum*, ST, and the *Compendium* are all contributions to theology conceived of as specifically different from philosophy, as essentially including the articles of faith among its principles. We can see most clearly just what that means in ST, where Aquinas seems most expressly concerned with the relationship between theology and philosophy, especially in the discussions with which he introduces the work.

In Aquinas's Prologue to ST, the work is presented as an innovative introductory textbook written by an educational reformer in the medieval university's faculty of theology, one who describes himself as a teacher of *catholica veritas* and describes his book as intended 'to impart the things that pertain to the Christian religion in a manner suited to the teaching of beginners'—not rank beginners, of course, but graduates of the arts faculty who are beginning their training in theology, 'those who are new to *this* teaching'.[12] If we take the reasonable view that the teacher's subject is the same as his book's, then the *catholica veritas* Aquinas teaches is identifiable with 'the things that pertain to the Christian religion'. And since the title of ST identifies its subject in a third way as 'theology', we seem to have been provided at the outset with a complex, but unsurprising, identification of three terms: the subject of Christian theology = everything that pertains to the Christian religion = *catholica veritas*.

I've been retaining the Latin for the third term because of the ambiguity of the word 'catholic', which, of course, isn't always used in its ecclesiastical sense, especially in Latin, and especially before the Reformation. In view of the readily understandable other two terms, however, it may seem pointless to hesitate between 'universal' and 'Catholic' (with a big 'C'), especially because reading '*catholica veritas*' as '*universal* truth' looks like smuggling a lot of theory into the characterization of ST on the basis of a single

---

[12] For a different view of the beginners for whom Aquinas intended ST, see Boyle 1982.

ambiguous phrase in its very first sentence. But when we take into account Aquinas's own carefully stated understanding of '*catholica*', the theory-laden reading of *catholica veritas* turns out to be exactly right. In his commentary on Boethius's *De trinitate* (In BDT), which he wrote before ST, he explains that the Christian faith deserves to be called '*catholica vel universalis*' in respect of *both* sets of its 'subjects (*materiae*)'—those in which it occurs (the believers), and those with which it is concerned (its topics). First, it is intended to occur in all human beings, and so is *catholica*—that is, universal—as regards its potential believing subjects. Second, catholicity—or, as Aquinas says at this point, 'universality'—'is found in the Christian faith also in respect of the things believed', because they have to do with 'a person's whole life and everything pertaining to a human being in any way' (In BDT 3.3c). I take it that the *catholica veritas* identical with the subject of theology and 'the things that pertain to the Christian religion' is, therefore, truth that is universal also in that second respect, in that way mandating the awesome scope of ST and warranting theology's inclusion under the genus of Grandest Unified Theory.

In his Prologue, Aquinas presents ST as innovative, but not in respect of its scope. Presumably he takes for granted the universality of theology's subject-matter.[13] The most important pedagogical innovation of ST, as he sees it, is in its organization. He says he has noticed that students new to theology have been held back in their studies by several features of the standard teaching materials, but especially 'because the things they have to know are imparted not in an order appropriate to a method of teaching'—an order he proposes to introduce in ST—'but rather in keeping with what the exposition of books required, or what an occasion for disputation called for'. He prefaces his review of pedagogical shortcomings by remarking that 'these matters' pertaining to the Christian religion 'have been written about by various people', but the pedagogical shortcomings he picks out also characterize other theological works of his own.

---

[13] Aquinas himself does not include the subject-matter of natural philosophy (the medieval precursor of natural science) within the scope of theology in this broad conception; but he omits it primarily because it isn't strictly *required* for the work of theology. The *relevance* of non-human nature to theology emerges occasionally, none the less, most strikingly in his various cosmological arguments for the existence of God. See sect. 8 below.

In the theology faculty of a medieval university, an 'occasion for disputation' gave rise to two sorts of formal exchanges employing the scholastic method. Every 'regent master' (professor) in theology was obliged to conduct 'disputed questions', something like a cross between a twentieth-century graduate seminar and a public debate, detailed disputations on particular topics selected and arranged by the master conducting the disputation. In addition, a master might subject himself to 'quodlibetal questions', occasions on which he would try to provide considered replies to any and all questions proposed by members of the academic audience—occasions made available twice each academic year, during the penitential seasons of Advent and Lent. When he began writing ST, Aquinas had already produced several important sets of both sorts of questions—disputed questions on truth, on power, and on the soul, as well as five quodlibets—and nothing he says here suggests that he means to denigrate them or the practices that gave rise to them, except as inappropriate for the training of beginners in theology.

As for the books regularly subjected to exposition and commentary in the theology faculty, they were the Bible and the *Sentences*, and it's even more certain that Aquinas is not repudiating such work generally or his own contributions to it except, again, as introductions to theology. As we'll see, his only earlier theological work, large or small, that is not set aside pedagogically by these considerations of organization is SCG.

5. *ST and* sacra doctrina

At the end of his Prologue, Aquinas introduces a fourth term into his complex identity claim, when he says that in ST he is going 'to pursue the things that pertain to *sacra doctrina*', thereby introducing his *preferred* designation for the subject of theology as he handles it in ST. The term may be, and sometimes has been, translated literally as 'holy teaching', and it's only natural that the designation he prefers for the subject-matter of this textbook should allude to teaching. But what Aquinas means exactly by *sacra doctrina* has been the subject of many learned studies and disputes, partly because he himself devotes the ten Articles of ST's first Question to considering 'what it is like and what things it covers'

(Ia.1, intro.).[14] I think that its status as a controverted technical term in ST warrants my leaving it in Latin, and that my purposes here excuse me from getting deeply involved in the controversy, which often loses sight of the plain fact that when Aquinas introduces *sacra doctrina* in the Prologue, he does so in a way that identifies it explicitly with universal truth and the things that pertain to the Christian religion, and implicitly with the subject of theology.

The very first Article of ST's very first Question makes it clear at once that it is not natural theology that ST is a *summa* of, since the Article begins by asking whether we need any '*other* teaching, *besides* philosophical studies (*philosophicas disciplinas*)', the studies that medieval beginners in theology would have just completed in the university's arts faculty. The question arises because philosophical studies are characterized not only as dealing with 'the things that are subject to reason' (obj. 1) but also as encompassing 'all beings, including God', as a consequence of which 'part of philosophy is called theology' (obj. 2). Although Aquinas of course accepts this characterization of philosophy's subject-matter as universal and as including a part that is properly called theology, he offers several arguments to support his claim that his *sacra doctrina*, specifically different from philosophy, is none the less not superfluous.

One particularly pertinent argument among those he offers makes no essential use of any religious considerations. He begins this argument by claiming that a thing's 'capacity for being cognized in various ways (*diversa ratio cognoscibilis*) brings about a difference between sciences'. He means that different sciences can reason to some of the same conclusions on the basis of different premises or evidence. In his example, he points out that in order to support the proposition that the earth is round, a naturalist uses empirical observations (*per medium circa materiam consideratum*), while a cosmologist supports that same proposition on a strictly formal basis (*per medium mathematicum, idest a materia abstractum*). 'And for that reason', he concludes, 'nothing prevents the same things from being treated by philosophical studies in so far as they can be cognized by the light of natural reason and also

---

[14] See e.g. van Ackeren 1952, which contains a very full bibliography of relevant literature; also Jordan 1986a, which contains a valuable bibliography of more recent relevant items.

by another science in so far as they are cognized by the light of divine revelation. That's why the theology that pertains to *sacra doctrina* differs in kind from the theology that is considered a part of philosophy' (ad 2). From my point of view, he is arguing in this passage for the academic legitimacy of revealed theology alongside the established philosophical study, natural theology, and he is taking the practitioner of revealed theology, who is dependent on the data of revelation, to be analogous to the empirical scientist. For all he says in this argument, he might appear to be willing to concede that revealed and natural theology differ *only* in this methodological respect, that they simply constitute two radically different ways of approaching the very same propositions about God and everything else.

But, of course, he wouldn't concede that. There are propositions that belong uniquely to *sacra doctrina*'s subject-matter just because of its specific difference from philosophy as regards starting-points and because of what one can get from those starting-points. This is clear from the body of Article 1, Aquinas's affirmative reply to the question of whether there is a need for another sort of teaching in addition to philosophical studies. He identifies the need in a peculiarly persuasive form, claiming that for human well-being, especially for human salvation,[15] it is necessary 'that there be teaching based on and in accord with divine revelation, in addition to philosophical studies, which are explored by human reason' without those special data. And as if to emphasize *sacra doctrina*'s reliance on revealed propositions, the first reason Aquinas gives as to why human well-being could not be left in the charge of unaided human reason is itself derived from revelation: 'The human being is designed by God for a final purpose of a sort that is beyond reason's power of comprehension, according to Isaiah 64[: 4]: "without you, O God, no eye has seen what you have prepared for those who love you".[16] But the final purpose has to be made known at the outset to human beings, who must direct their intentions and actions toward

---

[15] The Latin behind this bit of my paraphrase is just *ad humanam salutem*. I think the *humana salus* at issue here is broader than salvation as it is understood within Christian doctrine, but I also think that Aquinas's point depends on stressing that religious sense of the phrase.

[16] The Latin text Aquinas provides is: *oculus non vidit Deus absque te, quae praeparasti diligentibus te*. For *diligentibus* the Vulgate has *expectantibus*, which makes no difference relevant to Aquinas's point. The Douay translates *absque te* as 'besides thee', which strikes me as obliterating his point.

it.' So some propositions of Christian doctrine—for instance, that God became man—cannot be initially acquired by reason, yet are required for human well-being. Those propositions, at least, must be revealed to human beings by the one who, according to revelation, designed them for a kind of well-being that surpasses their reason's comprehension. And, of course, no doctrinal proposition that is initially available to human beings only in virtue of having been revealed by God can be part of natural theology's subject-matter.

On the other hand, no propositions appropriate to natural theology are excluded from revealed theology: the propositions that belong to natural theology form a proper subset of those that belong to *sacra doctrina*. 'It was necessary that human beings be instructed by divine revelation even as regards the things about God that human reason can explore. For the truth about God investigated by a few on the basis of reason [without relying on revelation] would emerge for people [only] after a long time and tainted with many mistakes. And yet all human well-being, which has to do with God, depends on the cognition of that truth. Therefore, it was necessary for human beings to be instructed about divine matters through divine revelation so that [the nature of human] well-being might emerge for people more conveniently and with greater certainty' (Ia.1.1c). Several features of this argument are worth picking out for my purposes.

Notice, for instance, that we now have plainly in view a traditional, unmistakable description of the subject of theology: 'the truth about God'. And, as he says a little further on, 'the discussion carried on in this science is about God, for it is called "*theo-logia*", which means the same as "discourse about God". Therefore, God is the subject of this science' (Ia.1.7, sc). Concern with God or the truth about God might seem too narrow for the conception of theology as a species of Grandest Unified Theory, but only until we find out what Aquinas thinks that that truth includes, as we've already done to some extent in seeing what he means by *catholica veritas*. When he sums up his examination of *sacra doctrina*, he says that its 'main aim . . . is to transmit a cognition of God, and not only as he is in himself, but also as he is the source of [all] things, and their goal—especially of the rational creature' (Ia.2, intro.). And so the subject-matter of *sacra doctrina*, the theology presented in this *summa* of theology, is the truth about *everything*, with two provisos. First, it is about God and about everything other than God as everything other than God relates to God as its source and its goal. Second, it is about everything other than God as related to God in those ways, but especially about human beings, whose study of theology should be motivated by the claim about the special nature of their well-being. Theology is about God considered in himself and considered in the fundamentally explanatory source-and-goal relationships—the relationships of efficient and final causation—to everything else, especially to the rational creature.[17] And so the business of theology is the single ultimate explanation of everything, the Grandest Unified Theory.[18] And, Aquinas insists, universal scope is just what one should expect in a rational investigation of the truth about God: 'All things are considered in *sacra doctrina* under the concept of God, either because they *are* God, or because they have an ordered relationship *to* God as to their source and goal. It follows from this that the subject of this science is really God' (Ia.1.7c), even though the intended explanatory scope of the science is universal.

We have already seen Aquinas referring more than once to *sacra doctrina* as a 'science', by which he means a systematic, reasoned presentation of an organized body of knowledge consisting of general truths about some reasonably unified subject-matter. And yet his argument supporting the need for *sacra doctrina* really supports, at best, a need only for revealed truths themselves, not also for a science devoted to expounding those truths and extrapolating from them. I'm inclined to think that he takes our need for the science to grow out of our rational nature, which impels us to try to understand what we're confronted with. (We'll soon be seeing some evidence for this view.) I'm also inclined to think that he uses the term *sacra doctrina* easily and naturally for either of those referents, primarily for the content of revelation itself in the first Article of Question 1, thereafter usually for the science constructed on the basis of that content.[19]

In the broad, broadly Aristotelian sense in which Aquinas uses

[17] See also his consideration of the theologian's special concern with human behaviour in ST IaIIae.7.2: 'Are the circumstances of human acts an appropriate concern for a theologian?'

[18] It is this conception of theology that warrants Aquinas's description of its practitioner as one 'whom all the other arts diligently serve' (IaIIae.7.2, ad 3).

[19] For a review of the controversy over the univocity of *sacra doctrina*, see van Ackeren 1952: ch. 1, 'Interpretations of the Meaning of *Sacra Doctrina*'.

the word 'science', it isn't obviously wrong to think of theology as a science (as it would be in the narrower twentieth-century sense of 'science'). But, says an objector, an Aristotelian science 'proceeds on the basis of principles known *per se*', and since *sacra doctrina* is *revealed* theology, it 'proceeds on the basis of the articles of faith, which are *not* known *per se*, since not everybody grants them. . . . *Sacra doctrina*, therefore, is not a science' (Ia.1.2, obj. 1). Aquinas defends *sacra doctrina* against this denigration by providing for revealed theology the status of a *subordinate* science, one whose starting-points are simply accepted on the authority of someone who has mastered the corresponding primary science. And every earthly instance of a primary science does proceed, he thinks, on the basis of 'principles known by the natural light of intellect. . . . Thus, just as music takes on faith (*credit*) [its] principles, passed on to it by the arithmetician, so *sacra doctrina* takes on faith [its] principles, revealed for it by God' (Ia.1.2c). Music is a science subordinate to the primary science arithmetic, but the music theorist in doing her work does not draw directly from the Aristotelian science of arithmetic. Considered simply as a music theorist, she has no access to that science itself, and so depends not on *arithmetic* but rather on 'the *arithmetician*', who authoritatively supplies—that is, reveals—the ratios the music theorist needs in order to get started. Analogously, Aquinas suggests, the practitioner of *sacra doctrina* is dependent directly on God, the consummate authority regarding *scientia Dei et beatorum*, relative to which *sacra doctrina* is a subordinate science. *Scientia Dei et beatorum*— the *scientia* to which only God and those who see God face to face have access—obviously could not be some celestial version of an Aristotelian science considered as an enterprise proceeding demonstratively on the basis of principles known *per se*.[20] It must be, instead, God's perfectly complete and ideally unified knowledge (*scientia*) of himself and everything else, aspects of which have been selectively imparted to practitioners of *sacra doctrina* as the starting-points for their enterprise.

Having received these authoritative principles through divine

---

[20] Any rational investigation, any enterprise of developing or mastering a network of propositions proceeding on the basis of principles, would be impossible in heaven—whether for God, who has the relevant *scientia* necessarily, immediately, essentially, eternally, or for the blessed, considered as direct participants in the beatific vision.

revelation, a theologian can engage in the subordinate science that is *sacra doctrina*. The first achievement of that enterprise will be dogmatic theology, extracting from Scripture the articles of faith and giving them an ordered formulation, summarized in creeds—as a music theorist might collect and suitably reformulate and organize the authoritatively revealed mathematical truths essential to her theorizing.

A further achievement within *sacra doctrina* is philosophical theology, supposedly analogous to music theory.[21] But I think Aquinas's analogy would have broken down if he had tried to extend it that far explicitly. The enterprise of philosophical theology can't be accurately characterized as simply accepting the divinely revealed propositions in order to do something else with them, as music theory produces something specifically relevant to music on the basis of the non-musical propositions supplied for it by the arithmetician. Instead, philosophical theology is devoted to clarifying, supporting, and extending the very propositions that are supposed to have been revealed as starting-points for theology. It's as if all that was left of mathematics was the bit contained in a primer of music theory, and someone (who would certainly not be acting as a music theorist in that case) were to try, on that meagre basis, to gain some understanding of the mathematics in the primer and to reconstruct portions of mathematics itself. Such attempts at understanding and reconstructing would be more nearly analogous to the operations that characterize philosophical theology: attempting to explain revealed propositions, providing generally acceptable evidence for them, and systematically working out their implications. So dogmatic theology appears to fit Aquinas's analogy pretty well, and philosophical theology doesn't.[22] But Aquinas

---

[21] Methodologically, the development of this subordinate science resembles that of an ordinary primary science: 'Arguments (*rationes*) derived from [the writings of] the saints to prove things that belong to the faith are not demonstrative but are, rather, persuasive arguments that show that what is claimed in the faith is not impossible. Alternatively, [such arguments] proceed on the basis of the principles of the faith—i.e. authoritative passages of Holy Scripture (as Dionysius says in *De divinis nominibus* 2). But from the believers' point of view something is proved on the basis of those principles in just the way something is proved from everybody's point of view on the basis of principles that are naturally known. It is for that reason that theology, too, is a science, as was said at the beginning of this work' (IIaIIae.1.5, ad 2).

[22] In a later Article of his Question on *sacra doctrina* Aquinas describes its dependence in a way that may avoid the difficulty of the original analogy. *Sacra*

had already observed elsewhere, in a passage that helps to present the need for a science of theology as natural to us, that in this respect the nature of *sacra doctrina* is not that of an ordinary subordinate science: 'For us, however, the goal of faith is to arrive at an understanding of what we believe—[which is] as if a practitioner of a subordinate science were to acquire in addition the knowledge possessed by a practitioner of the higher science. In that case the things that were only believed before would come to be known, or understood' (In BDT 2.2, ad 7).

6. Sacra doctrina *and natural theology*

Where do these considerations leave natural theology? Natural theology must be based, ultimately or immediately, on 'principles known by the natural light of intellect'. The possibility of developing a metaphysics of theism, of beginning a systematic presentation of philosophy with natural theology, depends on that feature of it, which it has simply in virtue of being one of what Aquinas calls the 'philosophical studies'. If natural theology when developed as a philosophical study in its own right is thought of as a science, it clearly can't be a science subordinate to *scientia Dei et beatorum*, just because as a philosophical study it can't be dependent on revelation. Only (Aristotelian) metaphysics, which, as we'll see, Aquinas sometimes presents as the science of the most fundamental truth, could be the primary science to which natural theology might be considered subordinate. Everything we've seen so far— everything we'll see in the rest of this investigation—suggests that Aquinas would have had no difficulty accepting natural theology in that role.

But perhaps Aquinas's arguments designed to show the need for *sacra doctrina* leave the impression that, at least in his own view, a full development of natural theology should appear foolhardy. It

doctrina, he says, 'gets its starting-points not from other sciences, but directly from God through revelation' (Ia.1.5, ad 2). And since Aquinas maintains that God's knowledge, the *scientia Dei et beatorum* to which *sacra doctrina* is subordinate, has God's own essence as its immediate object (Ia.14.5c), it may seem more illuminating to think of the practitioner of *sacra doctrina* as analogous to a biographer who has been supplied with some of his subject's letters and diaries and is endeavouring to verify claims made in those documents and to construct on their basis an account as full and coherent as possible.

may seem that natural theology transcending its traditional role as the perfunctory culmination of metaphysics and developing as a subordinate science in its own right would have to be viewed by him as both dangerous and pointless. It looks dangerous because it leaves the indispensable account of the essentials of 'all human well-being' up to 'a few', whose work would take 'a long time' and even then be 'tainted with many mistakes'. And it seems pointless because revealed theology is supposed to provide, authoritatively and at once, all the propositions essential to human well-being that natural theology could ever hope to provide, and then some. Even if I'm right in claiming that Aquinas's own SCG consists mostly in a novel attempt at a full development of natural theology in its own right, it's certainly possible that by the time he began ST, a couple of years after finishing SCG, he had changed his mind about such a project.

SCG itself will provide the best evidence on which to assess Aquinas's attitude toward natural theology. But ST offers help, too, when, well into its Second Part, Aquinas makes clear that any such condemnations he might have offered of natural theology on its own would be pertinent to it primarily as it had been carried out in Greek antiquity. Drawing heavily on Augustine's account of ancient natural theology,[23] he alludes to unnamed ancient (Stoic) philosophers who reasoned their way to pantheism, and also to (neo-)Platonists who 'maintained that there is one highest god, the cause of all things', among which are lesser superhuman, spiritual beings, some of whom they also called gods. He says that such views have been classified as *physica theologia*. This physical theology, he says, was a theology 'that philosophers used to speculate about (*considerabant*) in connection with the world, and to teach in their schools'; and he contrasts these ancient philosophers' physical theology with two other old pagan theologies that had nothing to do with philosophy: the one underlying the state religion ('civil'), the other embedded in the work of the poets and dramatists ('mythical'). All three of these ancient theologies he repudiates as idolatrous superstition, although physical theology, at least, doesn't deserve repudiation in those terms (IIaIIae.94.1c).

---

[23] In *De civitate Dei* VI.5. See also the discussion of Augustine's sources in Webb 1915: 10–15.

Now it's worth noticing that the repudiated ancient physical theology does not include anything attributed or attributable to Aristotle.[24] The sort of theology with which Aristotle's metaphysics culminates (and which he argues for also in his physics) is of course carefully distinguished by Aquinas from revealed theology; but it is repudiated by him neither here nor anywhere else. Formally, he says, the subject of Aristotelian metaphysics is *ens commune*—being, considered as broadly as possible. But since 'a cognition of the causes of a genus is the goal to which a science's investigation is extended', and since the only cause that could conceivably be uncovered for *ens commune* would have to be God, it's quite all right to call Aristotelian metaphysics 'theology', Aquinas says (In Met. Prooemium).[25] I don't want to make too much of what is probably a terminological accident, but it's clear that the repudiated *physical* theology, which went too far on the basis of misguided speculation about the natural world, is not to be confused with the sober Aristotelian *metaphysical* theology that appears to Aquinas as the inevitable logical consequence of the thoroughgoing rational investigation of *ens commune*. So not even all ancient, pagan varieties of natural theology are to be repudiated, considered as enterprises undertaken before the Christian revelation. Those efforts of ancient philosophers to provide philosophical backing for theological propositions in the absence of any knowledge of what Aquinas considers to be divinely revealed theology, those efforts at physical or metaphysical natural theology, surely did take a long time—600 years, at least—and in Aquinas's view their results surely were tainted with many mistakes. But what about the project of natural theology in his own time and place?

In thirteenth-century Western Europe the availability of divinely revealed truths was acknowledged in academic as well as ecclesiastical life, and in the arts faculty of the university as well as in its theology faculty. By Aquinas's day the (ecclesiastical) academic authorities had overcome their initial misgivings and officially acknowledged that a respectful study of Aristotelian physics and

---

[24] 'D'ordinaire, saint Thomas ne nomme Aristote que pour s'appuyer sur lui: il est la grande autorité de la *Somme contre les Gentils*, puisqu'il y est ainsi invoqué plus de 400 fois, environ 10 fois plus souvent que saint Augustin!' (Gauthier 1961: 76).

[25] For a fuller discussion of metaphysical theology and its formal relationship with revealed theology, see In BDT 5.4; also Wippel 1993a: 117 n. 5.

metaphysics with its integrated minor component of natural theology was compatible with the universally acknowledged availability of revealed truths about God. But no philosopher in Aquinas's circumstances could justifiably undertake the project of natural theology *heuristically*, as ancient pagan philosophers had done in their physical theology. Although the old pagans had failed, in the total absence of revelation their attempt to uncover truths about God on the basis of observation and reasoning alone was justified, even commendable, as no such attempt could have been seen to be in the high Middle Ages. The unavoidable dangers that the practitioners of physical theology had faced and eventually succumbed to would have made the enterprise of heuristic natural theology obviously irrational for philosophers who believed in revelation.

However, no such irrationality would attach to natural theology taken up *expositionally*, with the aim of beginning a systematic presentation of the truth about God and about everything else in relation to God in a particularly perspicuous and logically natural order. Such an enterprise, well suited to the model of an Aristotelian science,[26] could not, of course, include any revealed propositions among its starting-points or appeal to divine revelation for support in the course of systematically presenting its all-inclusive subject-matter. But there was no reason why it shouldn't (and every reason why it should) use revealed propositions as guides to the selection and ordering of the elements of its systematic presentation (see Introduction, sect. 3). Its aim would be not to develop theology from scratch, but rather to show, in the spirit of Romans 1: 19–20, the extent to which what had been supernaturally revealed could, in theory, have been discovered—the extent to which the invisible things of God might be clearly seen, understood by the things that are made. Such an enterprise is what I think SCG represents.

---

[26] 'Aristotle does not pretend to be offering guidance to the scientist—or, for that matter, to the historian or the philosopher—on how best to pursue his researches or how most efficiently to uncover new truths. . . . Rather, it [Book A of the *Posterior Analytics*] is concerned with the organization and presentation of the results of research: its aim is to say how we may collect into an intelligible whole the scientist's various discoveries—how we may so arrange the facts that their interrelations, and in particular their explanations, may best be revealed and grasped. In short, the primary purpose of [Aristotelian] demonstration is to expound and render intelligible what is already discovered, not to discover what is still unknown' (Barnes 1975: pp. x–xi).

7. The purpose of SCG

But why would any philosopher-theologian in thirteenth-century Christendom undertake what could well have looked like a risky *tour de force* at best? As far as I know, Aquinas is the only one who tried it. If I'm right about SCG, why would Aquinas have bothered to write it?

There is a familiar, still widely accepted, but hardly believable, reply to that particular question about Aquinas.[27] An early fourteenth-century chronicle, written about seventy years after Aquinas began SCG and more than half a century after he died, claims that he wrote it in response to a request from a prominent fellow Dominican for 'a work against mistakes made by unbelievers, a work by which the gloom of darkness might be dispelled and the teaching of the true Sun made manifest to those who refuse [simply] to believe'.[28] And since thirteenth-century Dominicans were serving as missionaries to Jews and especially to Muslims in Spain and North Africa, most scholars have supposed, on the basis of this chronicle, that SCG was intended as a manual for their use. If that's so, then SCG's presentation of natural, instead of revealed, theology in its first three books was dictated by the practical purpose of communicating the truth about God and everything else to people who would not have acknowledged the revealed texts which Aquinas would otherwise have cited as the source of that truth. As he says very near the beginning of SCG, 'It is difficult to argue against mistaken views associated with particular people, . . . because some of them—Mohammedans and pagans, for instance—do

---

[27] On this traditional account see R.-A. Gauthier's thoroughly informed, magisterial analysis in Gauthier 1961: 69: 'en un mot, . . . la *Somme contre les Gentils* n'est en aucune façon un ouvrage missionnaire.' (Gauthier 1993, by far the best available historical study of SCG, is a thoroughly reworked, separately published version of Gauthier 1961.) See also Jordan's penetrating critical review of the tradition in Jordan 1986*b*.

[28] The text as reproduced in the Leonine edn. of SCG (and trans. here) reads: . . . *ut opus aliquod faceret contra infidelium errores, per quod et tenebrarum tolleretur caligo, et veri solis doctrina credere nolentibus panderetur* (*Sancti Thomae Aquinatis . . . Opera iussu impensaque Leonis XIII P. M. edita* (Rome: ex Typographia Polyglotta, 1918), vol. XIII, p. vi). The same passage as reproduced in the (later) Marietti edn. (Turin: Marietti, 1967; vol. I, pp. 73 and 613) has *volentibus* for *nolentibus*, but with no indication that it is correcting the text quoted in the Leonine. (Gauthier expressly corrects *nolentibus* to *volentibus*: Gauthier 1961: 61 n. 146.) Either reading makes sense, but *nolentibus* strikes me as preferable, and not merely as the *lectio difficilior*.

not agree with us about the authority of any scripture on the basis of which they can be refuted. . . . And so it is necessary to have recourse to natural reason, to which everybody is compelled to assent,[29] even though natural reason cannot do the whole job of dealing with divine matters'—that is, with God and everything else as related to God (I.2.10–11).[30] He takes natural reason to be a sufficient basis on which to do a very large part of the job—from establishing the existence of God through working out details of human morality—in Books I–III, the books that contain what I'm treating as the paradigm of a fully developed natural theology. The insufficiency of natural reason he mentions at the end of this passage accounts for SCG's Book IV, in which Aquinas, beginning again with God and working his way down through human beings, addresses in particular just those propositions to which reason would have no access without the revelation he accepts—propositions such as the doctrines of the Trinity, of the Incarnation, of the resurrection of the body. He does this, he says, with the aim of showing that even those propositions 'are *not opposed* to natural reason' (IV.1.3348).

When we look carefully at what Aquinas himself says about his purpose in writing this *summa*, I think it becomes clear that what he wrote had at least its formal cause not in any consideration of missionary activities but instead within his thoughts about the interrelation of philosophy and Christianity.[31] He begins SCG by writing about the role of a wise person, one of those 'who give

---

[29] This, then, is a misrepresentation of Aquinas's position: 'On his account, therefore, argument is possible with regard to *sacra doctrina*. We are, so he thinks, in no position to argue with someone who accepts nothing in the body of revealed truth. But we can argue with someone who accepts some of it' (Davies 1992: 14).

[30] My many references to SCG are in this form. Since the vast majority of them are to SCG I, the initial Roman numeral indicating the book is often omitted from the references. The two subsequent Arabic numerals indicate the chapter and then the section as numbered in the best available edition of the Latin text: *S. Thomae Aquinatis, Doctoris Angelici, Liber de Veritate Catholicae Fidei contra errores Infidelium seu 'Summa contra Gentiles'* (Textus Leoninus diligenter recognitus), ed. C. Pera, OP, with the assistance of P. Marc, OSB, and P. Caramello, OSB, in 3 vols. (Turin and Rome: Marietti, 1961–7). In this book all quotations from Aquinas in English are my translations, and those taken from SCG are based on this Marietti edn. Appendix II below provides a complete table of parallel references in SCG I for readers who want to consult the only readily available complete English translation, in which the sections of the chapters are differently numbered. The first volume of the 5-vol. complete translation (Pegis 1975) contains SCG I.

[31] See esp. Chenu 1950: 247–51.

things an appropriate order and direction and govern them well'
(I.1.2). Obviously, such a person has to be concerned with purposes
and causes, goals and sources, and so the wisest person will be 'one
whose attention is turned toward the universal goal, which is also
the universal source' (I.1.3). Therefore, the highest, most universal,
explanatory truth must be wisdom's concern. And so anyone aspiring to wisdom will attend to metaphysics, since, Aquinas reports,
Aristotle rightly identified metaphysics as 'the science of truth—
not of just any truth, but of the truth that is the origin of all truth,
the truth that pertains to the first principle of being for all things'
(I.1.5). But since it is the business of one and the same science 'to
pursue one of two contraries and to repel the other, . . . the role of
the wise person is to meditate on the truth, especially the truth
regarding the first principle, and to discuss it with others, but also
to fight against the falsity that is its contrary' (I.1.6). The truth
regarding the first principle is the truth about God, supposing
God exists. The explanatory truth associated here with metaphysics
is, as we've already seen, the truth associated also with theology.
And so Aquinas is speaking as both a philosopher and a theologian
when he describes himself as intending in SCG 'to take up the
role of a wise person, though that may exceed my powers', in
order 'to clarify, to the best of my ability, the truth that the Catholic
faith professes, by getting rid of mistakes that are contrary to it'
(I.2.9).[32]

We've seen that when Aquinas is introducing ST, a textbook, he
naturally discusses his role as a teacher of theology. On that model,
his introduction to SCG, developed over its first nine chapters and
focused on the author's undertaking to perform the office of a wise
person, offers no support for the view that he conceives of it as a
manual for missionaries.

Neither is it a book he would recommend for beginners in theology. While SCG's topical organization is very broadly the same
as the one he advocates in ST for that pedagogical purpose, it is
crucially different in its details. To take just the first significant
difference of that sort, in ST the treatment of the doctrine of the
Trinity comes early in its First Part, immediately after the presentation of the divine attributes that are supposed to be accessible to

---

[32] '. . . ce que saint Thomas se propose en écrivant la *Somme contre les Gentils*,
c'est tout simplement de faire son métier de sage' (Gauthier 1961: 88).

natural reason. The plan of SCG, on the other hand, requires postponing all trinitarian discussions to Book IV. It obviously does make good pedagogical sense for a beginner in theology to take up all the knowable aspects of God's nature at the beginning of his study; but no aspect of God's nature that is knowable initially only via revelation could form part of natural theology.

What's more, the chapters of SCG—366 of them in the first three books alone—often consist almost entirely of arguments, one right after another—at least as many per page, I think, as in any of Aquinas's disputed questions. But in his Prologue to ST he cites the proliferation of arguments as another feature of thirteenth-century theology that renders most of its standard literature unsuitable for beginners. So for this reason, too, he would not recommend SCG as a textbook of theology.

But that very feature of SCG may seem to dispel any mystery there might have been about its purpose. This flurry-of-arguments approach, which Aquinas repudiates and carefully avoids in ST, seems to mark SCG as occupying one of the oldest niches in Christian theological literature: apologetics. And, by way of confirmation, in the historical section of the 'Apologetics' article in the *New Catholic Encyclopedia* the twenty-one lines devoted to the 'Medieval Period' do indeed start with these sentences: 'In the *Summa contra gentiles* Aquinas began with principles that he knew his opponents would acknowledge, the principles of Aristotelian philosophy. In the light of these mutually acknowledged principles Aquinas sought to answer objections to the faith' (Cahill 1967).[33] Aquinas is the only author and SCG the only book mentioned in that *Encyclopedia* article's tiny subsection on apologetics in the Middle Ages, and if what is said about it in those two sentences were correct, I suppose it would be satisfactorily classified as a medieval paradigm of apologetics. But at least the second sentence is mistaken. Neither Aquinas's professed aim nor his actual practice in the first three books of SCG is accurately described by saying

---

[33] Thomas Hibbs devotes the well-informed appendix ('Apologetics and the *Summa Contra Gentiles*') of Hibbs 1995 to considering and rejecting this characterization of SCG. I had written this book before Hibbs 1995 became available to me. It exhibits a wide acquaintance with relevant literature, but Hibbs's quite different approach yields an interpretation dramatically different from mine, as may be seen from these characteristic remarks: 'As we have seen, the understanding of the first three books as philosophy is violent and unfounded' (p. 181); 'Of course the believer is not a philosopher' (p. 184).

that he 'sought to answer objections to the faith'.[34] What he promises, it seems to me, is just what he delivers. And here's what he promises:

We will aim first [in Books I–III] at the clarification of the truth that faith professes and reason investigates, bringing in both demonstrative and probable arguments, some of which we have gathered from the books of the philosophers and of the saints—arguments on the basis of which the truth will be confirmed and its adversary overcome. Next, in order to proceed from things that are clearer to those that are less clear, we will move on [in Book IV] to the clarification of the truth that surpasses reason, dismantling the arguments of its adversaries, and elucidating the truth of faith by means of probable and authoritative arguments, as far as God grants it. (I.9.55–6)

Apologetics conceived of as answering objections to the faith is a reactive enterprise. But Aquinas's enterprise in SCG, even in its fourth book, is an activity he is initiating. His agenda is influenced far less by objections to Christian doctrine that have come his way than by revealed propositions, and he often ends a chapter in Books I–III by appending to the series of arguments a short paragraph or two designed, as he promises in his introduction, to show 'how the demonstrative truth is in harmony with the faith of the Christian religion' (I.2.12) (see Introduction, sect. 3). But his distinctive, primary aim in the first three books is the systematic presentation of that 'demonstrative truth', the argumentative clarification and confirmation of this 'truth that faith professes and reason investigates', relying only on reason's investigation of it, and sometimes approaching these tasks indirectly via the dismantling of arguments intended to support this truth's contrary.

8. The pedagogical motivation for SCG

Still, what motivates him to pursue that aim? Can we find him telling us SCG's practical purpose as plainly as he does ST's? I

---

[34] In fact, Aquinas explicitly disavows any intention of arguing 'against mistaken views associated with particular people (*Contra singulorum . . . errores*)', explaining that their *sacrilega* aren't so well known to him that he can extract from their mistaken views the arguments with which to refute them, and contrasting his situation in this regard with that of the Church Fathers (*antiqui doctores*), to whom such details were accessible 'because they themselves had been non-Christians (*gentiles*) or at least lived among them and were very familiar with their teachings' (I.2.10).

think so, although the clearest passages of this sort occur not in the first nine chapters of Book I, which introduce SCG generally, but in his introduction to Book II, where he shows plainly that the practical purpose of SCG also is pedagogical. The revealed theology which ST presents can be taught only to Christians, who will accept its doctrinal principles. What SCG teaches is theism. In Book IV, of course, this turns out to be Christian theism; but there is nothing distinctively Christian about it in Books I–III. SCG's overall subject-matter is identified not as *sacra doctrina*, but rather as *doctrina* (or *instructio*) *fidei Christianae* (e.g. II.2.863; 4.871), the appropriate audience for which is *non*-Christian. And, given SCG's highly argumentative, philosophically sophisticated presentation of *doctrina fidei*, its appropriate audience is made up of intelligent, educated non-Christians. A person who engages in teaching Christian theism in the style of SCG argues just as a philosopher ordinarily does, except, Aquinas says, that a philosopher presenting his view regarding created things of some sort 'draws his argument from the proper [immediate, natural] causes of the things', while the practitioner of *doctrina fidei* 'draws his argument [regarding the same things] from the *first* cause' (II.4.873), since he 'considers only those aspects of created things that are associated with them in so far as they are traced back to God' (872). On the basis of that description of this teacher's work, Aquinas shows that it's the very sort of work he envisaged for himself at the beginning of SCG, when he portrayed himself as essaying the role of a wise person. He points out that because the argumentation employed in this teaching of Christian theism is oriented as it is, 'it must be called the greatest wisdom, as considering the absolutely highest cause' (874).

Since what I've been calling philosophy generally and natural theology particularly seems to be what Aquinas in these passages calls teaching Christianity, I have some explaining to do. But not much. In saying what he says here, he is naturally thinking of SCG as a whole. But what he does in SCG can't count as teaching Christianity specifically without taking Book IV into account, and my characterization is meant to apply only to what he does in the first three books. It's true that the first three books can be described as teaching generic theism, constantly narrowing and refining the genus by further argumentation, and that may seem odd enough as a characterization of anything that could properly be called philosophy. But this superficial oddity in the notion of the metaphysics of theism can hardly come as a surprise. It is, after all, a presentation of philosophy differentiated from others by its beginning with arguments for the existence and nature of God.

The philosophical status of SCG I–III seems to be called into question more pointedly, however, when Aquinas carefully distinguishes in these same passages between *doctrina fidei* and philosophy, which in this context he sometimes calls *philosophia humana*. But just because the passages occur in his introduction to Book II, where he starts his systematic consideration of created things, the philosophy with which he is contrasting his approach in SCG is mainly natural philosophy (or what we would call natural science), as is clear from his examples. They focus on different accounts of fire that might be given by a (natural) philosopher and a practitioner of *doctrina fidei*, and the aim of those passages is to explain that it is no shortcoming in *doctrina fidei* that it does not provide detailed, systematic accounts of astronomy and mechanics (II.4.871–2). Contrasts of that sort don't at all set *doctrina fidei* apart from philosophy as twentieth-century philosophers conceive of philosophy.

The last of the contrasts Aquinas draws between them might, however, appear to go directly against what I've been saying about the metaphysics of theism: 'the two kinds of teaching do not proceed in the same order', he says. 'For in teaching philosophy (*doctrina philosophiae*), which first considers created things in their own right and leads on from them to a cognition of God, the consideration of created things is first, and the consideration of God is last. On the other hand, in teaching the faith (*doctrina fidei*), which considers created things only in their systematic relationship to God, the consideration of God comes first, the consideration of created things afterwards. And so it is more perfect, as being more like God's cognition, who observes [all] other things in cognizing himself' (II.4.876).[35] As I've been saying, I conceive of the metaphysics of theism as a particular systematic, argumentative exposition of philosophy. And, of course, such an exposition is just what 'teaching philosophy' amounts to—or might amount to, if we teachers of philosophy were more ambitious and our students had no other courses to take. But Aquinas here identifies the teaching of philosophy a little more precisely by specifying its standard

---

[35] For an account of God's apparently introspective cognition of everything else, see Stump and Kretzmann 1995.

format: philosophy from the bottom up. What I'm calling the meta-physics of theism, or philosophy from the top down, he identifies as *doctrina fidei*: 'sometimes divine wisdom proceeds from human philosophy's starting-points' (II.4.875).

I've already pointed out that my leaving SCG's Book IV out of account reduces that identification from teaching the faith to teaching an increasingly specified theism. Philosophy from the top down teaches theism but nevertheless counts as philosophical, because the starting-points and ultimate justifications of its arguments are all accessible to 'natural reason', and because it never uses revealed propositions as more than occasional guides to its agenda. Since Aquinas does this work at great length before taking up distinctively Christian doctrines in Book IV, it might look as if he must have considered it to be the most efficacious *introduction* to teaching Christianity to educated Muslims who, unlike heretics or Jews, share no acknowledged revelation with orthodox Christians. And, indeed, the topics covered in the natural theology of SCG I–III, all accessible to natural reason, are those he characterizes elsewhere as 'the *preambles* to the articles of faith' (ST Ia.2.2, ad 1). But nobody, and certainly not Aquinas, could suppose that Muslims needed to be argued into perfect-being theism of the sort developed in those first three books. As far as I know, they contain nothing contrary to Islam.[36] If Aquinas had intended SCG as a manual for missionaries to educated Muslims, Jews, or Christian heretics, he would have wasted the enormous effort represented in the 366 chapters of Books I–III.[37] For the practical purposes of proselytizing, he should have undertaken no more than the contents of Book IV. The appropriate audience for the teaching attempted in all the arguments of all those chapters in the first three books would be made up of intelligent, educated *atheists*, and I don't believe Aquinas ever met an avowed atheist.

[36] My views on Islamic doctrine are pretty ill-informed, and I would welcome correction on this point. But the explicit plan of SCG I–III and IV is such that if anything in I–III should turn out to be contrary to Islam itself, its occurrence there would, I think, surprise Aquinas, too. He does, however, argue against philosophical theses maintained by Islamic philosopher-theologians—e.g. in I.63–71.

[37] In commenting on this claim in 1994 Anthony Kenny offered me an interesting alternative: 'I don't think Books I–III are wasted even if the whole thing is meant for Jews and Muslims. They can be regarded as a softening-up exercise, designed to show how much the great monotheistic religions have in common. "You're with me so far? Now let me show you the little extra step you have to take in order to be saved." '

So, if my observations about SCG I–III are on the right track, it does seem to have been a risky *tour de force* for Aquinas, rather than the sober, eminently practical device it is standardly said to be. SCG I–III is his most unified, systematic contribution to the project of arriving at an understanding of what theists believe, of showing the extent to which what had been revealed might have been discovered, the extent to which the invisible things of God might be clearly seen, understood by the things that are made. But if SCG I–III had no discernible practical purpose when it was written, it may have acquired one since. Unlike Aquinas, I do know lots of intelligent, educated, avowed atheists.

9. Summa philosophica

No one knows what title, if any, Aquinas gave to SCG. In some of the medieval manuscripts it is entitled *Liber de veritate catholicae fidei contra errores infidelium*—'A Book About the Truth of the Catholic Faith, Directed Against Mistakes Made by Unbelievers'. That title strikes me as coming closer to an accurate representation of the book's aim and contents than the more pugnacious, traditional *Summa contra gentiles*—'*Summa* Against Pagans',[38] which became the accepted title perhaps in part because of the widespread perception of the book as a contribution to apologetics. During the nineteenth century, when ST was standardly called not *Summa theologiae*, the *summa* of theology, but *Summa theologica*, the theological *summa*, SCG was printed several times under the deliberately contrasting title *Summa philosophica*, the philosophical *summa*.[39] For reasons I've offered in this chapter, I think that this contrast, although potentially a little misleading, is broadly accurate,[40] as may be seen in Aquinas's plan for Books I–III of SCG: 'Since *we intend to pursue by way of reason the things about*

---

[38] On the authenticity and interpretation of these titles, see Gauthier 1961: 74–5.

[39] See Pera, 'Introductio' to the Marietti edn. of SCG, vol. I, p. 535 n. 2.

[40] For a sharply contrasting view see Gauthier 1961: 'la suprenante erreur de ceux qui ont voulu faire de la *Somme contre les Gentils* une "*Somme de philosophie*". Elle est, elle aussi, une *Somme de théologie*' (p. 90). 'Summa *of philosophy*' certainly would be misleading, and Gauthier offers no actual example of its use, although he does cite instances of '*Summa philosophica*' (p. 90 n. 252). See also Jordan 1993: 248 n. 3, where the designation *Summa philosophica* is provided as the paradigm case of 'gross re-titlings of his works'.

God that human reason can investigate, the first consideration is of matters associated with God considered in himself [Book I]; second, of the emergence of created things from him [Book II]; third, of the ordering and directing of created things toward him as their goal [Book III]' (I.9.57). And that is what I have been thinking of as the form of the metaphysics of theism.

Just as Aquinas is a philosophical theologian, so is he a theological philosopher. When he is writing as a philosopher in SCG, not merely as a philosophical commentator and certainly not as a philosophical theologian (in the technical sense identified above), he must and cheerfully does shun 'authoritative arguments' of any sort in Books I–III, although of course he must make use of them in Book IV. His tolerance of them there along with 'probable arguments' is just what distinguishes that book from its three predecessors.

As for the arguments he considers appropriate to what I'm calling philosophy from the top down, he shows good sense in not restricting himself to proofs, or 'demonstrative arguments'. They are the sort he will of course use when he thinks he has them, but, like almost all philosophers of any period, he recognizes philosophy's need for 'probable aguments' as well, citing Aristotle as having 'said very well that it is a mark of an educated person to try to get only as much conviction about anything as the nature of the thing permits',[41] and noting that Boethius endorsed this view[42] (I.3.13). A demonstrative argument can take as its premises only propositions that are, or can be, unconditionally, objectively known, and so it yields a conclusion with that same impeccable epistemic status. A probable argument—the sort that has always been most prevalent in philosophy—is one based on premises that are in fact widely accepted, or accepted by experts in the relevant field, and so it's possible for one group to be convinced by a probable argument that another group rejects. Consequently, while demonstrative arguments lead to genuine knowledge, probable arguments can at best produce more or less good reasons for accepting their conclusions.[43]

We've seen that Aquinas presents himself as pursuing wisdom in undertaking SCG. So it seems fitting to close this chapter in which

---

[41] *Nicomachean Ethics* I 1, 1094b23–5.   [42] *De trinitate* 2 (PL 64.1250A).
[43] See e.g. Aquinas's In PA, Prooemium, and SCG I.8.71 *bis*.

I hope to have encouraged the reader to join me in examining what he does in SCG by quoting his own appraisal of this undertaking: 'Among all human pursuits, the pursuit of wisdom is the most excellent, the loftiest, the most beneficial, and the pleasantest' (I.2.8).

TWO

THE GOD OF THE
SELF-MOVERS

1. The place of existence arguments in natural theology

Traditionally, the first item on natural theology's agenda is providing philosophically acceptable evidence in support of the proposition that God exists. For anyone willing to take natural theology seriously, that's a dispiriting prospect. Philosophers have for centuries been raising objections to every known argument for God's existence—a state of affairs that could, by itself, account for natural theology's decline. In such circumstances, can this project get started at all? Obviously it would have to be aborted if there were an airtight proof that God does *not* exist, but there isn't. The argument from evil is indisputably the most plausible candidate for that role, and it has, especially recently, given rise to rejoinders as numerous and at least as powerful as the many versions of the argument. It warrants all the attention it gets, but I think that the amount of attention it's been getting lately excuses me from devoting any time to its consideration here.[1] So, as I see it, starting natural theology is not impossible, just very hard.

While philosophers were finding fault with putative proofs of God's existence, they were, of course, also discovering comparable difficulties in producing proofs of the existence of other minds, for example, or of the reliability of sense-perception.[2] But no philosopher I know of has been dissuaded by such discoveries from undertaking a philosophy of mind or a theory of cognition. That familiar state of affairs has helped to show philosophers that what Aquinas would call 'probable' (rather than 'demonstrative') argumentation

[1] For important contributions to this literature see e.g. Stump 1985; Adams and Adams 1991; Peterson 1992; Howard-Snyder 1995.

[2] For a sophisticated and sensible appraisal of the status of arguments for the existence of God, see Ross 1969: esp. ch. 1, 'Arguments and Proof in Philosophical Theology'.

must be the norm in philosophy, which includes natural theology. It also helps to account for some recent attempts to show that no philosopher who in those circumstances goes on acknowledging the existence of other minds or the reliability of sense-perception can offer any principled objection to theism based on the state of the evidence for it.[3] But while no sane person can in practice sustain agnosticism regarding consciousness in fellow human beings or regarding the existence of the objects we apparently perceive, very many sane, bright people find no such practical difficulty in setting aside or rejecting the hypothesis that God exists. So even the rare philosopher who thinks that the inconclusiveness of the evidence for God's existence is on a par with the inconclusiveness of the evidence for the existence of physical objects and other persons might reasonably think herself practically justified in believing in bodies and minds other than her own while not believing in God. And *that* familiar state of affairs has helped to motivate the recent upsurge of anti-evidentialism in the epistemology of religious belief, most conspicuously expressed in the thesis of Reformed epistemology that 'it is entirely right, rational, reasonable, and proper to believe in God without any evidence or argument at all' (Plantinga 1983: 17; see also Introduction, sect. 4).

Unlike Reformed epistemologists, I'm not an anti-evidentialist. On the contrary, I think it's obvious that rational theism requires one to provide philosophically good evidence on the basis of which one can rationally believe that God exists. And philosophically good evidence typically comes in the form of arguments, though not in the form of airtight proofs.

2. How Aquinas sets the stage for natural theology in SCG

Aquinas himself adopts an especially stringent evidentialism when, in the concluding sentences of his introductory chapters, he lays down the following pre-condition of his philosophical investigation in Books I–III of SCG: 'among the things that have to be considered regarding God in himself [the business of Book I] there must be set out in advance—as, so to speak, the necessary foundation of the whole undertaking—a consideration by which it is demon-

---

[3] See e.g. Plantinga 1967; also Alston 1991.

strated that God exists. If that is not achieved, all consideration of matters having to do with God (*de rebus divinis*) is nullified' (9.58).

But this is *too* stringent. Aquinas here is following Aristotle's line regarding the need to establish the existence of the subject of a particular science (organized body of knowledge) before undertaking the development of that science.[4] And the science he has in view here is, of course, only natural, and not also revealed theology.[5] But establishing God's existence is clearly not logically prior to '*all* consideration of matters having to do with God'. If it were, the classical argument from evil could be thrown out on a technicality, since it depends on understanding that any being that could count as God would have to be omnipotent, omniscient, and perfectly good. What's more, any 'consideration by which it is demonstrated that God exists' must, similarly, presuppose an understanding of what could count as God, arrived at on the basis of some 'consideration of matters having to do with God'. I think we'll see that in Aquinas's own systematic natural theology acceptance of 'God exists' isn't really an all-or-nothing propositional attitude that depends solely on some argument or arguments offered at the outset. 'The necessary foundation of the whole undertaking' does have to include evidence of God's existence strong enough to make that proposition attractive as a working hypothesis, to make it intellectually worth one's while to engage in a philosophical investigation of 'God considered in himself'. But one's *acceptance* of the proposition 'God exists' can and should be allowed to develop on the basis of progress made in that whole undertaking.

On the way to arguing (in chapter 13) that God exists, Aquinas presents and rejects two quite different positions that are implicitly or explicitly in opposition to arguing for the existence of God as he proposes to do. In presenting and rejecting them (in chapters 10–12), he provides us with a clearer view of the sort of evidence he's committing himself to provide.

In the first place, he says (10.59–60), some of his predecessors

---

[4] See *Posterior Analytics* I 1, 71a1–b8; also Aquinas's commentary: In PA I: L2.14, 15, 18.

[5] For that reason an acceptable argument for the existence of God is essential to SCG as it isn't to ST, an introductory textbook of revealed theology. Theoretically, the inclusion of the famous Five Ways near the beginning of ST should constitute a digression from the project Aquinas is undertaking there.

and contemporaries reject out of hand the project of demonstrating God's existence just because the unimpeachable certainty attaching to the proposition 'God exists' puts it at the level of propositions used as first principles of Aristotelian demonstrations, on a par with 'Every whole is greater than any one of its parts'. A proposition of that sort is 'known *per se*', recognized to be true as soon as its terms are fully understood; and its contradictory or contrary is inconceivable. Such a first principle, far from needing to be demonstrated, simply cannot be demonstrated, because there is no more fundamental proposition from which to derive it.

Two of Aquinas's five illustrations of this radical position regarding 'God exists' are the two ontological arguments from Anselm's *Proslogion*. That's odd, because, of course, Anselm is there *arguing* for 'God exists', and so may seem *not* to be taking it as known *per se*.[6] In fact, Aquinas recognizes Anselm's arguments as arguments, and provides particular objections to both of them. His reason for taking them as illustrations of this position emerges in his general account of the trouble with any approach that takes knowledge of God's existence to be derivable from putatively *per se* knowledge of God's nature. He thinks that such an approach assumes a level of understanding that is theoretically unattainable by philosophers or theologians—a level at which it *would* be clear *per se* to natural reason precisely how God's nature entails, or simply is, God's existence. People attracted by such arguments, he says, 'do not distinguish between what is known *per se* considered on its own (*simpliciter*) and what is known *per se* as far as we are concerned (*quoad nos*). Of course, that God exists is known *per se* considered on its own, since the very thing that God is *is* his existence.[7] But

---

[6] Of course, a proposition may be self-evidently true and thus known (or knowable) *per se* even though not as far as we are concerned (*quoad nos*)—e.g. 'Goldbach's conjecture', the proposition that every even number larger than 2 is the sum of two prime numbers, which has until now been massively confirmed but neither proved nor shown to be undecidable. And although all arithmetical truths are knowable *per se*, many even mildly complicated propositions of that sort are not known *per se* at least as far as many of us are concerned, at least initially—e.g. 9,077/16 = 567.3125. Of course, in many such cases demonstrating the proposition's self-evident truth is something we can and should do. Might Anselm have been taking 'God exists' to be a proposition of that sort? In any event, Aquinas appears to be taking 'known *per se*' as equivalent to 'indemonstrable', which raises the possibility that he may be making only a technical point, tacitly acknowledging the possibility of a priori expository arguments for propositions known *per se*.

[7] In this sentence Aquinas takes for granted the very difficult proposition that 'the very thing that God is *is* his existence', but only for the sake of relevantly

because our minds cannot conceive of the very thing that God is, [his existence] remains unknown [*per se*] as far as we are concerned' (11.66).

Now this general indictment, too, may seem to miss Anselm by a mile. After all, the Anselmian formula identifying God as 'that than which nothing greater can be conceived of'—the formula on which the ontological arguments depend—is especially ingenious just because it seems to obviate any need to have a detailed conception of the very thing that God is in order to argue that God exists.[8] However, a careful analysis of those arguments of Anselm's, and especially of the more formidable modal version in *Proslogion* 3, shows that Aquinas is right to find this difficulty even in those arguments. In assessing them, the crucial question turns out to be whether the conception of God in the Anselmian formula is internally consistent, and that question can't be answered definitively if we cannot penetrate beneath the formula to assess all the details of that conception, if we 'cannot conceive of the very thing that God is'.[9]

But whatever we may think of Anselm's arguments or of Aquinas's treatment of them, the view that God's existence is known *per se* to human beings is bound to strike us, at the end of the twentieth century, as a most unlikely basis for objecting to Aquinas's procedure in SCG. Nobody *we* know is going to object to natural theology on *those* grounds. The second position Aquinas repudiates is one we're more likely to come across. 'Other people',

invoking the distinction between propositions known *per se* considered on their own and propositions known *per se* as far as we are concerned. He will provide reasons for considering that proposition to be true (see Ch. Four), but at this point he's not even proposing it. It will not become part of his natural theology until he has argued for it, just because he (very plausibly) maintains that it can't be known *per se* as far as we are concerned.

[8] It seems that the Anselmian formula's way of avoiding commitment to a detailed conception should have had special appeal for Aquinas, who maintains a little further on in SCG I that 'the divine substance is beyond every form our intellect acquires, and so we cannot apprehend it itself by discerning what it is' (14.117). Furthermore, the eliminative method he adopts when he begins his investigation of God's nature would seem to countenance the formula. (These moves on Aquinas's part are discussed in their own right in Ch. Three.)

[9] For an astute analysis and appraisal of Aquinas's criticism of the ontological arguments, see Matthews 1963. Matthews shows that Aquinas's treatment of the arguments in SCG is more effective than the better-known one in ST. For some explanation of the apparent vagueness of Aquinas's treatment of Anselm's arguments, see Davies 1992: 24 n. 17.

he says, 'have a view contrary to the position we have just been discussing, a view on the basis of which the effort of those who set out to prove that God exists would also be rendered useless. For these people say that God's existence cannot be discovered through reason, that it has, instead, been accepted by way of faith and revelation alone' (12.72).[10]

We in our day find that those who raise this objection to natural theology are motivated in one of two ways (and so did Aquinas in the thirteenth century). There are of course theists who are principled anti-intellectuals—those who would reject the very idea of natural theology as sacrilegious. The Christians among them sometimes share Tertullian's view—'After Christ Jesus, we have no need of curiosity; after the Gospel, no need of inquiry'[11]—taking their cue, perhaps, from St Paul's warning against being made foolish by philosophy (Colossians 2: 8). But, as Aquinas observes, there are others who 'have been moved to say this because of the weakness of the arguments that some people have presented to prove that God exists' (12.73). And these others, or at least their twentieth-century intellectual descendants, will, of course, include many who *deny* the proposition that God exists while *disdainfully* relegating it to unquestioning acceptance by way of faith alone.

In Aquinas's general rejoinder to this objection, the Christian anti-intellectuals who shun his approach are reminded of what they are religiously bound to consider as 'the truth in the Apostle's saying in Romans 1[: 20] that the invisible things of God are clearly seen, having been understood through things that were made' (12.77). Proceeding along the lines of that Pauline observation in support of natural theology turns out also to be perfectly suited to the development of an Aristotelian science as Aquinas conceives of it. It depends for its starting-points on sense-perception,[12] but 'teaches us how to draw conclusions about causes on the basis of their effects' (12.77). Thus, 'even though God transcends all sense-perceptible things and sense-perception, his effects, from which one draws a demonstration to prove that God exists, are sense-perceptible' (12.80).[13] And so, as SCG's very many chapters on

[10] The statement of this position is implausibly weak. It seems that 'must . . . be accepted' (*est accipiendum*) ought to replace 'has . . . been accepted' (*est acceptum*).
[11] *De praescriptione haereticorum* vii 12. See Kretzmann 1990.
[12] See *Posterior Analytics* I 18, 81b2–9.
[13] Here again it may seem that Aquinas is helping himself to an assumption he has no right to make. But these claims about God's transcendence of sense-perceptible

'God considered in himself' attest, Aquinas clearly does think that we are capable of reliably inferring a great deal about the nature and existence of God, that God's existence need not be '*accepted by way of faith and revelation alone*', but can also be 'discovered through reason'.

What Aquinas leads us to expect in chapter 13, then, is an a posteriori demonstration of God's existence in which he will argue that sense-perceptible things, events, or states of affairs cannot be satisfactorily explained otherwise than on the basis of the existence of a being that is plausibly identifiable as God.[14]

3. The arguments for God's existence in SCG I.13

What he actually provides there are five arguments presumably intended to fill that bill, introducing them in this way: 'having shown that it is not pointless to try to demonstrate that God exists, let us proceed to put forward arguments by means of which philosophers as well as Catholic teachers have proved that God exists' (13.81). The first four arguments are ascribed to Aristotle, the fifth to John Damascene and Averroës.

The fact that there are five arguments here is likely to make people think of Aquinas's much better-known cluster of a posteriori arguments for the existence of God, the Five Ways of ST Ia.2.3; and a comparison of the two groups is instructive. The Five Ways are based on considerations of various aspects of sense-perceptible reality: first, motion; second, efficient causality; third, contingency and necessity; fourth, degrees of perfection; fifth, purpose and directedness. The fourth and fifth SCG arguments clearly parallel ST's Fourth and Fifth Ways, and the third SCG argument parallels the Second Way. In none of those three pairings is the SCG member of the pair fuller than, or superior in any other respect to, its ST counterpart, and for present purposes I have no more to say about them.

things of which God is the cause are introduced here as part of Aquinas's development of Rom. 1: 20 only in answer to a religious objection to his project, not as part of his natural theology. His a posteriori arguments for God's existence will certainly not be taking it for granted that God causes sense-perceptible things or that he transcends them.

[14] On demonstrations of this sort as constituents of a science of theology, see MacDonald 1993: 176–8.

The situation is very different as regards the first two arguments in SCG's chapter 13. I'll label them G1 and G2. They are very nearly equally long, and each of them, with its supporting arguments, is more than ten times longer than any of the last three SCG arguments.[15] Aquinas introduces G1 and G2 as a thematically linked pair: 'But first we will present arguments by means of which Aristotle sets about proving that God exists. He undertakes to prove it on the basis of motion, in two ways' (13.82).

As for Aquinas's attributing G1 and G2 to Aristotle, it's certainly true that the appropriate passages in Aristotle's *Physics* and *Metaphysics* prefigure these arguments to varying degrees, sometimes in detail. But Aquinas's reworking and endorsing of them as arguments for the existence of God make him directly responsible for G1 and G2, and I'll treat them as *his* arguments without feeling obliged to comment on their Aristotelian background.[16] I will, however, make use of the helpful parallel passages in Aquinas's commentaries on the *Physics*[17] and the *Metaphysics*,[18] both of which he seems to have been writing within six years of finishing SCG (see Appendix I).

As for Aquinas's identifying 'motion' as the basis of these arguments, his use of the Latin word *motus* in them parallels Aristotle's broad, generic use of the Greek word *kinesis* to mean either change of location (local motion) or qualitative change (alteration) or quantitative change (increase or decrease). In this discussion I'll continue to use the words 'motion', 'move', 'mover', and so on, taking that broad, generic interpretation of them for granted.[19]

Aquinas says that both G1 and G2 proceed 'on the basis of motion' (*ex parte motus*), the very words with which he later characterizes ST's First Way. Do both G1 and G2 correspond to the First Way, then? No. The correspondence between the First Way and the main argument of G1 is quite close. In each of them the

---

[15] G1 takes 170 columnar lines in the Marietti edn. of SCG; G2, 174. (Sects. 109–12 of I.13 contain a special appraisal of G2.) The third argument takes 17 lines, the fourth, 13, and the fifth, 14.

[16] For helpful commentary of that sort see e.g. Gerson 1990*b*.

[17] See also van Steenberghen 1971.

[18] See also van Steenberghen 1974.

[19] G1 is presented by Aquinas as if local motion alone might be basis enough for the argument, while in ST's closely similar First Way his single paradigm of motion is a case of alteration. In G2, on the other hand, a consideration of all the genera and species of motion is essential to the structure of the argument, as we'll see.

same two premises require support. G1 provides the support in six separate, detailed arguments (three for each of the dangling premisses); the First Way provides it succinctly in two sub-arguments incorporated into the main argument. As Aquinas's apparent favourite among the Five Ways, the First Way, the *manifestior via*, has received a great deal of critical attention. G1, its more complicated ancestor, has been comparatively neglected; but a recent article by Scott MacDonald (1991*a*) does a beautiful job of examining G1 and the First Way together and, more important, of answering the well-known objections to this sort of argument from motion. For the practical purpose of starting natural theology with a good argument for the existence of God along the lines provided in SCG, I could simply present G1 as analysed and defended by MacDonald. But, partly because he has already ably done that work on G1, I want to focus on the almost totally neglected and misconstrued G2. MacDonald's main thesis is that the argument from motion which Aquinas develops in G1 and in the First Way is incomplete in itself, but valid if completed by certain modal considerations, and that Aquinas himself realized this. The requisite modal considerations, MacDonald maintains, are supplied for the First Way in the Third Way (1991*a*: 154). In an allusion to G2, he suggests that it may have been intended to play a corresponding role in support of G1.[20] Perhaps he's right about that, but I want to consider G2 on its own as nearly as possible.

The principal difference between G1 and the First Way is that G1 offers alternative supporting arguments and spells out everything in more detail. It is more complex than the First Way, but only extrinsically and accidentally. G2, on the other hand, is intrinsically and substantively a more complex argument from motion than either the First Way or G1, and G2 has no counterpart among the Five Ways.[21] Despite Aquinas's clearly treating it as a second

[20] MacDonald 1991*a*: 152: 'In his presentation of the second "Aristotelian" proof [G2], he [Aquinas] acknowledges that the claim that there is a primary mover that is not moved by anything exterior to it does not entail that there is a primary mover that is completely unmovable [as G1 concludes]. . . . It seems to me plausible . . . to suppose that he was aware of the parasitic nature of the first "Aristotelian" proof and that he left it unremarked in view of the forthcoming supplementary discussion.'

[21] G2 is altogether the most complex of all Aquinas's arguments for God's existence. Its complexity appears to have been the principal consideration that led van Steenberghen, astonishingly, to omit any detailed treatment of it from his big book devoted entirely to Aquinas's arguments for God's existence, where he characterizes it as a complicated, scientifically antiquated reprise of G1—too complicated in

argument in chapter 13, some have taken G2 to be simply continuous with G1, forming one huge argument from motion.[22] But because, as the reader may have noticed, no counterpart for the Third Way appears among the four other arguments of chapter 13, it has sometimes been supposed that G2 must fill that particular gap— not merely relating to G1 as MacDonald claims that the Third Way relates to the First, but prefiguring the Third Way itself. In an article on Aquinas's arguments from motion the Polish logician Jan Salamucha presents an instructively mistaken version of this view of G2.[23] He writes: 'The second proof *ex motu* given in the *Summa contra Gentiles*, is connected with that of *ex contingentia mundi* [the Third Way]. For this reason, St. Thomas himself is not satisfied with this proof and closed it with the remark, *Praedictos autem processus duo videntur infirmare . . .* ["Two things appear to weaken the lines of reasoning we have been considering . . ."]. He then gives explanations stressing the weak points of the proof. It is possible that later this second proof *ex motu* was reformulated, elaborated and presented in the *Summa Theologiae* as the proof *ex contingentia.*'[24] G2 does resemble the Third Way in its concern with modalities, but that resemblance is superficial in view of the essential differences between the two arguments. Most notably, the Third Way, like the First Way and G1, must take on the notoriously hard job of trying to block an infinite regress of moved movers, while G2 not only tolerates but systematically incorporates such a regress.[25]

its structure and implausible in its assumptions to be worth examining closely: 'Une fois de plus la preuve est développée avec un luxe de considérations qui se situent au niveau de la science aristotélicienne dans ses éléments les plus caducs. *Il faudrait des pages nombreuses pour analyser et critiquer en détail cette démonstration, sans profit notable pour le lecteur*' (van Steenberghen 1980: 117–18; emphasis added).

[22] See e.g. Baisnée 1952; also van Steenberghen 1966: 120; also Martin 1988: 99– 100. Martin, indeed, seems to think that *all* of SCG I.13 constitutes one single argument.

[23] Salamucha 1958; repr. in Kenny 1969.

[24] Salamucha 1958, Kenny 1969: 177; cf. MacDonald 1991*a*: 149 n. 56.

[25] SCG contains another argument that has been described as prefiguring the Third Way very closely, one that appears in a later chapter of SCG in a version designed to serve as an argument for God's eternality (15.124). Van Steenberghen argues (1966: 126–7) that the Third Way is unsatisfactory as it stands, but can be improved by revisions drawn from this SCG argument, which he describes as 'the more satisfactory formula' of the argument from contingency (p. 149). The argument in 15.124 will be considered in Ch. Three, but not as a version of the Third Way.

What Salamucha takes to be 'explanations stressing the weak points' of G2 are actually Aquinas's reassurances regarding two aspects of it that someone might *mistakenly* suppose to be grounds for objecting to it. In examining G2, we'll see reasons why Aquinas might very well have become dissatisfied with it eventually; but he certainly shows no dissatisfaction with it in SCG. On the contrary, he promotes G2 as being in at least one respect 'the most efficacious way (*via efficacissima*) of proving that God exists' (13.110). In his final appraisal of G2, the first of the two aspects of it that Aquinas says '*appear* to weaken' it is the fact that it is constructed 'on the basis of [Aristotle's] hypothesis of the eternity [i.e. the beginninglessness] of motion, which among Catholics is taken to be false'. However, he points out, 'the most efficacious way of proving that God exists is on the hypothesis of an eternal [i.e. beginningless] world, [just because] on that hypothesis it seems *less* evident that God exists. For if the world and motion did have a first beginning, then, plainly, we must posit some cause that produces the world and motion to begin with. For everything that comes into existence for the first time must get its start from some originator, because nothing brings itself from potentiality to actuality, or from non-existence to existence' (13.109–10).[26] G2, then, seems to have been designed to show that there must be a being whose existence and nature account for the world's existence, even when the world is viewed as having existed *always*.[27]

4. The structure of G2

The being that argument G2 has in its sights is a sempiternal, transcendent ('separated'), absolutely unmoved, cosmic first mover—that is, a beginningless, everlasting, ultimate source of all

[26] Cf. In Phys. VIII: L1.970: 'This way of proving that there is a first source [viz. on the hypothesis of the beginninglessness of motion] is the most efficacious way, which cannot be resisted. For if it is necessary to suppose that there is one first source in case the world and motion exist sempiternally, it is much more so if their sempiternity is ruled out, since it is evident that everything that is new needs an originating source. Therefore, it is only if things exist from eternity that it could seem unnecessary to posit a first source. And so if it follows that a first source exists even on that hypothesis, it is shown to be altogether necessary that a first source exists.' For this passage and other relevant data about the text of Aquinas's appraisal of G2, see the note to 13.110 in the Marietti edn. of SCG (vol. II, app. I, p. 286).

[27] The second of the two features of G2 that appear to weaken it is discussed in sect. 5, stage III, below.

change, a source that is itself necessarily unchangeable in any respect and extrinsic to everything it changes. With some justification, Aquinas considers himself entitled to identify such a being as God. But in view of all he does in the immediately following chapters of SCG to argue for such a being's possession of traditional divine attributes, we might think of G2 as, even in Aquinas's own view, only the first instalment of his argument for the existence of a being that theists would recognize as God.

Aquinas moves toward G2's conclusion in several stages.[28] But, despite its complexity, G2 is unified by its focus on the concept of a mover, which should be understood through the first three stages of the argument as the efficient cause of whatever moving is ascribed to it.

G2's stage I (13.97–100) is intended to show the untenability of the position that every mover is moved by another mover, and to yield the preliminary conclusion that there is a first mover that is not moved by anything extrinsic to it. Stage II (13.101–2) begins with the acknowledgement that such a first mover might be a *self-mover*, a mover that is moved by something intrinsic to it, rather than an entirely immovable mover. Stage II then proceeds via an analysis of the concept of a self-mover to argue that introducing this concept only postpones the inevitable, since a self-mover's intrinsic mover must be immovable. Stage III (13.103–7) reconsiders self-movers, this time from the standpoint of empirical observation, and draws conclusions about the nature of anything that could count as a cosmic first self-mover. Stage IV (13.108), finally, is intended to show that even a cosmic first self-mover would presuppose a sempiternal, transcendent, immovable, absolutely first mover, 'which', Aquinas says, 'is God'.

5. *The stages of G2*

Stage I

In stage I Aquinas confronts an 'adversary', presumably anyone who defends the thesis that '*Every* mover is a moved mover'. He

[28] I suppose this composite structure of G2 warrants his referring to it in the plural as 'lines of reasoning' and even 'demonstrations' in his final appraisal of it. Since the appraisal follows both G1 and G2, it's natural to interpret its plurals, *praedictos processus* (13.109) and especially *praedictis demonstrationibus* (13.111), as referring to both those arguments as wholes. But the two features picked out in the appraisal characterize only G2. See my discussion of Salamucha's view in sect. 3 above.

presents his adversary with a destructive dilemma: if your thesis is true, it must be true either (1) *per accidens* or (2) *per se*; but it is true neither *per accidens* nor *per se*; and so your thesis is false.[29] Stage I divides naturally into two parts, then. If the first of these parts, Ia, succeeds, it destroys the first, *per accidens* lemma. Part Ib is intended to finish the job by destroying the second lemma, the *per se* lemma.

Stage Ia

If every mover is moved, then this proposition is true either *per se* or *per accidens*. If *per accidens*, then it is not necessary, for what is true *per accidens* is not necessary.[30] Therefore, that no mover is moved is contingent. But if a mover is not moved, it does not act as a mover (*non movet*) (as the adversary says).[31] Therefore, that   5 nothing is moved is contingent, since if nothing acts as a mover, nothing is moved. This, however, Aristotle considers to be impossible—namely, that there be a time when there is no moving.[32] Therefore, the first was not contingent, since what is false and impossible does not follow from what is false and contingent. And so the propo-   10 sition 'Every mover is moved by something else' was not true *per accidens*. (13.97)[33]

I think that the first lemma, which stage Ia is designed to reject, is an unlikely interpretation of the adversary's thesis anyway, because if a mover is moved only *per accidens*, then it isn't moved *qua* mover, in its capacity as a mover. That this is what Aquinas means by being moved *per accidens* can be seen in a parallel passage in his

---

[29] What makes a proposition true *per se* is that its predicate holds of its subject just because the subject is correctly characterized by the subject term—e.g. 'Every whole is greater than any proper part of it'; 'A human being is a mammal'; '17 is a prime number'; 'Water is H_2O'. A proposition true on any other grounds is true *per accidens*.

[30] In the parallel passage in Aquinas's commentary on Aristotle's *Physics*, he provides an explanation that might be attached to this second premiss: 'Nothing that is *per accidens* is necessary; for what is in anything *per accidens* is not in it necessarily but can fail to be in it—like musicianship in a builder.' That is, if it's true that the builder is a musician, it's true not *per se* but *per accidens*. 'Therefore, if movers are moved *per accidens*, it follows that they can fail to be moved [without failing to be movers]' (In Phys. VIII: L9.1043). See also In Phys. VIII: L9.1042, quoted just below.

[31] Cf. the parallel: 'But since you [the adversary] claim that every mover is moved, it follows that if movers are not moved, they do not act as movers' (In Phys. VIII: L9.1043).

[32] *Physics* VIII 1, 250b11–252a4.

[33] Cf. *Physics* VIII 5, 256b3–13; In Phys. VIII: L9.1042–3.

Physics commentary, where he presents the distinction not in terms of truth, but in terms of the inherence of properties: 'If everything that is moved is moved by something that is moved—i.e. if every mover is moved—this can occur in two ways. In one way, so that a mover's being moved is found in things *per accidens*—I mean, so that the mover does not do its moving *on account of* its being moved (as if we were to say that a musician is a builder not *because* he is a musician but *per accidens*)—or [in the second way] so that it is not *per accidens* that the mover is moved, but *per se*' (In Phys. VIII: L9.1042).[34] On this interpretation, I think, any worthy adversary of the sort Aquinas is envisaging would disown the *per accidens* lemma without a fight.

If I'm right in suggesting that the rejection of the first lemma is a mere formality, then the fact that stage Ia is flawed has less practical importance than it would have otherwise. As Aquinas reads his adversary's thesis, in maintaining that every mover is moved, the adversary must be maintaining either that every mover is, by its very nature as a mover, something that is itself moved in its moving something, or that every mover is, merely as it happens, something that is itself moved whenever it moves something. But no worthy adversary would accept that reading of the thesis. The first premiss of Ia (in lines 1–2) is, no doubt, intended to be tautological, unobjectionable to the adversary; but the only interpretation on which it is so is this one: 'Every mover is moved either *per se* or *per accidens*.' Aquinas's casting the exhaustive disjunction in terms of the truth *per se* or *per accidens* of the adversary's universal thesis leaves the first premiss highly implausible.

Still, if we ignore the dubious moves and the unnecessary technicalities of stage Ia, we might be able to make out an acceptable line of argument here, one that could be sketched this way: if the adversary's thesis is true *per accidens*, then a mover's being moved is contingent, in which case it is possible that no mover is moved. But if no mover is moved, then—on the adversary's thesis—nothing acts as a mover, and in that case there is no moving. So, if the adversary's thesis is true *per accidens*, it is possible that there be no moving at all. But, as Aristotle claims, that there be no moving at all is *im*possible. Now, what is impossible does not follow from

[34] The translation of this passage in Blackwell *et al.* 1963: 516 leaves the words *ut movens moveatur* untranslated, and mistranslates the words *propter id quod movetur*.

what is contingent, and so a mover's being moved cannot be contingent. Therefore, the adversary's thesis is not true *per accidens*.

It's in the announcement that Aristotle considers it to be 'impossible . . . that there be a time when there is no moving' (lines 7–8) that Aquinas springs his trap for the adversary, who is plainly expected to be in this respect an Aristotelian. This is the hypothesis of beginningless motion whose inclusion in G2 is a necessary condition of its being characterized as 'the most efficacious way'. Attributing it explicitly to Aristotle is important dialectically, but the explicit attribution is important also because Aquinas himself thinks it's *not* impossible that there once was no motion at all. He believes, of course, that in fact all motion began with creation (although he argues, contrary to most of his contemporaries, that that cannot be known except by recourse to revelation, which is off limits here[35]). For purposes of G2, then, Aquinas, like his adversary, fully accepts this Aristotelian hypothesis.

The proposition embedded in the conclusion of Ia, 'Every mover is moved by something else', isn't expressly identified as the adversary's thesis—which is called 'the first' in line 9—but Aquinas's use of the past tense in lines 9 and 11 strongly suggests that he is taking 'Every mover is moved' as simply an abbreviation for 'Every mover is moved by something else'.[36] This fuller version of the adversary's thesis can be inferred from the abbreviated version along with the Aristotelian principle 'Everything that is moved is moved by something else (*Omne quod movetur ab alio movetur*)'—OQM, I'll call it. The OQM principle is tacit and underived in G2, but it occurs explicitly as the first premiss of G1, where it is supported by three sub-arguments; and so Aquinas is

---

[35] For Aquinas's position in the medieval controversy over the possibility of a beginningless universe, misleadingly (but universally) designated *de aeternitate mundi*, see e.g. SCG II.30–8. See also Wippel 1984*b*; Wissink 1990; and, more generally, Dales 1990; Dales and Argerami 1991; Kretzmann 1985.

[36] In the parallel passage in his *Physics* commentary he retains the original version of the adversary's thesis: 'Therefore, it follows that at some time nothing is moved. However, that is impossible, because it was shown above [VIII 1, 250b11–252b6] that it is necessary that there always be motion. But this impossibility does not follow from our having supposed that movers are not moved. For if it is *per accidens* that a mover is moved, it will be possible that movers not be moved; and nothing impossible follows from the positing of what is possible. Therefore, we are left with the conclusion that the other thing from which it follows—I mean, that every mover is moved—is impossible' (In Phys. VIII: L9.1043).

within his rights to be assuming it here.[37] I consider the tacit OQM to be acceptable within G2, especially because MacDonald's published analysis and appraisal of G1 and the First Way shows the acceptability of the OQM principle in this context (MacDonald 1991*a*: 128–32).

Consequently, although there are good reasons to worry about some features of stage Ia, I think we can extract an acceptable line of argument from it, at least for the sake of argument G2. I wish I could say the same of the much more important stage Ib, which focuses on the second lemma, the stronger, likelier interpretation of the adversary's thesis.[38]

Stage Ib

But if the aforementioned proposition ['Every mover is moved by something else'] is true *per se*, then, similarly, something impossible or absurd follows. For the mover must be moved either with the same species of motion as that with which it acts as a mover, or with another. If with the same, then it will have to be the case that what 5 alters is altered, and, further, that what heals is healed, that what teaches is taught—and with the same knowledge. But this is impossi-

---

[37] The OQM principle has been much discussed. For a good critical review of the literature and a very well-informed account of the OQM principle in medieval philosophy generally and Aquinas particularly, see Weisheipl 1965; also Lobkowicz 1968 and Weisheipl 1968 (a reply to Lobkowicz 1968).

[38] As I read SCG I.13, stages Ia and Ib of G2 are separated by what may be considered an *ad hominem* supplement to Ia: 'Again, if any two [characteristics] are conjoined *per accidens* in something, and one of them is found without the other, it is probable that the other can be found without that one. For example, if being white and being musical are found in Socrates, and in Plato one finds being musical without being white, it is probable that in some other man one can find being white without being musical. Therefore, if being a mover and being moved are conjoined in something *per accidens*, while being moved is found in something [else] without its being a mover, it is probable that being a mover is found [in some third thing] without its being moved. And one cannot raise as a counter-instance against this a case of two things of which one depends on the other and not vice versa (as is clear in the case of substance and accident), for [*ex hypothesi*] these [characteristics under discussion] are conjoined not *per se* [as accident is conjoined with substance] but *per accidens*' (13.98; cf. In Phys. VIII: L9.1044). Since this argument concludes to the probability of an unmoved mover, which is not something Aquinas wants to deny, I would bring out its *ad hominem* character by continuing it along the following lines: many things are moved although they are not movers, and so if 'Every mover is moved' is true *per accidens*, then, probably, there is a mover that is not moved. But the adversary flatly denies that there is an unmoved mover, and so the adversary must also deny that 'Every mover is moved' is true *per accidens*.

ble; for it is necessary that the one who is teaching have the know
ledge, but it is [also] necessary that the one who is learning not have it.
And so the same thing will be had and not had by the same thing—   10
which is impossible. But if [the mover] is moved in accordance with
another species of motion—e.g. so that what alters is moved locally,
and what moves something locally is increased, and so on as regards
the others—then, since there are finitely many genera and species of
motion, it will follow that this cannot go on *ad infinitum*. And so there   15
will be a first mover that is not moved by something else. Unless,
perhaps, someone might say, 'Suppose there is recapitulation of this
sort: once all the genera and species of motion have been used up,
there must be a return to the first again, so that if what moves something locally is altered, and what alters it is increased, then what   20
increases that is, again, moved locally'. But from this will follow the
same as before—namely, that that which acts as a mover in accordance with some species of motion is moved in accordance with the
same species, albeit not directly, but indirectly (*non immediate sed
mediate*). Therefore, we are left with having to posit some first   25
[mover] that is not moved by anything extrinsic [to it]. (13.99–100)[39]

The genera of motion at issue here are just the three I mentioned
earlier: locational change, quantitative change, and qualitative
change (or alteration). After picking out alteration as the genus,
the case developed in lines 5–7 picks out two subaltern species of
alteration—healing and teaching—and then a most specific species
of teaching: teaching some particular item of knowledge. For the
argument to have any chance of deriving the absurdity it aims at, it
must focus on most specific species of motion, as Aquinas himself
insists in his commentary on the relevant passage in Aristotle's
Physics: 'It is plainly impossible that a mover be moved with the
same species of motion [as that with which it acts as a mover]. For
it is not enough to stop at some subaltern species [of motion];
instead, one will have to go on through the process of division all
the way to the individuals—i.e. to the most specific species. For
example, if someone is teaching, he is not just being taught, he is
teaching and being taught the same thing. I mean that if he is
teaching geometry, he is being taught that same [bit of geometry]
(*hoc idem*)' (In Phys. VIII: L9.1046).

There is no logical absurdity in your being altered in one way
while altering something else in another way—in, for instance, your

---

[39] Cf. *Physics* VIII 5, 256b27–257a14; In Phys. VIII: L9.1046–9. The textual material quoted in the immediately preceding note intervenes between stages Ia and Ib.

hearing the clock chime as you're helping the student understand the theorem you're teaching her. The intended absurdity is associated with a case in which the mover is being moved with the very same, most specific species of motion as that with which the mover is doing its moving—a case in which, for example, you are being taught the very same theorem you're teaching in the very same way you're teaching it at the very same time you're teaching it (not even a little earlier). For in that case you would (as teacher) *have* and (as learner) *not have* the very same thing in the very same respect at the very same time, which is absurd.

Well, all right, *that* can't happen. But even if we grant, for the sake of the argument in stage Ib, that there are only three genera of motion, we're bound to say that there must be infinitely many most specific species of those three genera. Just think, for instance, of all the propositions that might be taught. It is simply false—or, at any rate, unbelievable—that 'there are finitely many genera and species of motion' (lines 14–15) in the sense of 'species of motion' required for stage Ib. And so it's illegitimate to try running the argument by merely ringing the conveniently few changes on the three genera, as in lines 11–14 and 19–21.

But suppose someone were to push the teaching example harder (trading on what must be admitted to be favourable features peculiar to it) and claim that if you are teaching theorem 45 now, you must once have been taught that very theorem. Thus, in moving your student in accordance with the species of motion that is teaching-theorem-45 you are 'moved in accordance with the same species, albeit not directly, but indirectly' (lines 23–4). Clearly there is a sense in which your once having been moved with that most specific species of motion is a moving of you that would be most explanatory of your being able now to move your student with that same species of motion. But in view of the fact that the simultaneity condition is not satisfied in this case, it doesn't violate the principle of non-contradiction, as the first one did. So, what's supposed to be absurd about the mover's being moved *not* at the very same time—one legitimate interpretation of being moved *in*directly—by the very same most specific species of motion in the very same respect? We are not told. And so the general point cannot be made even on the basis of what seems to be its most advantageous sort of example.

Perhaps there is an even simpler objection to stage Ib. For even if there were something intolerable about recycling species of motion all the way back to the species instantiated in the terminating motion (as Aquinas claims there is, in lines 16–24), why couldn't there be cases in which only the other two species are recycled, thereby avoiding the outcome he thinks is absurd? Let Z be the last moved mover in a beginningless series of moved movers. And suppose that Z is moving whatever it moves locally and that it is the only local mover in the series, and that Z is moved by Y, which is moving Z by alteration and is moved by X, which is moving Y by increase and is moved by W, which is moving X by alteration and is moved by V, which is moving W by increase . . ., and so on, *ad infinitum*.[40]

Of course, there's much more that could be said about G2's stage Ib, and some of what could be said might be favourable; but there's no point in going further with it now. As it stands, it can't be saved. So stage I's a priori argument—not the sort of argument Aquinas has led us to expect in this chapter—does not succeed in reducing 'Every mover is moved by something else' to an absurdity. Consequently, G2 has not established the existence of 'some first mover that is not moved by anything extrinsic to it'. I think Aquinas would have done better to leave this argument where he found it, in *Physics* VIII 5.[41]

Stage II

Considered as an argument for the existence of God, G2 is spoiled by the failure of its first stage. But in its subsequent analysis of the notion of a first mover, it makes a contribution that is perhaps unique among Aquinas's existence arguments. He calls attention to the fact that stage II involves a fresh start. Here's how he makes the transition from stage I to stage II in the parallel argument in his *Physics* commentary: 'But that first [mover]'—the one inferred in stage I of G2—'must be either immovable or a self-mover', since stage I's conclusion is only that there is a first mover that is not moved by anything *extrinsic* to it. 'Therefore, we have to consider

---

[40] The version of this argument in the parallel passage (In Phys. VIII: L9.1046–7) is fuller, but no better.

[41] There is a second Aristotelian argument in VIII 5 to this same effect (beginning at 257a4), and Aquinas develops it in his commentary (VIII: L9.1048), though not as part of G2 in SCG I.13. It strikes me as illuminating some features of what I'm calling stage Ib, but not as a better argument to the same conclusion.

that which moves itself, on this basis making another beginning of our consideration' (In Phys. VIII: L9.1049).

But because when we have the conclusion that there is a first mover that is not moved by something else that is extrinsic to it, it does not follow that it is immovable inwardly (*penitus*), Aristotle goes further, by saying that this can occur in two ways. In one way, so that the first [mover] *is* immovable inwardly. If we suppose that, then we have the thesis—namely, that there is an immovable first mover. In the other way, so that the first [mover] is moved by itself. (And that seems probable, because what occurs on its own is always prior to what occurs in virtue of something else. That is why as regards moved things, too, it is reasonable that the first thing moved be moved by itself, not by anything else.)

But, given this, the same thing follows again.[42] For it cannot be said that [in the case of] a self-mover the whole is moved by the whole, because then absurdities discussed earlier would follow—I mean [such absurdities as] that someone would at the same time be teaching and be taught (and similarly as regards other motions), and, again, that something would be in potentiality and actuality at the same time [and in the same respect]. (For what is acting as a mover, considered just as such, is in a state of actuality, but what is being moved [considered just as such] is in a state of potentiality.) We are left, therefore, with the conclusion that one part of it is a mover only, and the other part [is what is] moved. And so we have the same as before—namely, that something is an immovable mover.

But one cannot say that both parts are moved, the one by the other [and vice versa], or that the one part moves itself and moves the other, or that the whole moves a part, or that a part moves the whole, because absurdities brought out earlier would follow—I mean [such absurdities as] that something would at the same time move something and be moved in accordance with the same species of motion, and that it would at the same time be in potentiality and actuality, and, further, that the whole would not be moving itself first but rather by reason of a part. We are left, therefore, with the conclusion that in the case of a self-mover one part must be immovable and the mover of the other part. (13.101–2)[43]

Any mover that at least sometimes moves something when it is not being moved by anything extrinsic to it is on such occasions, and in virtue of that fact alone, a *first* mover. And nature certainly seems

5

10

15

20

25

30

---

[42] i.e. 'even if one should arrive at a first [mover] that is a self-mover, one must none the less come to a first [mover] that is immovable' (In Phys. VIII: L10.1050).

[43] Cf. *Physics* VIII 5, 257b13–258a5; In Phys. VIII: L9.1049; L10.1052–61.

to include innumerable series of movers and moved things in short causal chains whose first links are movers that are moved intrinsically if at all. MacDonald calls such familiar, apparent first movers 'mundane' (1991a: 147). You, for instance, are a mundane first mover whenever you do something just because you feel like doing it. The notion won't be left at that uncritical level for long, since Aquinas is heading toward the consideration of just such familiar, mundane, first movers in the a posteriori stage of G2.

Animals, the mundane first movers we're familiar with, seem to be self-movers on many ordinary occasions. But anyone who, like Aquinas, subscribes to the OQM principle must take the very notion of a *self*-mover to be incoherent theoretically. If 'Everything that is moved is moved by something *else*', then, strictly speaking, '*nothing* moves itself', as Aquinas expressly concludes in the course of supporting OQM as the first premiss of argument G1 (13.89). However, the conclusion of G2's stage II speaks less strictly, appearing to countenance the notion of a self-mover as long as it is analysed in just one particular way of the six ways considered in stage II.[44]

According to the first, and only strict, analysis of self-mover, (1) if X can be considered a self-mover, then, of course, X is the mover, and X is what X moves; and so 'the whole [of X] is moved by the whole' of X (line 13). But, alluding to two 'absurdities discussed earlier',[45] Aquinas here dismisses this first analysis (which yields what might be called *strict* self-moving) as entailing an impossibility. And I think he's clearly right to do so on either basis, though it may be more instructive in this context to see how he means to do it on the basis of the discounted stage Ib. For although, as I've claimed, X's moving something else, Y (which is what's at issue in stage Ib) with a most specific species of motion M_1 is not incompatible with X's being moved with M_1, at least indirectly, there are no ways out of incompatibility when it's the whole of X itself that's doing the moving and the whole of X itself that's then being moved. You cannot be at once both altogether the one teaching and alto-

[44] This provisional approach to the notion of a self-mover is plainly and succinctly expressed in the clause of his *Physics* commentary immediately prior to his taking up this analysis: 'on this basis making another beginning of our consideration—I mean, so that *if* anything moves itself, we might consider how that is possible' (VIII: L9.1049).

[45] The first is in G2's stage Ib, the second in the strongest of the sub-arguments supporting principle OQM in G1 (13.89).

gether the one learning theorem 45, both the one who already understands it and the one who doesn't understand it yet.[46] And so any analysis of self-mover that might be taken seriously will have to begin by allowing an *un*strict interpretation of the concept.

Aquinas says (lines 20–2) that already at this point we're left with the conclusion that one part of X is a mover only, while the other (complementary) part of X is what is moved by that moving part of X. But he's really anticipating the final conclusion of stage II, which he restates (lines 32–4) after dismissing four other possible analyses of self-mover, broadly conceived of. These analyses of X as a 'self-mover' are (2) that the whole of X moves a part of it, (3) that a part moves the whole, (4) that one of two complementary parts moves itself and the other part, and (5) that two complementary parts move each other. Besides the two absurdities he used in dismissing analysis 1, Aquinas alludes here (lines 31–2) to a third previously derived absurd conclusion.[47] It may be intended as the basis on which to rule out analysis 5, which might also be dismissed simply on the grounds that it offers a circular explanation of motion.[48] Either of the two absurdities already invoked will do the job for analyses 2–4.

The last analysis of 'self-mover' X is the one Aquinas favours here: (6) that one of two complementary parts of X is 'a mover only'—that is, is an immovable mover—and the other part is what that first part moves.[49] Not only does analysis 6 steer clear of the

---

[46] 'In this way, therefore, it will follow, further, that a person will be teaching and being taught at the same time with respect to one and the same knowable object'— which is absurd (In Phys. VIII: L10.1052).

[47] This absurdity, too, is found in argument G1 in support of principle OQM (13.85).

[48] The only reason for taking the notion of a self-mover seriously at this stage of the argument is that such a thing may seem to provide a viable alternative to an altogether unmoved mover for the role of a cosmic first mover that might count as God. But, as Aquinas explains in the parallel passage, 'If each of the two [complementary] parts of a whole self-mover moves the other part reciprocally, one of them is no more a mover than the other is. But a first mover is more of a mover than a secondary mover is. Therefore, neither of those [parts] will be a first mover. That is absurd, because in that case it would follow that that which is moved from within itself (*ex seipso*) would be no nearer [an approximation] to the first source of motion—the one that is second to none (*quod nullum sequitur esse*)—than that which is moved by something else' (In Phys. VIII: L10.1055).

[49] In his *Physics* commentary Aquinas is a little more forthcoming about the status of the part that does the moving: 'If regarding the part of a self-mover that does the moving we are given [the hypothesis] that it moves itself as a whole, then it follows, on the basis of things already proved, that, again, one part of that part

absurdities that bring down the other five; it also appears most likely to be suited to animals, which he has earlier described as apparently 'moved from within themselves (*ex se mota*)' (13.88), in which the part that does the moving is called the soul (or some more precisely identified faculty of the soul). In argument G1, where Aquinas applies only the strict sense of 'self-mover', he *denies* that animals move themselves (13.88). In argument G2, on the other hand, he is ready, after the second stage we've just been examining, to consider animals as self-movers, broadly speaking. This way of considering animals occupies stage III, which is illuminated by stage II, the results of which might be summarized in this way.

Stage II begins by disclosing a fork in the argument. We're looking for a first mover of movable things, and it's already clear that such a thing can't be 'moved by something else that is extrinsic to it' (line 2). But we can't suppose at once that we're closing in on an immovable first mover, because 'if one were to consider which is the first cause of motion in the genus of movable things—that which moves itself, or something movable that is moved by something else—everyone would agree that it is probable that the first mover [among movable things] is a self-mover. For a cause that operates on its own is always prior to one that operates via something else' (In Phys. VIII: L9.1049). And so stage II goes on to examine a first *self*-mover as a possible alternative to the immovable first mover.

Considered as a self-mover, X has two complementary parts, of which one, X_1, is X's intrinsic mover that moves X_2, X's other complementary part. X's moving itself = X's being moved by itself = X_1's moving X_2. X can be considered a *first* self-mover if X moves something else, Y, as a result of X's moving itself, and if, in X's moving itself and thereby moving Y, X_1 itself is immovable considered just as a mover. You, presumably, count as a first self-mover on this analysis if, for instance, you pick up a pencil and put it down again just because you feel like it.

does the moving and the other part of it is moved. For it has already been shown above [VIII: L10.1052] that the only way a whole moves itself is that one part of it does the moving and the other is moved. . . . We are, therefore, left with the conclusion that the part that does the moving in a self-mover is altogether immovable' (VIII: L10.1061). Aquinas's Aristotelian analysis of self-movers is carried forward throughout VIII: L11.1062–8 in ways that illuminate the analysis in L10, but without adding anything essential to argument G2.

But as this analysis leads us to think of the self-movers we know at first hand, it shows us features of them that enable us to focus more clearly on the requisite characteristics of some self-mover that could, conceivably, count as the cosmic first mover we're seeking. On this basis we turn to stage III, the beginning of G2's a posteriori argument.

Stage III

However, in the self-movers that exist among us—in animals, I mean—the part that does the moving—the soul—is moved *per accidens* even if it is immovable *per se*. And so Aristotle shows, further, that in a *first* self-mover the part that does the moving is *not* moved, neither *per se* nor *per accidens*.[50]   5

For since the self-movers that exist among us—animals—are destructible, the part in them that acts as a mover is moved *per accidens*. Now it is necessary that destructible self-movers be traced back to some first self-mover that is sempiternal. Therefore, it is necessary that some self-mover have a mover that is not moved, neither *per se*   10 nor *per accidens*.[51]

Now it is clearly necessary from Aristotle's point of view that some self-mover be sempiternal. For if motion is sempiternal, as he supposes, the generation of self-movers that are generable and destructible must be perpetual. But none of those self-movers can be the cause   15 of this perpetuity, because none of them exists always. Nor [can] all of them together [be its cause], both because there would be infinitely many of them and because they do not exist simultaneously. We are left, therefore, with the conclusion that there must be some perpetual self-mover that causes the perpetuity of generation as regards those   20 inferior self-movers. And so its mover is not moved, neither *per se* nor *per accidens*.[52]

Again, as regards self-movers, we see that some of them begin to be newly moved because of some motion with which the animal is not moved by itself, as when it is awakened from sleep by digested food or   25 a change in the air[53]—a motion with which that self-mover itself is, of

---

[50] Cf. In Phys. VIII: L12.1069.

[51] Cf. *Physics* VIII 6, 258b10–16; In Phys. VIII: L12.1069–71

[52] Cf. *Physics* VIII 6, 258b23–259a21; In Phys. VIII: L12.1074–6.

[53] The editors of the Marietti edn. add the words *cum excitatur a somno* ('when it is awakened from sleep'), omitted by the Leonine editors, although they appear in all but two of the manuscripts used for the edn. The inclusion of those words is further justified by the parallel passage in In Phys. VIII: L13.1080, as the Marietti editors point out in a note at this point.

course, moved *per accidens*. From this we can gather that no self-mover whose mover is moved either *per se* or *per accidens* is moved always. A first self-mover, however, is moved always; otherwise motion would not be sempiternal, since every motion other than a first 30 self-mover's motion is caused. We are left, therefore, with the conclusion that a first self-mover is moved by a mover that is not moved, neither *per se* nor *per accidens*. (13.103-6)[54]

I think it's clear that human beings are among the animals under consideration in stage III. In the parallel passage of the *Physics* commentary Aquinas indicates plainly that both human and non-human animals are included.[55] In any case, I propose to consider stage III in terms of human beings.

Stage II's analysis shows that in anything that might be strictly considered a self-mover the part that does the moving, considered just as such, must be immovable, both *per se* and *per accidens*. Stage III begins by observing that this is *not* what we find in the only 'self-movers' we are familiar with, including ourselves. A human being's rational soul, its intellect and will, is the part that does the moving of the human being, and it is movable *per accidens*.

What he means here by a soul's being moved *per accidens* is best determined by the evidence he provides, the most accessible of which is based on ordinary observation (lines 23-7). Human sleeping and waking are most particularly states of the rational soul (of the sensory soul to a lesser degree, and of the nutritive soul not at all). The waking of a human being 'by digested food or a change in the air' involves the rational soul's being moved *per accidens* intrinsically by a motion in the nutritive or the sensory soul, which was in turn moved *per accidens* extrinsically. And the fact that the being moved is from sleep to wakefulness helps to ensure that the

---

[54] Cf. *Physics* VIII 6, 259b3-28; In Phys. VIII: L13.1080-1. I'm omitting these immediately following lines: 'And it does not count against this argument that the movers of the lower spheres move a sempiternal motion and yet are said to be moved *per accidens*. For they are said to be moved *per accidens* not by reason of themselves but by reason of the things movable by them, which follow the motion of a higher sphere' (13.107; cf. *Physics* VIII 6, 259b28-31; In Phys. VIII: L13.1082).

[55] In In Phys. VIII: L12.1070-1 Aquinas introduces the parallel to G2's stage III with allusions to intellect that help to show that he takes the argument to apply to, if not to focus on, human animals. And by his reference to animals with destructible souls in the same context, he indicates that it is intended to apply also to non-human animals: 'in connection with the self-movers we are familiar with—I mean, destructible animals—it can be the case that the part that does the moving in the self-mover—the soul—is destructible and is moved *per accidens*' (VIII: L12.1069).

part of the human being that does the moving on such an occasion isn't somehow the rational soul itself. In this way even the inde-structible rational soul proves to be relevantly movable *per accidens*, so that in its own active moving (of the body) it is to some extent passively subjected to the vicissitudes of the external world via the nutritive or the sensory soul. And if not even the rational soul, the distinctively human intrinsic mover, is an immovable in-trinsic mover, then there are no genuine self-movers among the things we are familiar with. Anything that might count as a cosmic first self-mover would have to be unlike the 'self-movers' we know, in being immovable even *per accidens* as regards the part that does the moving, in the sense that it would have to be impervious to any extrinsic efficient causation.

The absolute unmovedness of any first mover that might count as (or come close to counting as) God is only one of two points aimed at in stage III. The other is the beginninglessness of any viable candidate. The Aristotelian thesis that motion is sempiternal (line 13) is of course crucial to this aspect of stage III. But it is only the beginninglessness and continuity implicit in sempiternity that are relevant here (and not also its endlessness), and so we can focus our attention appropriately by reading Aquinas's 'sempiternal', 'per-petual', and 'always' as 'beginningless' or 'beginninglessly', and his 'perpetuity' as 'beginninglessness'.[56]

Stage III is developing the hypothesis that motion is to be ex-plained in terms of self-movers, and that all motion is ultimately to be explained in terms of a cosmic first self-mover. Aquinas says that if motion is beginningless, then the generation of self-movers that are generable and destructible must be beginningless (lines 13–15). For my purposes in this strand of stage III we can generalize the Aristotelian hypothesis to something like this: the generative series of generable and destructible natural things—that is, the physical universe considered diachronically—is beginningless. That hypoth-esis is, I think, compatible not only with stage III but also with all varieties of cosmic evolution.[57]

---

[56] He uses *sempiternum* in 13.104–7, *perpetua* and *perpetuitas* in 105, *semper* in 105 and 106, and *aeternitas* (as synonymous with *perpetuitas* or *sempiternitas*) in 109 and 110.

[57] Even if empirical data render the Big Bang hypothesis undeniable, a beginningless universe with a beginningless process of cosmic evolution is not thereby ruled out, as cosmologists' considerations of a 'concertina' universe indicate.

Notice that this strand of the argument is concerned not with the source of any element or elements of the generative series, or even directly with the cause of the series itself, but rather with the cause or explanation of its *beginninglessness* (cf. lines 15–16, 19–20). What could account for there having been movers *always*? Aquinas is surely within his rights to suppose that if X accounts for Y's existing beginninglessly, then X itself cannot have begun to exist (lines 15–16). But suppose we do think of the beginningless generative series as the physical universe itself. We will then recognize that, in view of its beginninglessness, none of the infinitely many generative events making up the series lacks an explanation in the form of an extrinsic moved mover. And so the presupposition here is that there is some explanation of the very fact that there is this beginningless series of moved movers. Why is there what there is, rather than something else or nothing at all? Those who share my view that this question is not merely rhetorical will find that presupposition unexceptionable. As for those who say they don't share that view, I find it very hard to believe that they aren't kidding themselves, especially because they, like all the rest of us, recognize that rational inquiry, if not quantum physics, depends on taking particular instantiations of that question seriously in every other context. Every cosmological argument depends on some version of the principle of sufficient reason, and the version on which this one depends strikes me as prima facie irresistible and pragmatically defensible: 'if there is a cause of the generation and destruction of things that move themselves, there must also be a cause of the fact that their generation and destruction is perpetually continuous' (In Phys. VIII: L12.1074).

The rest of this strand of stage III is devoted to ruling out (a) any element or elements of the beginningless series (lines 15–16) and (b) all its elements taken together (lines 16–18) as possibly explanatory of its beginninglessness, and I see no good grounds on which to object to this development. The familiar objections raised by Hume and Russell against this line of reasoning in cosmological arguments have been decisively answered in well-known work by William Rowe,[58] some of which we'll be considering in another connection in the next chapter. But the exclusion of those other possibilities isn't all that goes on in the rest of stage III, which

[58] See e.g. Rowe 1975c.

strikes me as particularly likely to be misleading. I think I can most effectively offer my view of it by taking a broad approach based on details already uncovered.

Stage III is the heart of G2, and G2 is an argument from motion the main line of which might be sketched up through stage III in this way. Things obviously get moved, and everything, Z, that gets moved is moved by something else, Y, that explains Z's motion. If Y itself is a moved mover, then Y's motion in moving Z is explained by X, the mover that moves Y in its moving of Z. So if *every* mover is a moved mover, this explanatory regress of movers is infinite, and the general fact that things get moved is left unexplained.

But some movers of other things are *intrinsically* moved. Since being intrinsically moved must be explained in terms of having a part that does the moving and a complementary part that is moved by that intrinsic mover, it doesn't constitute an exception to the OQM principle. Unlike ordinary, extrinsically moved movers, such self-movers could serve as termini of explanations of motion, but only if their own intrinsic movers were themselves immovable.

However, animals are the only self-movers of which we have any experience, and souls, the intrinsic movers of animals, are all movable extrinsically *per accidens*. Moreover, every animal gets generated and destroyed, and so no motion produced by any animal or animals, or by any self-mover relevantly like them, could explain the infinite explanatory regress or, what in this case is the same thing viewed otherwise, the beginningless generative series of movers.

Any self-mover that could serve as the source of such an explanation, that could count as absolutely first, or what I'm calling a cosmic first self-mover, would have to be sempiternally and continuously operative as an extrinsic mover of other things. And just as any first self-mover's intrinsic mover is immovable, so a cosmic first self-mover's intrinsic mover would have to be immovable, since whatever is movable in any way is, in some respect, to some degree, dependent on something else's moving it (lines 27–9),[59]

[59] Some such claim must be the intended point of the otherwise mysterious clause in lines 30–1, 'every motion other than a first self-mover's motion is caused'. As we've seen, it is one of Aquinas's principles that every motion, without exception, is caused. Furthermore, stage IV of argument G2 is intended to reveal what must be the cause of a cosmic first self-mover's motion. It seems to me that Aquinas might have meant to say that every motion other than a first self-mover's motion is initiated—*incipitur*, or something like it. But the word in the text is *causetur*.

and thus not a viable basis for the explanation of the beginninglessness of the generative series. So, if the beginningless generative series of movers is to be explained by a cosmic first self-mover, that self-mover must itself be moving other things beginninglessly and continuously, and so it must itself be 'moved by a mover that is not moved, neither *per se* nor *per accidens*'(lines 32–3). That is, if X is a cosmic first self-mover, capable of serving as the basis for the explanation of the beginningless generative series of movers, X must be a first self-mover that moves other things beginninglessly and continuously. Since the self-movers we are, and are familiar with, are (a) generable and destructible, and (b) only occasionally first self-movers, of course no ordinary self-mover could fill the bill of cosmic first self-mover.

I've been treating a cosmic first self-mover as a purely hypothetical and pretty unlikely entity, one that must be examined for the sake of completeness but that can be discarded thereafter. Aristotle seems to have thought of such an entity, identified as the outermost celestial sphere, as a cosmological necessity,[60] but I think Aquinas takes a more ambivalent position in his final appraisal of G2. The second of the two features of G2 that 'appear to weaken the lines of reasoning we have been considering' is that 'in the demonstrations that have just been presented it is assumed that the first thing moved, a heavenly body, is moved from within. From this it follows that it is animate, which many people do not grant. In reply we have to say that if [that] first mover is not assumed to be moved from within, then it must be moved directly by something immovable [that is extrinsic to it]. That is why even Aristotle introduces this conclusion under a disjunction: that one must either arrive directly at a separated, immovable first mover or [arrive] at a self-mover, from which, in turn, one arrives at a separated, immovable first mover' (13.109, 111–12).[61] And so we've returned to the fork in the argument. The plainer, and only really satisfactory, way to go is directly towards a sempiternal, separated, immovable first mover as the ultimate explanation of the beginninglessly, continuously moving Aristotelian universe. Anyone who follows the other way, via consideration of a possible cosmic *self*-mover, will arrive (a little later) at the same destination, as G2's stage IV is designed to show.

[60] See e.g. *Metaphysics* XII 7, 1072a21–7.
[61] Cf. *Physics* VIII 5, 258a5–8; In Phys. VIII: L11.1062.

Stage IV

But God is not a part of any self-mover. And so Aristotle, on the basis of the [sort of] mover that is *part* of a self-mover, further investigates, in his *Metaphysics*, another, altogether *separate* mover, which is God. For since every self-mover is moved through appetite, a mover that is part of a self-mover must move on account of its appetite for some 5 appetible object. That appetible object is superior to that mover as regards moving, for what has appetite is in some respect a moved mover, while what is appetible is an altogether unmoved mover. Therefore, there must be a separated, altogether immovable first mover, which is God. (13.108)[62] 10

All the movers we encountered in argument G2 before stage IV can and should be considered efficient causes of whatever motion is attributed to them, as I said earlier. It's only in case we take seriously the possibility of a cosmic self-mover (as Aristotle did) that we have to recognize final causation, the other sort of motive force in Aquinas's world, the sort of motive force presupposed by the very notion of a self-mover, the only sort that can move a self-mover when it's behaving as such and not merely being pushed around. Without stage IV, argument G2 points to a cosmic first mover that sempiternally and extrinsically sustains nature's beginningless motions and drives them. Stage IV adds the image of a cosmic first mover toward which are drawn the motions that have their sources within nature's self-movers—cosmic (if any) or merely mundane, like us. As might be expected, final causation is very important in Aquinas's natural theology generally, and, as we'll see, it gets fuller treatment later, when some of the questions raised by its use in stage IV of argument G2 will get answered.

With all its labyrinthine complexities, redundancies, and digressions, G2 is certainly not the more elegant or the stronger of SCG's two arguments from motion. Though it's far from being Aquinas's best, however, I think it clearly is his most intricate argument for God's existence. It has fatal flaws, as we've seen, but it also contains lines of thought that illuminate later developments in his natural theology. And I'm sure I haven't yet seen clearly all there is, bad or good, to see in it.

[62] Cf. *Metaphysics* XII 7, 1072a26–30; In Met. XII: L7.2519–22.

THREE

THE EXISTENCE OF ALPHA

1. Orientation

As we've seen, Aquinas ends his general introduction to SCG by making a claim he seems to think is obvious, since he offers no support for it. He declares that his project of a natural theology based on Aristotelian metaphysics could not get started without a satisfactory argument for God's existence (9.58). He then duly begins the natural theology proper by devoting a long chapter to the presentation of five arguments, mostly Aristotelian, by means of which, he says, it has been proved that God exists.

The first of those arguments—G1, as I've been calling it—does look promising, if it's appropriately supplemented along the lines proposed in MacDonald's recently published (1991a) analysis of it and its younger relative, the more famous First Way (of ST Ia.2.3). But I haven't provided an appraisal of argument G1 as part of my project in this book, so I consider myself entitled to view it only as an intriguing logical object shimmering on the horizon.

G2, the second of chapter 13's arguments, is the only existence argument I've examined so far. And we've seen that it's too flawed to be considered philosophically acceptable evidence for the existence of a primary, universally explanatory being—the sort of being the argument has in its sights. None of the remaining three arguments in the chapter is as impressive a candidate as G1 (or, in some respects, even G2) is for being an argument of the sort Aquinas thinks he has to have in order to get his project started. From my point of view, then, we're about to move on into natural theology's investigation of the nature of God without having been expressly provided with an acceptable argument for the existence of anything extraordinary, let alone God. The naturally suspect character of such a move lends plausibility to Aquinas's claim that the project can't be pursued any further in these circumstances.

But, as I suggested in Chapter Two, I think he overstates his project's need for an existence proof at the outset. Like any feasible natural theology, it really requires no more to begin with than *the working hypothesis* that there is an appropriately, broadly characterized sort of explanatory being, which needn't be identified as God and, in the absence of a more detailed characterization, really shouldn't be identified as God.

This required hypothetical being is of a sort Aquinas already has in view well before the arguments of chapter 13. For he begins SCG by saying that in it he intends 'to take up the role of a wise person' (2.9), and, as he conceives of wisdom here, 'considering the highest causes is part of what it is to be a wise person' (1.3).[1] Therefore, the most fundamental truths making up the profoundest explanations involving primary (or ultimate) things, events, and states of affairs must be wisdom's concern. And this means that the one subject-matter indispensable to anybody intending 'to take up the role of a wise person' is the subject-matter of metaphysics as Aristotle and Aquinas envisage it. For, Aquinas says, Aristotle 'intends [metaphysics or] first philosophy to be the science of truth—not of just any truth, but of the truth that is the origin of all truth, the truth that pertains to the first source (*primum principium*) of being for all things' (1.5).[2] (It seems clear that Aquinas sees his natural theology as the extension of metaphysics understood along these lines— Aristotelian metaphysics extended into the metaphysics of theism—and that his taking up the role of a wise person consists primarily in his developing that extension.) So, if God exists, then, of course, God will be this broadly characterized universal source, the first source of being for all things. That's simply part of what it is to be God, considered pre-theoretically, and any natural theology that aims at being taken seriously by theists would have to present God in that guise. It certainly seems possible, however, that there should be a universal first source of being, but no God— possible that metaphysics, even when conceived along these Aristotelian lines, should not culminate in *theology*, as Aristotle himself

---

[1] See also Aristotle, *Metaphysics* I 1, 981a28–b6; and Aquinas's commentary In Met. I: L1.24–8; also *Metaphysics* I 2, 982a30–b4; In Met. I: L2.49. For a full account of Aquinas on wisdom see Stump, forthcoming.

[2] *Metaphysics* II 1, 993b29–30 (translating the medieval Latin text): 'For that reason it is necessary that the principles (*principia*) of existing things be absolutely true (*verissima*), for it is not the case that they are true at some times and not true at other times. Nor do they have any cause for their existence; instead, they [are the causes for the existence] of other things.' See also In Met. II: L2.298.

thought it did. Any entity that could count as the first source of being for all things would have to be breath-takingly extraordinary, but even breath-takingly extraordinary isn't yet divine.

2. How to proceed

So, taking ourselves to be without a good argument for the existence of God or of anything else that might count as the universal first source of being, suppose we proceed by thinking not in terms of natural theology as ordinarily understood (and as Aquinas evidently understands it) but more broadly—meta-cosmologically, it might be said—in terms of what I've been calling the Grandest Unified Theory, the theoretically developed answer to the big question, Why is there this sort of world rather than another sort, or nothing at all? Now if we assume that there is an answer to that question—and we're certainly not in a position to declare that there *can't* be one[3]—then simply in making that assumption we are adopting the working hypothesis that there is an ultimate explanatory principle, what Aquinas identifies as 'a universal source', 'a first source of being for all things', whatever would have to be at the heart of the answer to the big question. And we understand that this hypothesis is not to be taken as equivalent to the hypothesis that God exists. For instance, among other considerations that weigh against the equivalence, it's conceivable that there should be an irreducible plurality of ultimate explanatory principles. I'll take up that possibility in Chapter Five; but meanwhile, for the sake of handy reference, I'll suppose that there is at most one, and I'll use 'Alpha' to designate this hypothetical first source, whether it's one or many.[4] As far as I'm concerned, the development of this natural theology can then proceed as an inquiry into the sort of thing an ultimate explanatory principle would have to be, into what sort of thing Alpha would have to be. If that inquiry turns up evidence for the existence of Alpha, so much the better; but in this development the question of Alpha's nature precedes the question of its existence.

---

[3] See Rowe's helpful discussion of the criteria for a question's being meaningful and for its having an answer (1975c: 140–3).

[4] For the sake of handy reference, even an irreducible plurality of ultimate explanatory principles can be thought of as one.

Aristotle thought, naturally enough, that in the systematic presentation of a topically unified inquiry, in the development of an Aristotelian science, the question of the subject's existence would have to be settled at the outset.[5] As he and Aquinas, the consummate Aristotelian, conceive of a particular science, its principal concern—developing the detailed answer to the question of *what* the subject of the science is—does require, first, an affirmative answer to the question of *whether* that subject is. Now if the Aristotelian science at issue is zoology, say, or astronomy, this ordering of questions about the subject's existence and about its nature seems just right, as long as we understand that in most such cases an affirmative answer to the question of the subject's existence would be so uncontroversial that the question would be asked and answered perfunctorily if asked expressly at all. And this may seem especially clear when the Aristotelian science under consideration is metaphysics, the science that has as its primary subject beings considered simply as beings. There can't be a serious question of whether there are beings, especially if they're being considered simply as *beings*. On the other hand, since the goal of metaphysics is the ultimate explanation of beings considered simply as beings, it might be said to have as its ultimate subject the universal first source of being, and evidence for the existence of that mysterious subject really is called for. But just because that subject isn't anything familiar to us, it seems best to let the evidence for (or against) its existence emerge in the course of considering what its nature would have to be. After all, Aristotle himself offers his most fully developed arguments for the *existence* of the first mover only in the *last* books of his *Physics* and his *Metaphysics*. The fact that Aquinas undertakes to *launch* his project in SCG with his adaptations of those culminating Aristotelian arguments is part of my reason for thinking of his project as the metaphysics of *theism*, or as philosophy from the top down, as I explained in Chapter One. I've been proposing to try following the trail he blazed, but I'm prepared to go ahead *without* an affirmative answer to the question of whether a first cause exists. And so I'm proposing to construe this stage of the investigation as taking up not the question of existent God's nature but the question of what can be justifiably said about the nature of hypothetical Alpha.

<hr/>

[5] *Posterior Analytics* I 1, 71a1–b8; In PA I: L2.14, 15, 18.

3. *How Aquinas proceeds in SCG*

But Aquinas himself, after all, insists that the investigation he intends to carry out can't be begun without a good argument for the existence of God. So it's only reasonable to expect that the moves he makes in the chapters immediately following chapter 13 will be based, explicitly or implicitly, on what he considers to be the just-proved proposition 'God exists'. And so, surely, going ahead without taking that proposition to have been established can't count as following Aquinas in this enterprise. Well, we'll see.

But before looking directly at what he does in the chapters immediately following chapter 13, we can helpfully remind ourselves that his project in SCG is different from all his other large-scale projects in theology, in that he expressly declares that in the arguments of SCG I–III he will not base any conclusions on any data derived from any source other than those available to human experience and human reason apart from any putative revelation. So, even if we suppose for a moment that every one of his five existence arguments in chapter 13 succeeds, then, if Aquinas observes his own rules, in the immediately following chapters he should not be setting out to investigate the nature of an entity any more God-like than is warranted by the conclusions of the existence arguments in chapter 13. And those conclusions, taken one by one, describe the entity whose existence is inferred as 'an immovable first mover' (G1), 'a separated, altogether immovable first mover' (G2), 'a first efficient cause' (G3), 'something that is a being in the fullest possible sense (*aliquid quod est maxime ens*)' (G4), and 'someone by whose providence the world is governed' (G5).[6]

The G5 conclusion does unmistakably describe *God*, a supernatural, knowing, universally governing person. However, in the chapters immediately following chapter 13, Aquinas never draws on or alludes to argument G5; nor does he use the G5 description to pick out the being whose nature he is investigating. Since G5's conclusion is more unmistakably theistic, and thus presumably more to his purpose than any of the other four, the most likely explanation for his not making use of it would be that he considers

[6] 13.83 (G1); 108 (G2); 113 (G3); 114 (G4); 115 (G5).

G5 a weak argument.[7] And although it appeals to evidence that might be developed more persuasively, G5 *is* a weak argument.[8] But Aquinas introduces all five as 'arguments by which philosophers as well as Catholic teachers *have proved* that God exists' (9.81), and he provides no explicit indication that he thinks less of G5 than of the others. I have no fully satisfactory explanation for his ignoring it after having gone to the trouble of including it among the arguments of chapter 13.

To varying extents, Aquinas does use the descriptions in the conclusions of the other four arguments, as we'll see, and some of them are more detailed than others, a little more nearly theological than merely cosmological. But none of them is full enough to provide an unmistakably sufficient condition for deity, and so I'll adopt the further working hypothesis that when Aquinas uses the word 'God' in the chapters immediately after chapter 13, we could, without giving up information we're entitled to, read 'God' as 'Alpha'.[9]

Aquinas ends the first nine chapters of SCG, his general introduction, by describing the rest of Book I as devoted to 'the consideration of matters having to do with God considered in himself' (9.57), as distinct from the consideration of other things in relation to God, the business of Books II and III. And so, in keeping with the Aristotelian programme we've already noted, he thinks of the rest of Book I as divided into two main parts, the first consisting of four chapters devoted to the question of God's existence, culminating in chapter 13's arguments, the second consisting of eighty-eight chapters devoted to the question of God's nature. But the first part

[7] In these circumstances it may be worth remembering that G5 is the only one of the arguments in ch. 13 that isn't drawn from Aristotle. Aquinas attributes it to John Damascene and Averroës. So it's the only one that can be characterized as an argument 'by means of which . . . Catholic teachers have [or, more precisely, one Catholic teacher has] proved that God exists' (13.81).

[8] 'It is impossible that contrary and discordant things coexist (*concordare*) in a single order always or for the most part except under someone's governance, on the basis of which all and each will be brought to tend toward a definite goal. But in the world we see things of diverse natures coexisting in a single order, not rarely or by chance, but always or for the most part. Therefore, there must be someone by whose providence the world is governed, and him we call God' (9.115).

[9] Naturally, I don't intend this claim of replaceability to extend to the use of 'God' (or 'Lord') in the scriptural passages he appends near the ends of some of those chapters—e.g. 14.119, 15.126.

is separated from the second by a short chapter 14, which provides presuppositions for the rest of his natural theology.

4. Two presuppositions of Aquinas's procedure

The presupposition I want to consider first is Aquinas's explicit statement of the only basis he thinks he really needs, now that he is about to start the new investigation. And it's interesting that the basis he cites is not an explicitly existential claim. Instead, he merely ascribes to the subject of his investigation a single characteristic, the one associated particularly with argument G2: 'let us take as a starting-point (*principium*) that which is already manifest from the above [arguments]—I mean, that *God is altogether immovable*' (14.119). Since by 'altogether immovable' (*omnino immobilis*) he means incapable of being changed in any way,[10] there's nothing unmistakably divine about this characteristic. As we saw in examining G2, some of its argumentation does offer good grounds for denying mutability to anything that, like Alpha, could count as an ultimate explanation of change. But I think it's in any case self-evident that Alpha can count as the *ultimate* explanation of change only if it is itself altogether unchangeable in at least the aspect of it that is supposed to account for all change. We'll be seeing more of this immutability, but for now it seems right to say that following Aquinas in taking the absolute immutability of the ultimate explanatory principle as an already established starting-point for the investigation of Alpha's nature does not involve either accepting an existence claim or associating with Alpha a characteristic that only God could have.[11]

In the order in which I'm considering them, the second of chap-

---

[10] This may be seen in the variants of this claim used as premises in later chapters: 'altogether without motion' (15.122); 'altogether impassible and immutable' (16.132; cf. 23.215 and 217). The claim itself is invoked in e.g. 15.121, 17.138, 19.152, 20.156, 23.215.

[11] Aquinas does open ch. 14 with an announcement of an existential result: 'Therefore, having shown that there is a first being (*est aliquod primum ens*), . . . we have to investigate its characteristics' (14.116). But I think it's clear that this particular existence claim is important to him only as an announcement that he has fulfilled the Aristotelian pre-condition for going on to investigate the *nature* of the first being that is his science's subject. What makes me think it's clear is that at the end of ch. 14 it is only immutability, not existence, that he deliberately cites as the basis from which to go on.

ter 14's presuppositions is an epistemological observation that I consider uncontroversial, whether applied to God or to Alpha. Aquinas puts it this way: 'in virtue of its immeasurability the divine substance is beyond every form our intellect acquires, and so we cannot apprehend it itself by discerning (*cognoscendo*) what it is' (14.117). He hasn't provided any argument for the first being's 'immeasurability', nor does he claim to have done so. What he's noting here really amounts to no more than our inability to locate Alpha within any of our taxonomic schemes or conceptual frameworks, which have all been developed, naturally, as means of knowing the ordinary phenomena of which Alpha is supposed to be the ultimate explanatory principle. This comes out more clearly when he argues a little later that God (or Alpha) can't be found in any of the nine Aristotelian categories of accident (chapter 23) or in the first Aristotelian category, substance (25.236), and that God (or Alpha) can't be given a full-fledged definition (25.233). What's uncontroversial here is the underlying idea that anything that could count as the ultimate explanation of physical reality could not be apprehended, measured, or classified in any of the ways human beings have discovered or could devise for apprehending, measuring, or classifying things in nature. Quarks, gluons, the strong force, and all the other ingredients in currently fundamental physical explanations conform to or manifest natural laws, the basic conceptual framework in which standard scientific explanations terminate. But anything that could count as an ultimate explanation would have to explain natural laws as well.

This epistemological presupposition of Aquinas's can also seem to defeat his purpose in going on to investigate the nature of ultimate reality. For what could be the goal of that investigation if not to 'apprehend it itself by discerning what it is'?

5. A third presupposition: the eliminative method

Aquinas's answer to that question is the third and last presupposition provided in chapter 14. 'We have a kind of knowledge of' the first being, he says, 'by discerning what it is *not*, and we come closer to a knowledge of it to the extent to which we can through our intellect *eliminate* more [characteristics] from it; for the more fully we observe anything's differences from other things, the more completely do we discern it' (14.117). And, of course, he's right. Negative discoveries do carve out affirmative information. Just think of the assured progress you'd be making in a game of Twenty Questions by getting nothing but negative answers to your cleverly framed series of questions. 'For example, if we say that God is not an accident'—that is, doesn't belong in any of the nine categories of accident—'he is on that basis distinguished from all accidents.' Therefore, if God can be fitted into the Aristotelian categories at all, he belongs in the first category: substance. 'If we then add that he is not a body, we will distinguish him also from some substances' in the first category, and we will know that God is an incorporeal substance, if he is a substance at all (14.118). And so on.

So the third of chapter 14's presuppositions is methodological, and Aquinas himself calls this indirect route to cognition 'the eliminative method (*via remotionis*)' (14.117, 119). It is, I think, exactly suited to the project of acquiring cognition of the characteristics of the hypothetical Alpha, coming 'closer to a knowledge of it to the extent to which we can through our intellect eliminate more [characteristics] from it'. That's why Aquinas introduces as his new starting-point only the already accomplished *elimination* of the characteristic of being in any way subject to change: 'Therefore, in order to proceed by the eliminative method as regards the cognition of God, let us take as a starting-point that which is already manifest from the above [arguments]—I mean, that God is altogether immovable' (14.119).

It may be reassuring as regards the further development of this natural theology to point ahead to two facts about the eliminative method that will emerge as we go on. First, it's not the only method Aquinas uses in building up an indirect cognition of the nature of ultimate reality. After he's prepared the ground with a series of eliminative moves, through chapter 28, he begins to argue in a different way for a special sort of *affirmative* conclusion, as we'll see in Chapter Five.

Second, the entirely negative and presumably meagre results of the eliminative method are not his only resource even in these early chapters. In applying the method (and indeed throughout SCG) Aquinas freely introduces as premises of his arguments not only propositions he has argued for earlier but also many propositions he treats as *principles* of this subordinate science, as needing no support within this project itself. It's not hard to pick out more than ninety such principles in chapters 14–28, for instance. Some of them would be certified as axiomatic by anyone's philosophical intuition—e.g. 'What doesn't exist can't accomplish anything'; 'Parts are incomplete in respect of their whole'; 'A continuum is potentially divisible *ad infinitum*'. Many others should be readily accepted in these circumstances as Aristotelian commonplaces—e.g. 'Every definition is made up of a genus and differentiae'; 'What is common to many things is something over and above those many only conceptually'. A few of these principles would be hard or impossible for most of us to accept—e.g. 'Intellect is not a corporeal power'. But Aquinas's procedure in SCG typically involves such a proliferation of arguments for each conclusion important to his project that we're seldom, if ever, forced to choose between accepting an implausible principle and bypassing an important conclusion.

Where does Aquinas get these principles? Almost entirely from Aristotle, of course, although his explicit attributions are rare and seem to have been reserved for theses Aquinas probably takes to be distinctively Aristotelian, such as 'Time is the measure of motion' and 'There is no infinite magnitude'. And what entitles him to use them as unsupported premisses? No doubt he takes some of them to be self-evidently true, and surely he's sometimes within his rights to do so—e.g. 'A conditional proposition with an impossible antecedent can be true', or 'Substance does not depend on accident, although accident depends on substance'. I believe that he takes all the others to have been successfully argued for by Aristotle. For instance, when he invokes the Aristotelian thesis of the incorporeality of the human intellect, he justifies doing so by pointing out that '*it has been proved* that intellect is not a corporeal power' (20.183).[12] Nothing of the sort has been even discussed in the preceding chapters of SCG, so his claim that it has been proved must be an allusion to Aristotle's own arguments to that effect in *De anima* III (an allusion of a sort that his thirteenth-century academic contemporaries would have had no trouble picking up). But since the natural theology Aquinas is developing evidently has, by his own lights, the status of a science subordinate to metaphysics

---

[12] [P]*robatum est quod intellectus non est virtus corporea*, which Pegis translates: '*we have proved* that the intellect is not a corporeal power' (1975: 113; emphasis added), thereby misleadingly implying that such a proof is to be looked for in the preceding chapters of SCG I.

proper, to *Aristotelian* metaphysics, there's every reason why he should—indeed, must—help himself to Aristotelian principles and argued theses in developing his subordinate science. Still, in assessing any of his arguments, we will of course have to ask about the acceptability of his apparently unsupported premisses.

Drawing on the arguments of chapter 13 for no more about the first cause initially than that it must not be subject to any change, Aquinas carries his investigation of its nature forward by applying the eliminative method again and again in chapters 15–28, arguing for the elimination of at least nineteen characteristics that an altogether immutable first cause couldn't have. In doing so, he regularly draws on propositions of that sort that were argued for earlier (as well as on the Aristotelian principles I've just been talking about). I'll examine several of those derivations and their results in Chapter Four. For my present purposes a look at his very first arguments in this series will be helpful.

For instance, Aquinas's opening move in chapter 15 is to show that anything 'altogether immutable', regardless of any causal function it might have, would also have to be beginningless and endless, since, as he says, 'everything that does begin or cease to exist undergoes it through motion or change' (15.121). Immutability's incompatibility with ceasing to exist is more obvious than its incompatibility with beginning to exist. Still, even though a thing's beginning to exist can't count as a change in that thing, which didn't exist until then, it must count as a change in the way the world is. And so Alpha, which is by hypothesis the ultimate explanation of all change and of the way the world is, could never have begun to exist any more than it could ever cease to exist.[13]

But, as Aquinas goes on to observe in that same chapter 15, the world that Alpha is supposed to be the explanation of is full of things that do, and therefore can, begin and cease to exist. On the basis of that observation he develops another argument, one that focuses on Alpha's causality as the earlier argument focused on its immutability. As we'll see just below, he presents this argument simply as another application of the eliminative method, not as an argument for the existence of anything. But I think that part of it

---

[13] The argument in 15.123 is perhaps clearer than the one in 15.121 as regards beginninglessness, but I think that it's less clear as regards endlessness, and that the argument to the same conclusion in 15.121 is generally the better of the two.

can and should be considered as an argument for Alpha's existence, and that's how I will now consider it. The part I'm interested
in I'll call argument G6.

6. The existence of Alpha

a. Argument G6

We see things in the world that can exist and can also not exist (*sunt
possibilia esse et non esse*)—I mean those that can be generated and
can be destroyed. Now everything that can exist [and can also not
exist] has a cause. For since on its own it is related indifferently to
those two—existing and not existing—if existing is its status (*ei*   5
approprietur), that must be on the basis of some cause. But one cannot
go on *ad infinitum* in [a series of] causes, as was proved above on the
basis of Aristotle's reasoning. Therefore, one must posit something
the existing of which is necessary (*aliquid quod sit necesse esse*).[14] Now
everything necessary either has the cause of its necessity in something   10
else, or it doesn't but is, instead, necessary through itself. But one
cannot go on *ad infinitum* in [a series of] necessary beings that have
the cause of their necessity in something else. Therefore, one must
posit some first necessary being that is necessary through itself.
(15.124)

b. General observations

The sentence with which I end my translation of this passage, the
conclusion of argument G6, is not the final conclusion of Aquinas's
argument, which, like the other arguments of chapter 15, is intended to show that God is eternal. Accordingly, his complete
argument includes these two additional sentences: 'And that is
God, since he is the first cause, as has been shown. Therefore, God
is eternal, since everything necessary through itself is eternal.' I'm
leaving out the first of those two sentences because I'm now concerned with Alpha rather than with God, and because I'm only

---

[14] The editors of the Marietti edn. of SCG suggest that this Latin expression stems
from Avicenna's Arabic, and they distinguish it typographically (although not in all
its occurrences). See their note to this passage. But they offer no evidence that
Aquinas derives the expression from the medieval Latin translation of Avicenna,
and I see no reason why he should have had to do so.

supposing that there is a first cause, not claiming that it has already been shown.[15] The second sentence omitted, Aquinas's final conclusion for this argument, is what makes the argument appropriate for chapter 15. His complete argument is a product of the eliminative method, because 'eternal' as used in that final conclusion must mean existing beginninglessly, endlessly, and probably also timelessly.[16] G6, the argument I'm now interested in, is only the part of Aquinas's argument that purports to show that 'one must posit some first necessary being that is necessary through itself'. I'm not interested now in deriving another characteristic from that kind of necessity.[17]

G6's 'first necessary being that is necessary through itself' is inferred as the explanation for the existence of all the things 'we see . . . in the world that can exist and can also not exist', the things that make up the observable world. So the entity to which argument G6 concludes is Alpha, the hypothetical first cause of the existence and nature of the observable world.

The fact that G6 deals in possibilities and positings might give the impression that the argument is merely hypothetical, concluding only to a necessity that Alpha would have to have if Alpha really does exist. But G6 clearly is an inference to the explanation of the most familiar kind of actual existence, the kind exemplified by ordinary things that 'we see . . . in the world'. And so the conclusion of G6 is to be read as a claim that a certain extraordinary sort of thing must actually exist, and that it must exist differently from

---

[15] Aquinas's claim here that it has been shown that God is the first cause should perhaps be construed as going beyond the starting-point he cites at the end of ch. 14, in which case he may be drawing here on G3 more directly than on G2 (or G1).

[16] 'Eternal' means only sempiternal (beginningless and endless) in 15.121 and 123. In 15.125 God is not called eternal at all, but only sempiternal. Only in 15.122 is there an argument explicitly and unmistakably for God's atemporality. But argument G6 as I interpret it may indeed imply the atemporality of the being whose existence it argues for; see n. 30 below.

[17] Although the title of ch. 15 contains the proposition 'God is eternal' and although the chapter contains five arguments (including the one in 15.124) concluding either that God is eternal or that God is sempiternal, the derived propositions in ch. 15 that matter most to Aquinas in the following chapters are the conclusion (lines 13–14) and the sub-conclusion (lines 8–9) of G6 (as distinct from the full argument in 15.124). He uses these G6 results as premises at least eleven times in chs. 16–28: 16.130 (twice), 18.143, 19.150 (twice), 19.151, 22.203, 22.205, 22.206, 24.223, and 26.240. In those same chapters he cites 'God is sempiternal' just once (16.128) and 'God is eternal', meaning no more than that God is sempiternal, twice (16.127 and 26.242). See further discussion in Ch. Four.

the way the things we see in the world exist, just in virtue of its serving as the ultimate explanation of their existence.

Considered in this way, as an argument for Alpha's existence, G6 is clearly within the extended family of the 'cosmological' arguments, those that attempt to argue from the undoubted existence or occurrence of ordinary things, events, or states of affairs to the existence of an extraordinary being whose existence and nature constitute the ultimate explanation of the existence or occurrence of everything, including itself.[18] That observation about G6 invites comparisons between it and others of Aquinas's cosmological arguments for God's existence. It will become clear that G6 is specifically different from any of the three cosmological arguments in chapter 13 (G1, G2, and G3). As for the cosmological arguments among ST's Five Ways, what I'm calling G6 has been described in the literature, much too simply, as 'the version of the *Third Way* given in the *Summa contra Gentiles*' (van Steenberghen 1966: 126).[19] Since the Third Way, too, is an argument based on the contingency of ordinary existence, it might count as G6's closest relative among the Five Ways. But there are more than enough significant differences between the two arguments to rule out taking G6 to be merely a version of the Third Way, differences that warrant considering G6 on its own.

c. Double dependence

G6 begins with propositions immediately inferable from commonplace observations about familiar things. We regularly observe the more impermanent things around us being generated and being destroyed, and we have good reasons to think that all the less impermanent things we see, such as mountains and planets and

---

[18] The literature on the cosmological argument(s) is vast. The best philosophical treatment of it I know is Rowe 1975*a*. Craig 1980 provides a very helpful historical account.

[19] Van Steenberghen considers this 'version' clearly better than the Third Way itself and useful in refurbishing it: 'When set right with the help of the *Summa contra Gentiles*, the *Third Way* doubtless gives us a satisfactory proof' (1966: 127). 'Why St. Thomas ever abandoned the simpler and more satisfactory formulation of the proof given in the *Contra Gentiles* (begun in 1258) to become involved in the curious and complicated considerations of the *Third Way* (written towards 1266) is a historical enigma to which we shall return' (ibid. 127 n. 9; cf. pp. 149–50). For a later, more detailed discussion along these same lines, see van Steenberghen 1980: 126–30, 187–205.

stars, have been generated and will be destroyed. The world is full of existing things that *can* also not exist, things that did not always exist but have been (and so 'can be') generated and *can* be destroyed—in short, contingently existing things (lines 1–3).

As G6 implies, Aquinas thinks that a contingent being's present existence is dependent in two respects: first, it has been generated, and so depends on something else for having come into existence; second, it depends on something else for existing, because it has no intrinsic tendency to continue to exist: 'on its own it is related indifferently to (*de se aequaliter se habeat ad*) . . . existing and not existing' (lines 4–5).[20]

The dependence of a contingently existing thing in this second respect may at first seem overstated, because it entails the denial of an altogether natural, practically universal background belief, which might be thought of as the assumption of existential inertia— the assumption that many or most contingent beings *do* have a tendency to continue to exist, other things being equal. And there's nothing objectionable in that assumption, as long as it's recognized that a contingent being is by definition something the existing of which is utterly dependent on other things' being equal, on the fulfilment of many necessary conditions.[21] Aquinas's denial of existential inertia applies only to such an utterly dependently existing thing considered 'on its own', not within a context normal for its existing. So the cause or causes inferred in lines 3–6 must be whatever it takes to explain some contingent being's presently existing despite its doubly dependent existential status. What it takes is answers to these two questions, into which the question about a thing's existence can be analysed: (Q1) What explains its having come into existence? and (Q2) What explains its presently existing? The causes inferred in lines 3–6, then, may at first seem to

[20] Being related indifferently to existing and not existing must apply only to an *existing* contingent thing considered on its own, as is suggested in the wording of lines 5–6—'if *existing* is its status, *that* must be on the basis of some cause'—and even by G6's opening words: 'We *see* things *in the world*'. Aquinas is not suggesting that any non-existent contingent being considered on its own, such as my twin brother, could suddenly show up among existing things. My existing must have some explanation; no explanation is needed to account for the non-existence of my twin.

[21] For this reason the contingent things Aquinas describes as being 'related *indifferently* to . . . existing and not existing' (lines 4–5) might be described more precisely as having no inherent tendency *to exist*, a characteristic strongly suggested by his going on to claim only as regards the *existing* of such a thing that *that* 'must be on the basis of some cause' (line 6).

be both generating and sustaining causes. But, as we'll see, generating causes are not at issue in argument G6.

The natural sciences provide answers to Q1 and Q2 about very many sorts of dependently existing things, and their answers are in terms of other dependently existing things. But, of course, both questions can and, at least from the standpoint of metaphysics, should be asked again about each dependent explanatory being referred to in such explanatory answers, no matter what level of generality they're formulated at, no matter how pervasive or simple may be the dependent things, events, or states of affairs they refer to. And the crux of Aquinas's line of reasoning in G6 is his denial that it is theoretically possible to trace back explanatory beings in this way *ad infinitum* (lines 6–7). What does he mean by that?

d. A series of generating causes

He might mean that it is theoretically impossible for the series of explanatory dependent beings to be beginningless, theoretically impossible for Q1 to be correctly answered again and again in terms of generating causes that 'go on *ad infinitum*' into 'the dark backward and abysm of time' (*The Tempest*, Act I, sc. ii). He might; but he doesn't. As I pointed out in Chapter Two, Aquinas argues elsewhere in SCG and in other works *against* the impossibility of the infinite temporal and causal regress entailed by the notion of our world's having existed always.[22] In doing so, he sometimes expressly supports the theoretical possibility of a regress that is infinite, as he says, only accidentally (*per accidens*). For instance,

in connection with efficient causes a regress that is infinite *accidentally* is *not* considered impossible—if, that is, all the infinitely many causes have the order of only one cause, but their being many is accidental. A carpenter, for example, acts by means of accidentally many hammers because one after another of them breaks; and so it is an accidental characteristic of this hammer that it acts after the action of another hammer. Similarly, it is an accidental characteristic of this man, in so far as he begets, that he has been begotten by another; for he begets in so far as he is a man and not in so far as he is the son of another man, since all men considered as begetters have a single status among efficient causes, the status of a particular begetter.

---

[22] See e.g. SCG II.31–8 and ST Ia.46; also, specifically, his very short, polemical treatise *De aeternitate mundi, contra murmurantes*.

And so it is not impossible that a man be begotten by a man *ad infinitum*. (ST Ia.46.2, ad 7)

For many things to 'have the order of only one cause (*non teneant ordinem nisi unius causae*)' or 'to have a single status among efficient causes (*habent gradum unum in causis efficientibus*)' is for their plurality to be irrelevant to the causal activity of any one of them, whether or not they are elements in a single causal series. The many hammers successively owned and used by the carpenter, one at a time, are not elements in a single causal series, but are altogether causally independent of one another: each of them does its hammering without in any way depending on its predecessors. On the other hand, each human begetter in a single line of biological descent is causally dependent on his immediate predecessor in that causal series in one respect—for his having been begotten. Even so, each of them does his begetting without depending on any of his predecessors in *that* respect. A father's begetting, considered just as such, is no more dependent on his father's begetting him than this hammer's hammering is dependent on the most recently discarded hammer's hammering. Since the plurality of these independently operating causes is entirely accidental to the causality of any one of them, there is in theory no reason why the series of hammers, or even the series of begetters, should not have been beginningless, should not constitute a temporally infinite regress.

So, when Aquinas says in lines 6–7 that 'one cannot go on *ad infinitum* in [a series of] causes', he doesn't mean that if we start with any doubly dependently existing thing, we can't in theory answer question Q1 *ad infinitum* in terms of a beginningless series of generating causes—an infinite regress of dependently existent, independently explanatory beings. In considering argument G2, we saw that Aquinas is occasionally willing to adopt the hypothesis of this world's beginninglessness for the sake of argument. Quite rightly, he takes the inclusion of that hypothesis to strengthen an argument for the existence of a first cause just because it poses a stiffer challenge to such an argument. So I propose adopting that hypothesis here in G6. I will suppose that for each and every thing that comes into existence the answer to Q1—the explanation of that dependent being's coming into existence—can be correctly given in terms of the causality of at least one earlier dependent being. In other words, I'm supposing, for the sake of argument G6, that there actually is a beginningless series of dependent beings generated by earlier dependent beings. I'll call that series S. Theories of biological, geological, and cosmological evolution have given us good reasons to think that the uncountably many concurrent generatively causal series of dependent beings tend to converge as they are traced back in time, that these series branch only in one 'direction'—from past to future. For simplicity's sake I will suppose that we are dealing with just one many-branched causal series S, in which can be found the answer to Q1 for any and every dependently existent thing to which Q1 applies.[23] S contains the hypothetically beginningless history of the natural world.

But Q1 obviously couldn't apply to the series S itself, because, by hypothesis, S never came into existence. If S itself is in some respect a dependently existent being, it isn't a *doubly* dependent being as I've been using that designation, because the question 'What explains S's having come into existence?' has no application.

e. Sustaining causes

And now a closer look at G6 should show that the kind of dependence at issue in this argument really is not every ordinary thing's dependence on something else for its having come into existence, but rather its dependence on something else for its remaining in existence, for its existing now, for its now becoming a component of the immediate future, which as of right now *isn't* yet. In some of Aquinas's cosmological arguments he clearly is focusing on generative dependence, as he shows in ST's Second Way when he explains that nothing can cause *itself* in the respect relevant to that argument, because, in order to do so, it would have to have existed before it began to exist. In G6, although he alludes to generability in order to establish the contingency of ordinary things, the kind of dependence he's concerned with is brought out in his denial of existential inertia and his claim that, consequently, a contingent being's presently existing requires an explanation (lines 4–6): 'if *existing* is its status, *that* must be on the basis of some cause' (lines 5–6). Besides, since Aquinas expressly grants the possibility of an

---

[23] This sort of convergence is at least in keeping with an Aristotelian proposition Aquinas invokes as an unsupported premiss in 18.147: 'Prior to every multitude [of things some] unity must be found.'

infinite regress of generating causes, we should, if we can, avoid interpreting his denial of an infinite regress here as if it concerned generating causes. And we can. I will, then, take argument G6 to be concerned not with generating, but with sustaining causes.

The dependence of ordinary contingent things on sustaining causes is beyond dispute. But does series S itself need sustaining? Does it make sense to ask what explains beginningless S's remaining in existence, getting from the present instant into the immediate future? Does it make sense to ask why the world doesn't come to an end right now? Putting question Q2 in the form suggested by Aquinas's line in argument G6, does it make sense to ask what explains S's sempiternality, its beginningless, continuous ongoingness?

Question Q2 applied to series S seems ambiguous as between diachronic and synchronic considerations of S's persistence. The diachronic consideration—What explains S's having for ever had new members?—is addressed in the answers to all the instances of Q1 asked about the generation of the particular doubly dependent beings that are the members of S, and so it doesn't constitute a question to be asked separately about S itself.[24] The synchronic consideration—What explains S's going on right now?—is a different question, one that amounts to a genuine application of Q2 to series S. As such, it may seem to require conceiving of S itself as a dependent being.

f. S's instantaneous, synchronic, present phase

Well, *is* series S a dependently existent thing in the sense of requiring a sustaining cause? Is it a thing at all? Since S's existence is successive, since there is no time at which all its members exist together, we might feel uncomfortable about regarding S as a thing in its own right.[25] I don't think worries of this sort are justified, but

[24] It is this diachronic consideration that lies behind the extensive, sophisticated medieval discussions *de aeternitate mundi*—on the possibility of a beginningless universe. (See Ch. Two, n. 35.) Participants in that discussion who, unlike Aquinas, denied the possibility—and that includes most of them—would not have taken this view of the applicability of Q1 to S.

[25] This sort of question has been admirably dealt with in Rowe's analysis and appraisal of the metaphysical status of a beginningless causal series in Rowe 1975*a*, and esp. 1975*c*, and my discussion here owes something to his. In private correspondence (1993) Bernard Katz has suggested to me that, despite Rowe's worries on this score, there is no particular difficulty associated with treating the exhaustive

the issue doesn't have to be settled here. In asking about the explanation of S's going on right now, we're asking about the explanation of S's now having any members, rather than none at all. And so in this case we're asking not for an explanation of S as a beginningless diachronic whole, but rather for an explanation of its instantaneous, synchronic, present phase, which I'll label Sn. Unlike S itself, Sn is not at all successive; all of Sn's members exist at once. And since each of Sn's members is, by hypothesis, a being that depends for its existing on the present operation of sustaining causes, the explanation of Sn can be construed as simply the sum of all the explanations of the existing of the dependent beings that are Sn's members. If such a construal makes sense, then the sum of all those particular explanations would explain S's now having not merely any elements at all, but even the very elements it now has.

Such an explanation of S's going on right now in terms of explaining Sn would be enormously more complex than is needed for purposes of argument G6. And, besides, it may seem that all those particular explanations are too disparate to be summed into an explanation of Sn. After all, beings that depend on other beings for their existing have very different necessary conditions. Your presently existing needs the earth's atmosphere as part of its explanation; a mountain's or a star's presently existing doesn't. But Sn converges when traced up its chain of sustaining causes as S converges when traced backwards in time. Moving up several levels in the explanation of your continuing to exist, the existing of the earth's atmosphere requires earth's gravity, and so does the mountain's continuing to exist—though not the star's. And, moving up many more levels of explanation all at once, the continuing existence of earth's gravity and of the star and of every other dependent

collection of dependent beings as an object. I'm inclined to share Katz's view: '[I]t is quite plausible to regard the universe as a mereological sum of . . . the dependent beings that make up or made up the natural universe. . . . In fact, it seems to me that is exactly what the universe is, the mereological sum of all the things that make it up. (What else could it be? Surely not something set-theoretic?) Moreover, it would be quite reasonable to suppose that the mereological sum of dependent beings would itself be a dependent being. But what about your objection that there is no time at which all of S's members exist together? . . . [W]e can raise the very same question about things that we clearly do regard as concrete objects but which also seem to lose and gain parts: for example, an automobile or, for that matter, any persisting physical object. . . . So, I don't think that the observation that S's existence is successive, or that there is no time at which all its members exist together, is a good reason for concluding that S cannot be construed as a concrete being.'

being '[w]e see . . . in the world' has the continuing existence (or obtaining) of natural laws as a necessary condition. For my immediate purposes, I can pause there, at the level of explanation at which a general reference to natural laws is the most (or the only) appropriate move to make. And, naturally, part of any generally correct answer to the question of what keeps the world going will have to be that natural laws continue to obtain. (By 'natural laws' here, I mean nature's actual governing regularities, of course, not anybody's up-to-the-minute codified best estimate of what those regularities might be.)

So I maintain that Q2 does apply to S in virtue of applying to Sn, and that Q2 applies to Sn in virtue of applying to each of Sn's members in such a way as to lead, through repeated applications, to an identifiable single condition necessary for S's going on right now: the persisting efficacy of natural laws. I am definitely not maintaining that the persistence of natural laws needs no explaining. At this point I want only to claim that although (in lines 6–7 of argument G6) Aquinas issues his denial of the theoretical possibility of going on *ad infinitum* only as regards applying Q2 to the existing of a particular observable dependent being, the denial can and should be construed as applying also to explaining S's presently continuing. But how, exactly?

g. A synchronic regress of explanations

We've seen that Aquinas elsewhere accepts the possibility of a diachronically infinite regress of explanations in answer to repeated applications of Q1. Here he is denying the possibility of a synchronically infinite regress of explanations in answer to repeated applications of Q2. Aquinas thinks that a causally linked series of efficient causes does not admit of an infinite regress just in case, for each cause in the series, its causally operating is required for its immediate successor's causally operating, so that the effect is not achieved unless all the causes in the series are operating simultaneously: 'in connection with efficient causes a regress that is infinite *essentially* (*per se*) is *impossible*—if, that is, the causes that are essentially required for some effect were infinitely many. For example, if a stone were moved by a stick, the stick by a hand, and so on *ad infinitum*' (ST Ia.46.2, ad 7). If in asking question Q1 about S we picture a horizontal series of generating causes, stretching back infinitely into the past, then the series of sustaining causes we're considering now in asking question Q2 about Sn should be pictured as vertical, the series of causes all of which must be operating at once, right now, in order to explain the present existing of anything that is 'on its own . . . related indifferently to . . . existing and not existing'.

Aquinas says that the impossibility he's alluding to here 'was proved above on the basis of Aristotle's reasoning' (lines 7–8). At this point in SCG, anything 'proved above' has to have been proved in chapter 13, and chapter 13 does contain not just one, but four, Aristotelian arguments against infinite causal regresses—three as sub-arguments in argument G1 and one in G3. But only one of those four, the third one in G1, is clearly relevant to our case here: 'That which is moved instrumentally cannot move anything unless there is something that moves it initially (*principaliter*). But if one goes on *ad infinitum* as regards movers and things moved, all of them will be moving instrumentally, so to speak, because they are posited as moved movers; but nothing will be [operating] as the initial mover. Therefore, nothing will be moved' (13.95).

Like the Aristotelian example of the hand, the stick, and the stone, this argument has to do with causes of motion, rather than with sustaining causes as such. But the relevant sort of causes of motion, considered just as such, obviously is a species of sustaining cause: the stone stops moving as soon as the stick stops moving, and the stick stops moving as soon as the hand stops moving. This sub-argument from G1 insists that in such a synchronic causal series all the intermediate causes, however many there may be, must be merely *instrumental*, dependent for their causal operation on the causally prior, but temporally simultaneous, operation of some cause that is causally first in that series. So this inferred first cause cannot itself be an instrumental cause in the series, but must instead be the originally operative cause relative to which all the others in the causal series are instrumental. Aquinas does not, and need not, concern himself with how many intermediate instrumental causes may be involved in explaining a dependent being's presently existing. When he says that 'one cannot go on *ad infinitum*' in such a series, he means that it must be traceable to a first (or ultimate) cause, even if the causal distance between the first cause and the sustaining of the dependent being were *infinitely* divisible into simultaneously operating intermediaries.

*h. The impossibility of a synchronically infinite regress
of explanations*

But what entitles Aquinas to deny the possibility of going on *ad
infinitum* in such a causal series? The most fully satisfactory answer
I know is the one developed by Rowe. Suppose that A is a dependent being whose existing right now is explained by B's current
sustaining activity, and that B's sustaining of A is explained by
reference to C. 'Can we now say', Rowe asks, 'that the explanation
for the fact that the causal activity of causing A to exist is now going
on might be found in B? It seems clear we cannot' (1975*a*: 33).[26] In
keeping with a later medieval tradition, Rowe calls a causal series
of this sort 'essentially ordered'. 'Now', he says,

if C is causing B to be causing A to exist, then since we are operating within
an essentially ordered series it also will be true that C is now causing A to
exist. C, therefore, will be exhibiting that very sort of causal activity we
are trying to explain. And if C is the first member of the series, we might
be able to explain why the causal activity *causing-A-to-be-now-existing*
is now going on by reference to C.[27] However, if C is an intermediate
cause, if some other thing is now causing C to be causing A to exist,
then we cannot find the explanation for the fact that this activity is going on
by reference to C. What then if the series progresses to infinity? Each
member of the series will be right now exhibiting the causal activity we are
trying to explain. It will be true that every member of the series is exhibiting the causal activity in question and also true that the fact that the
causal activity is going on cannot be explained by any member of the
series. For any member we select, it will be true that it is caused to exhibit
the activity in question by some other member and, therefore, true that we
cannot explain the fact that this sort of causal activity is going on in the
universe by reference to that member. . . . [I]f the series proceeds to infinity there will be no explanation of the fact that a certain sort of causal
activity [causing A to be now existing] . . . is going on in the world. (Ibid.
34–5)

---

[26] In the passages I'm drawing on, Rowe is in fact developing an interpretation of
Aquinas's attempt to block an infinite regress, but the attempt Rowe is focusing on
is the one in the Second Way, which can be read along these lines only if the Second
Way is interpreted as concerned not with coming into existence but rather with
remaining in existence, an interpretation Rowe adopts, ascribing it to G. H. Joyce
(Rowe 1975*a*: 27 n. 9). I think Joyce's line of interpretation is badly suited to the
Second Way, but fits G6 well; so I think Rowe's explanation of the blocking of the
infinite regress of sustaining causes is better suited to G6 than to the Second Way.

[27] Only the first two hyphens in the italicized phrase occur in Rowe's text; I've
supplied the others.

And therefore, I would add, there could not in that case be a philosophically satisfactory, metaphysical explanation of the fact that A—or S—is now continuing to exist.[28] A's—and, therefore, S's—existing now would be a brute fact, theoretically inexplicable, '*if* the essentially ordered series of causes resulting in A's present existence proceeds to infinity, lacks a first member' (ibid. 35–6).

Aquinas doesn't take the brute-fact alternative seriously, whether in G6 or anywhere else. As Rowe quite rightly observes (ibid. 36–7), that fact about Aquinas shows that he assumes or considers self-evident some form of 'the Principle of Sufficient Reason [PSR], a principle that in its strongest form maintains that no thing can exist and no fact can obtain without there being an explanation for that thing's existence or for that fact's obtaining' (ibid. 37). Rowe argues convincingly that PSR is untenable in its strongest form (Rowe 1975*b*), and I agree. But I also agree with his claim that 'no one has put forth any convincing argument for the falsity of PSR$_2$', this weaker form of PSR: '*Every existing thing has a reason for its existence either in the necessity of its own nature or in the causal efficacy of some other beings*' (Rowe 1975*a*: 261). I subscribe to PSR$_2$, interpreting the expression 'a reason for its existence' in the sense of a reason for its presently existing. Not only the history of science, but even a fundamentally rational attitude towards ordinary reality, presupposes PSR$_2$. And since there is no ordinary existing thing about which we could tolerate the blithe announcement that there simply is *no* reason for its existence, rationality forbids our abandoning the principle when the existing thing in question is extraordinary or all-pervasive—a thing such as the universe, or matter.

---

[28] Rowe carefully distinguishes between 'two different items: *i. the fact that A now exists*, and *ii. the fact that a certain sort of causal activity (causing A to exist) is now going on*' (ibid. 33). His apparent reason for doing so is that 'Someone might argue that, even though B is not the first member, we can still explain item (i) by reference to B and B's causal activity vis-à-vis A. I do not wish to dispute this point. To say that we have not really "explained" the present existence of A until we explain why B is causing A to exist, tracing each step backward until we arrive at an ultimate first cause, may be nothing more than a confusion as to the nature of explanation' (ibid.; see also the sentence on pp. 34–5). But the situation Aquinas is concerned to characterize as no explanation at all is not one in which an ordinarily adequate sort of first-level explanation has been captiously rejected as insufficient. It is, instead, one in which the first-level explanation is in terms of something that is itself theoretically inexplicable. In such a situation no one with a philosophical interest in understanding A's presently existing could consider its being referred to B's causal activity to constitute any explanation at all.

It may already be apparent, but it will become clearer, that the form of PSR presupposed in G6 is PSR$_2$. Even at this point it should be clear at least that in G6 Aquinas is assuming that '*Every existing thing*' that is related indifferently to existing and not existing '*has a reason for its existence . . . in the causal efficacy of some other beings.*'

It seems to me, then, that argument G6 is acceptable as far as the sentence ending in line 8. In any essentially ordered series of causes invoked to explain the presently continuing existence of any and every dependent being, there must be something that serves as a first, non-instrumental, independently operating cause.

Could that something be the natural laws themselves? Their persistence is a necessary condition common to the existing of all the dependent beings we've been considering, but the persistence of the laws—or, more precisely, of the natural dispositions or governing regularities represented in them—certainly isn't self-explanatory. The necessity that has sometimes been ascribed to them isn't *logical* necessity, but rather a kind of conditional necessity. Nor do the laws themselves, even sublimated and unified in the Theory Of Everything, or the Final Theory, seem to constitute a plausible candidate for the role of first, non-instrumental, independently operating cause.[29] Anything that could count as Alpha would, obviously, have to have some intimate sort of relationship with natural laws, but identity goes too far.[30] Pointing to the laws

[29] A paradigm of the distinction between a necessary condition and the sustaining cause that supplies the condition is (a) nourishment as a necessary condition of life and (b) the source of the nourishment as the cause sustaining life.

[30] Cf. Davies 1983: 45: 'The God who is outside time is regarded as "creating" the universe in the more powerful sense of "holding it in being at every instant". Instead of God simply starting the universe off (a belief known as deism rather than theism), a timeless God acts at all moments. The remote cosmic creator is thus given a greater sense of immediacy—he is acting here and now—but at the expense of some obscurity, for the idea of God being above time is a subtle one.

The alternative roles of God in time, causing the creation, and a timeless God holding the universe (including time) in being, are sometimes illustrated schematically in the following way. [End-note citing Swinburne 1979: ch. 7, q.v.] Imagine a sequence of events, each one causally dependent on the preceding one. They can be denoted as a series . . . E_3, E_2, E_1, stretching back in time. Thus, E_1 is caused by E_2, which in turn is caused by E_3 and so on. This causal chain can be denoted as follows:

$$\ldots \to E_4 \overset{L}{\to} E_3 \overset{L}{\to} E_2 \overset{L}{\to} E_1$$

where the 'L's remind us that one event causes the next through the operation of the laws of physics, L.

The concept of a causal God . . . can then be illustrated by making God, denoted G, the first member of this series of causes:

counts as indicating part of the answer to the big question—Why is there this sort of world rather than another sort, or nothing at all?—but only the part that has to do with there being this sort of world rather than another, not at all the part that has to do with there being something rather than nothing.

i. Dependently necessary beings

Now, what about the sub-conclusion in lines 8–9 of the argument? It infers that 'one must posit something the existing of which is necessary'. A review of G6 up to this point shows that at least part of what can legitimately be meant here by saying of something that its existing is necessary is that it exists, but it couldn't have been generated and it can't be destroyed. We've already seen that 'altogether immutable' Alpha could never have begun to exist and can never cease to exist. Could Alpha on those grounds be identified as this necessarily existent thing that 'one must posit'? No—or, at any rate, not yet.

Aquinas understands generation and destruction as including all the natural processes of being brought into and taken out of existence. And in his Aristotelian view of nature, some actually existent things—the sun, for instance—exist necessarily in the special, narrow sense of not being subject to any natural processes of beginning and ceasing to exist, and yet they exist dependently. Unlike all the other things '[w]e see . . . in the world', a dependently necessary being is independent of all natural originating and sustaining causes. But the sun's nature doesn't entail its existence any more than the nature of the carrot I'm about to eat entails its existence. The (Aristotelian) sun's existing independently of natural generation and destruction warrants its being described as necessary in this special sense, while the fact that its nature does not entail its

$$G \to \ldots \to E_4 \overset{L}{\to} E_3 \overset{L}{\to} E_2 \overset{L}{\to} E_1$$

By contrast, if God is outside time, then he cannot belong to this causal chain at all. Instead, he is above the chain, sustaining it at every link:

$$\begin{array}{ccc} G & G & G \\ | & | & | \\ L & L & L \end{array}$$
$$\ldots \to E_4 \to E_3 \to E_2 \to E_1$$

and this picture could apply equally well whether the chain of causes has a first member (i.e. a beginning in time) or not (as in an infinitely old universe). With this picture in mind, we may say that God is not so much a cause of the universe as an *explanation*.' See also Braine 1988.

existence dictates its being described as having 'the cause of its necessity in something else' (lines 10–11)—something else that sustains it in an existence that is not subject to the vicissitudes of nature.[31]

Although at least many, maybe all, of Aquinas's dependently necessary beings are scientifically discountable, his introduction of them in lines 9–11 of G6 is justified dialectically. The argument aims at showing that 'one must posit some first necessary being that is necessary *through itself*'. But since Aquinas and his contemporaries believed in '*necessary* beings that have the cause of their necessity *in something else*' (lines 12–13), he has first to rule out those lesser necessary beings. He does so by denying the possibility of an infinite regress of dependently necessary beings (in lines 11–13) along the lines of the analogous denial in lines 6–7—the one we've already looked at. If we then move directly to G6's conclusion that 'one must posit some first necessary being that is necessary through itself', we have arrived justifiably at an entity that can and must be identified with altogether immutable, beginningless, and endless Alpha.

j. Alpha as existing independently

But what does it mean to say that Alpha is necessary through itself (*per seipsum necessarium*)? It means that Alpha—that is, whatever ultimately explains the present continuing of S (the beginningless series of generating causes and their effects)—must itself exist *independently* as well as immutably, beginninglessly, and endlessly. The possibility of Alpha's depending on something for having come into existence can't arise, because Alpha's having in any way begun to exist has been shown to be impossible. And Alpha considered simply in its explanatory relationship to S can't depend on anything else for its existing, because it has been identified as the requisite first cause in the essentially ordered series of causes that explains Sn's existing and thus S's going on right now. Such a first cause was shown to be required by the nature of an essentially ordered series of causes and PSR₂. Invoking PSR₂ in order to get to

---

[31] Human souls and angels are among the things that Aquinas thinks exist necessarily in this sense, because he takes them to involve no matter, and therefore to be invulnerable to natural disintegration. But since their natures do not entail their existence, they, too, exist dependently. For a helpful critical survey of Aquinas's views on this topic, see Brown 1964.

Alpha's existence in G6 and then discarding it would be unjustifiable, and Aquinas obviously has no inclination to declare Alpha's necessary existence inexplicable. All necessary existence is explicable, either on the basis of extrinsic necessitation or on the basis of intrinsic necessitation (lines 9–11). And the necessary existence that must belong to Alpha, the first cause, must of course be explained intrinsically (lines 11–14). Putting it in terms of PSR$_2$, Alpha must have *a reason for its existence*, and cannot have it *in the causal efficacy of some other beings* and so must have it *in the necessity of its own nature*. Putting it as the conclusion of G6 puts it, a 'first necessary being' must be 'necessary through itself'.

k. Summing up G6

Summing up, let A be some existing thing that can also not exist—you, or this planet, or this galaxy, or all the galaxies taken together—something that does actually exist but that on its own, in its own nature, is related indifferently to existence. And suppose that A is a present member of a beginningless series of generating causes and their effects. Then, since *every existing thing has a reason for its existence either in the necessity of its own nature or in the causal efficacy of some other beings*, there must be some reason for A's existing. That reason cannot be in the necessity of A's own nature, since A on its own is related indifferently to existence; and so the reason for A's existing must be in the causal efficacy of other beings. However many other beings may in their causal efficacy be contributing instrumentally to A's existing now, their operating causally would not constitute the reason for A's existing now if there were not some first cause at the head of that essentially ordered series of causes. Therefore, since A does exist, such a first cause—Alpha—must exist. As such, Alpha must be not an instrumental but an altogether independent cause, dependent on absolutely nothing else for its present causal operation, which actualizes simultaneously the causal efficacy of all the instrumental causes in the series.

The Alpha whose necessary existence is argued for in G6 is a first sustainer; but I introduced Alpha into this discussion as the hypothetical first mover, the ultimate explanation of all change. Can Alpha the first mover and Alpha the first sustainer be one and the same? I think so. Since we have an argument for the first sustainer's existence, it's only natural to take the primary identification of Alpha to be that of first sustainer. What makes it also the first mover is that its sustaining of nature (involving all the natural laws) is what makes possible all the natural changes that occur when and as they do because of the natures of things. Alpha the first mover considered in this way need not initiate any change, but must serve as the essential co-operating, enabling cause of every natural (and even volitional) change.

So, if Alpha the first sustainer is also the first mover, then it is as such altogether immutable, and therefore beginningless and endless. Alpha, by our initial hypothesis the first cause, must as such be at the head of an essentially ordered series of causes that explains the existing of any and every dependently existing thing. And, as the first sustaining cause, Alpha must be a first necessary being that is necessary through itself—that is, must exist altogether independently, in the sense that Alpha's existing is to be explained solely on the basis of Alpha's nature. Alpha's existing, then, is obviously independent of natural laws. But since those laws are inevitably referred to at some relatively elevated stage in the explanation of any dependent being's existing, natural laws must be intimately related to the nature of Alpha in some way. We will look at the nature of that relationship in Chapter Six below.

The last word of this chapter must be that even if, as I think, we now have good evidence for the existence of Alpha, what we have does not constitute an argument for the existence of God, simply because the characteristics essential to the entity in the conclusion of G6 don't constitute a condition sufficient for deity.

FOUR

FROM INDEPENDENCE TO PERFECTION

1. Reorientation

Aquinas claims that his project in SCG I–III can't get started unless the existence of God has been established at the outset. I've been disagreeing, on two grounds. First, with one negligible exception, even his own arguments in chapter 13, which he says establish God's existence, conclude at most that there is a first, immutable cause, an extraordinary entity the existence and nature of which constitute an ultimate explanation of all change and all existence.[1] Any atheist could accept that proposition; some atheists no doubt do accept it. Identifying such an acknowledged first cause as God requires further argumentation to show that this extraordinary entity must have characteristics that pick out the supreme being of the monotheistic tradition, to show that it must be the transcendent, personal, omniscient, omnipotent, perfectly good creator and governor of the universe. In drawing up that list of necessary and sufficient conditions, even a project in natural theology must rely on traditional doctrinal accounts of God that have their source in putative revelation—not for evidence, of course, but merely for the list of specifications to be met. Argumentation designed to identify some existent entity as God presupposes good evidence for the existence of an entity extraordinary in respects that at least qualify it as a candidate for the role of God, but it clearly does not presuppose that the existence of *God* has been established.

Second, all we really need to begin this natural theology is the

---

[1] As I pointed out in Ch. Three, only G5, the fifth of the existence arguments in ch. 13, concludes to the existence of something that would have to count as God, under the description 'someone by whose providence the world is governed'. But G5 is also the only one of the arguments in ch. 13 that Aquinas never makes use of in applying the eliminative method in chs. 15–28 (and even beyond those chapters, where, as we'll see, he uses a different method).

hypothesis that there is an ultimate explanation, an answer to the big question, Why is there this sort of world rather than another sort, or nothing at all? I've been using 'Alpha' as the designation for the entity or entities at the heart of that hypothetical ultimate explanation. And, since it's part of the notion of a working hypothesis that it gets confirmed or disconfirmed as the work goes on, I said near the beginning of Chapter Three that the most sensible way to get at the answer to the question of Alpha's *existence* was to let the answer emerge from the investigation into the *nature* of whatever might count as first cause.

Aquinas begins his version of that investigation in his chapter 15, and my consideration of it in my Chapter Three had barely begun before I claimed to have found good evidence for the existence of Alpha, in an argument embedded within his investigation of eternality. I'll briefly review that result below. Because of it, I can say now that in this project the most sensible way to get at the answer to the question of *God*'s existence is to let it emerge from the continuing investigation into the nature of Alpha.

In the first stage of Aquinas's investigation into the nature of the first cause, he proceeds by what he calls the 'eliminative method'. Such an approach is appropriate to his project, and perhaps initially unavoidable at any level of explanation involving concepts more specific than causation itself. Nothing that could count as the ultimate explanation of the observable world could be cognized, measured, or categorized in any of the specific, natural-scientific ways human beings have discovered or devised for cognizing, measuring, and categorizing things and changes which that ultimate explanation is supposed to explain. As a consequence, any more specific cognition we might be able to acquire of the first cause will have to be indirect to begin with. As Aquinas points out, 'we cannot apprehend it *itself* by discerning what it *is*' (14.117). His eliminative method, then, is designed to start us finding out about Alpha's nature 'by discerning what it is *not*'. '[W]e come closer to the knowledge of it to the extent to which we can through our intellect *eliminate* more [characteristics] from it; for the more fully we discern anything's differences from other things, the more completely do we discern it' (ibid.).

In Aquinas's own view, he's using the eliminative method in chapters 15–28 to acquire knowledge indirectly by picking out many characteristics that could not belong to *God*. But, in keeping with my initial supposition in introducing the Alpha hypothesis, I want to try interpreting those results of his as providing indirect knowledge about *Alpha*.

Even before the concept of Alpha is subjected to the eliminative method, however, some things that must be true of Alpha can be brought out just by reflecting on the hypothesis that introduces it as the (hypothetical) ultimate explanatory entity. (We have to have *some* minimal positive identification of the subject of the inquiry in order to get started on considerations of its nature and existence, even by means of the eliminative method.) We're entitled to some claims that are obviously entailed by the hypothesis alone—for example, that Alpha would have to be (1) first (in more than one sense), (2) a cause, and (3) immutable. And it is in fact just those three characteristics that Aquinas considers himself entitled to use as the positive identification on the basis of which to start applying the eliminative method, though he extracts them from the conclusions of some of his arguments for the existence of God in chapter 13.[2] I take them to be only corollaries of my working hypothesis, but even that status is enough to make them available as starting-points for the eliminative method. This first stage of the inquiry into Alpha's nature, then, will be a process of figuring out what sort of entity an immutable first cause of everything could not be.

In chapters 15–28 Aquinas applies the eliminative method in many arguments, taking for granted only those three starting-points and, as I pointed out in Chapter Three, certain logical and metaphysical principles (as well as conclusions of Aristotelian arguments). Naturally, as he goes along he also uses some results of earlier arguments as premises for further eliminations.[3] Before

---

[2] Arguments G1 and G2 obviously involve claims 1, 2, and 3. Argument G3 involves 1 and 2. Argument G4 involves 1 and, a little less obviously, 3. Argument G5 seems to involve only 1.

[3] It isn't surprising that those premises sometimes are *variants* of the propositions that were actually argued for earlier, but there is seldom if ever room for real doubt about which earlier result is intended. I've found only one instance of an absolutely unwarranted premise of this sort, where, in one of seven arguments for the elimination of any kind of composition, Aquinas relies on the premiss that God is the first and highest good (18.146)—a proposition that wasn't even introduced previously, let alone argued for, in any version. There are also some peculiar instances of his invoking as a premiss in one chapter a proposition that he doesn't argue for until later—e.g. that God is most excellent (invoked in 20.159 and 27.154, argued for in ch. 28)—and this expressly labelled instance of the same sort: 'But there aren't any accidental characteristics in God, as will be shown [in ch. 23]' (21.198). See also nn. 9 and 23 below.

considering the plausibility and utility of any of those eliminative claims about Alpha, I want to review briefly the results of argument G6 and its leading role in the application of the eliminative method.

2. The eliminative method and argument G6

The argument I labelled G6 concludes that 'one must posit some first necessary being that is necessary through itself' (15.124). And since one must posit this as a consequence of considering what is required to explain the undoubted existence of ordinary real things that '[w]e see . . . in the world', the conclusion of G6 is to be read as a claim that a certain kind of extraordinary thing must really exist, and that the way it exists must be very different from the way the things we see in the world exist, just in virtue of its serving as the ultimate explanation of their existence. And so if G6 is an acceptable argument, as I've claimed it is, it provides us with good grounds for maintaining that Alpha does really exist, necessarily, through itself.

The conclusion of my extracted argument G6 is not the final conclusion of the full argument Aquinas himself develops at that point in chapter 15. The full argument concludes finally that 'God is eternal', at least in the sense of being beginningless and endless and probably also in the sense of being timeless. That proposition, which implicitly eliminates beginning, ending, and temporality, is just the sort of thing we'd expect as a result of the eliminative method Aquinas is employing here, especially as compared with G6's affirmative conclusion about 'some first necessary being that is necessary through itself'. And so the extraction of G6 as an existence argument to be considered on its own, although unquestionably a legitimate move logically, may seem to thwart Aquinas's intentions and to give separate expression to a conclusion quite extraneous to his own purposes at this stage of his project.

This impression is accurate in only one unimportant respect, however, and that is that Aquinas himself doesn't designate the G6 portion of his argument as an argument for the *existence* of anything. But, of course, in his view his project needs no additional existence arguments after chapter 13. And it's worth noticing that G6 is like those arguments of chapter 13 and unlike all the other arguments of chapter 15 in depending not at all on any of the three given starting-points for the eliminative method but only on pre-theoretic observations regarding ordinary reality. What's more, Aquinas clearly does consider just this G6 *portion* of his argument to have produced results very important to his project. In fact, the results of the G6 portion have more practical value for him than does the eternality conclusion reached at the end of this argument of his (and at four other points in the chapter), since in the many subsequent arguments up to and including chapter 28 he invokes these G6 results in one form or another at least a dozen times, but eternality—or, more precisely, sempiternality—only once or twice.[4]

The salient result of G6 is, of course, the one in its positive conclusion: there is 'some first necessary being that is necessary through itself'. I've discussed that result in Chapter Three, and I'll have more to say about it in this chapter. Here I want just to point out that even Alpha's *per se* necessity, despite the affirmative look of it, is to be interpreted in the context of Aquinas's chapters 15–28 as the *elimination* of every sort of *dependence*.

Summing up my review of G6, I claim that it is an acceptable cosmological argument for the existence of Alpha; that it provides, in a mildly surprising form, what turns out to be a very important premiss for Aquinas's subsequent applications of his eliminative method; and that the apparently affirmative attribution in its conclusion is an appropriate result of the eliminative method when the conclusion is understood as eliminating from Alpha every sort of dependence.

3. Applying the results of the eliminative method to Alpha generally

Now, what else is achieved in Aquinas's application of the method, and how well do those results apply to Alpha as delineated so far?

---

[4] G6 results: 16.128, 16.130 (twice), 18.143, 19.150 (twice), 19.151, 22.203, 22.205, 22.206, 24.223, and 26.240; sempiternality: 16.128 and 26.242 (also mentioned in a merely introductory passage in 16.127). (Atemporal eternality, argued for in 15.122 and implied in 15.124, is not invoked in any subsequent chapter up to and including I.28.) The use of sempiternality in 16.128 clearly harks back to G6, and could be just as well, or even more accurately, counted as another use of results of G6: 'whatever *can* exist can [also] *not* exist. But God *secundum se* cannot not exist, since he is sempiternal.' The only reason I can see for stipulating here that we're talking about God in himself (*secundum se*) is to call to mind the *de se* in G6. Contingently existing things *considered in themselves* (*de se*) are related indifferently to existing and not existing, whereas existent God *considered in himself* is *not* related indifferently to those two states but, rather, *cannot* not exist.

In Aquinas's application of the eliminative method in chapters 15–28 there are more than eighty arguments that are intended to eliminate nineteen predicates from the concept of Alpha—that is, to show, in the following order, that Alpha could not be

(A) anything that begins or ceases to exist (15.121, 123–5)
(B) temporal (15.122, 124?)
(C) dependent for its existence on anything other than itself (15.124)
(D) anything that has any passive potentialities (16.128–33)
(E) matter, or anything material (17.134–6)
(F) the universal material cause (prime matter) (17.137–40)
(G) composite in any way (18.141–7)
(H) subject to anything unnatural, violent, or coercive (19.149–52)
(I) corporeal, whether a body or a power in a body (20.154–86)
(J) other than its own essential nature (21.197–201)
(K) anything whose being is other than its nature (22.203–8)
(L) anything that has any accidental characteristics (23.214–19)
(M) specified by differentiae (24.223–6)
(N) classified within any genus or category (25.228–32, 235–6)
(O) defined (25.233)
(P) the subject of an a priori demonstration (25.234)
(Q) a universal formal cause (26.238–47)
(R) the form of any particular thing (27.251–8)
(S) imperfect (28.259–66).

I believe that all nineteen of these predicates are properly eliminable from the concept of Alpha. And, of course, if I'm right about that, then Alpha gets much more sharply delineated as a consequence of all those eliminations. I'll look more or less briefly at each of them, less briefly at the more controversial or more illuminating ones. I can't claim to offer full support for any of them now, but working on them has led me to think that the material Aquinas supplies in his several arguments for each elimination can be made to yield at least a very plausible case for each. It's clear that the elimination of some of these predicates has the effect of making Alpha look more like God. But it remains to be seen whether or not eliminating even all of them could count as unveiling Alpha to reveal God unmistakably.

In Chapter Three I said all I think I need to say about the elimination of predicates A and C. I said less there about M, N, and

O, but there's nothing unexpected or controversial in the observation that anything that could count as the ultimate explanation of the observable world could not be classified or defined by means of categories, genera, and differentiae—the taxonomic devices we've found to be indispensable to our detailed understanding of the things and events that make up the observable world. As for the closely associated predicate P, Aquinas derives its elimination immediately from the elimination of predicate O on the basis of an Aristotelian technicality. The entity under consideration cannot be the subject of an a priori demonstration 'because the starting-point of [such] a demonstration is the *definition* of whatever is the subject of the demonstration' (25.234). But the rest of what he says on this score in that same passage is untechnical and readily acceptable regarding Alpha at this stage of the investigation, when it is cognized only indirectly. He says that we can't frame any demonstration regarding the ultimate explanatory principle except on the basis of its effects, and so, if it can be the subject of demonstrative argumentation at all, it can be the subject of only a posteriori demonstrations.[5]

Aquinas argues for the elimination of predicate B, temporality, on the grounds of immutability. Temporality is ruled out by immutability only if immutabilty is understood super-strictly, the way Parmenides seems to have understood it, as ruling out getting older even when that sort of change involves no other sort of change in the thing that is getting older—the way Caesar's assassination is getting older. But the immutability justifiably associated with Alpha at this stage seems not obviously super-strict, and the mode of existence that really should be eliminated from Alpha here is spatio-temporality. It may be eliminated on the grounds that to be spatio-temporal is to be subject to this world's natural laws, a condition that can't characterize whatever it is that is supposed to account for this world's natural laws (in some way yet to be disclosed). And if Alpha could not be spatio-temporal, then, clearly, Alpha could not be matter, or anything material (E), or corporeal, whether a body or a power in a body (I).[6] The elimination of E

---

[5] 25.234: *Patet etiam quod non potest demonstratio de ipso fieri, nisi per effectum: quia principium demonstrationis est definitio eius de quo fit demonstratio.*

[6] Ch. 20, 'God is not a body', is much the longest of the chapters in which the eliminative method is applied. It contains ten arguments, more than any other chapter, but most of the chapter is devoted to one very complex argument (20.161–

leads naturally, perhaps irresistibly, to the elimination of F, the possibility that Alpha is the universal *material* cause of things. But I want to consider F later, in another connection.

Since Aquinas's concept of matter is the Aristotelian concept of it as passive potentiality, it isn't surprising that the route he takes to the elimination of E runs through the elimination of D, passive potentiality. In the elimination of D itself two kinds of passive potentiality are at issue. One kind is potentiality for existence and for non-existence, dependence on something else for beginning to exist and for continuing to exist: 'everything that has potentiality mixed into its substance can, to the extent to which it has potentiality, not exist' (16.128). This kind of passive potentiality is eliminated, naturally, on the basis of Alpha's absolutely independent existence, which was argued for in G6.[7] The other kind is passive potentiality in an existing thing, regardless of the necessity or contingency of its existence: 'Just as anything whatever is naturally suited to act [or to move something] in so far as it is in an actualized state, so is it naturally suited to be affected [or to be moved] in so far as it is in a state of potentiality' (16.132). In other words, mutability varies directly with passive potentiality. Following Aquinas in adopting this unproblematic Aristotelian principle, we may conclude with him that Alpha 'has no potentiality—that is, no *passive* potentiality—at all' (ibid.), since Alpha's immutability is one of the starting-points of the eliminative method.

On that basis it's easy to eliminate H as well, since an entity with no passive potentiality at all is clearly an entity invulnerable to anything violent, coercive, or otherwise unnatural to it.[8] Moreover, an entity without passive potentiality must likewise be without

84). It's not clear to me why Aquinas takes the elimination of corporeality so seriously (especially since the elimination of predicate I is never invoked as a premiss in chs. 21–8), or why none of his arguments for it rely on the earlier elimination of E, since eliminating materiality seems to be the most obvious basis on which to eliminate corporeality. Does he, perhaps, avoid using the materiality–corporeality connection because the universal hylomorphism maintained by some of his contemporaries requires incorporeal matter and so would reject that connection?

[7] Arguments against potentiality for existence and non-existence occur in 16.128, 129, 130, and 133. (For 16.128, see n. 4 above; for 16.130, see sect. 4c below.)

[8] Aquinas doesn't employ the elimination of D directly in the elimination of H, arguing instead from the elimination of G (19.149), from *per se* necessity (19.150 and 151), and from immutability in the form of the condition of being altogether immovable (19.152). The elimination of D has an indirect role, however, since it was used to support the elimination of G (18.141).

components of any kind, since composition by its very nature entails a theoretical susceptibility to decomposition, which is a kind of passive potentiality (18.141). And since anything theoretically susceptible to decomposition can cease existing, anything that exists necessarily through itself must be simple, not composite in any way (18.143). And so predicate G can apparently also be eliminated from the concept of Alpha.

4. Eliminating the distinction between Alpha's nature and being

a. The cautious and bold interpretations of the elimination

But agreeing to the elimination of G becomes harder when we see how radically thorough Aquinas's elimination of compositeness is. For the elimination of real components entails the elimination of all real distinctions within Alpha. And it turns out that when Aquinas rules out all real distinctions in this way, he is especially concerned to rule out *metaphysical* distinctions, as in the eliminations of predicates J, K, and L. The eliminations of predicates J and L are relatively easy. Alpha's immutability entails that it could not be anything that has any accidental characteristics (L) since, as Aquinas points out, 'an accidental characteristic is naturally suited to inhere and not to inhere' in a subject at different times (23.217). And since there can't be accidental characteristics in Alpha, 'there is, therefore, nothing in it other than its essential nature' (21.198)[9]—that is, Alpha could not be other than its own essential nature (J).

But the metaphysical distinction Aquinas is most concerned to eliminate from the extraordinary first entity is the ordinary distinction between a thing's essential nature and its existence, or being.[10]

---

[9] This line of argument in support of the elimination of J in ch. 21 is so natural that it's no wonder that Aquinas borrows the elimination of L from ch. 23 in order to use it in ch. 21: 'Therefore, only accidental characteristics are in a thing besides its essential nature. But there aren't any accidental characteristics in God, as will be shown' (21.198).

[10] In discussing this *essentia/esse* issue in SCG and other works, Aquinas uses several words and expressions interchangeably with *essentia*, including *natura*, *quidditas*, *quod quid est*, and *substantia*. I use 'nature' or 'essential nature' for this element of the issue. For the other element Aquinas uses only the nominalized infinitive *esse*, which is best translated in different ways in different places—as e.g. 'being', 'existing', or 'existence'.

His view of the theoretical importance of that result is brought out in his referring to it after the elimination has been carried out as 'this sublime truth' (22.211), and we'll soon see why he calls it that. But its practical importance to his project is also striking: within the six remaining chapters in which the eliminative method is applied he invokes this result in one form or another nineteen times, more often than any other in his entire application of the method.[11]

The distinction he wants to eliminate from the first entity is one we can readily recognize in connection with contingent entities, though it's so pervasive that we wouldn't ordinarily notice it. For instance, if I want to know whether there is such a thing as a marsupial bat, I want to know whether or not anything with that essential nature exists, to know whether or not that nature is instantiated, or has being. I know, roughly, what nature a marsupial bat must have, but I don't know whether it has being. And the same distinction characterizes every contingent thing: if and when it actually exists, it instantiates some essential nature that could also be uninstantiated or that could be, and very often is, instantiated also by the existing of some other individual. We couldn't know that unicorns don't exist if we didn't know, roughly, their essential nature; but the essential nature of unicorns doesn't entail their non-existence. We need to know a lot more than what sort of thing a unicorn must be in order to know that there aren't any. In short, a contingent thing's being is other than its essential nature.

Now, what would it mean to say of Alpha that its being 'is *not* other than' (22.202) its nature? 'Not other than' may seem unambiguous, but that claim admits of two interpretations, one cautious, the other bold; and I think both interpretations can be found in Aquinas.

The cautious interpretation is the one lying behind the remarks I was just making about unicorns. It can be drawn out of the conclusion of argument G6, where Alpha emerges as something that is 'necessary *through itself* (*per seipsum necessarium*)' (15.124), as something the necessary existence of which is explicable on the basis of its own nature and nothing else besides. In chapter 22, where this elimination takes place, Aquinas sometimes describes the entity whose being is not other than its nature in terms that fit that G6 conclusion perfectly, as when he says of it that it 'exists

---

[11] See 23.214, 24.223, 24.224, 24.225, 24.226, 25.229 (twice), 25.230, 25.231, 25.232, 25.236, 26.239, 26.240, 27.251 (twice), 27.252, 28.259, 28.260, and 28.266.

through its own essential nature (est per essentiam suam)' (22.210). For even without any means of knowing Alpha's nature fully, or even directly, we are entitled by the conclusion of G6 to say that the explanation of Alpha's necessary being must lie in Alpha's own nature, which must be such that merely on the basis of knowing it fully we would know that Alpha must exist.

We can get some idea of what that might be like by considering mathematical entities, which can serve as analogues for Alpha, if only in this respect. No mathematical entity could qualify as a candidate for the role of Alpha, because the necessary being of a mathematical entity couldn't explain the existence of contingent things. Mathematical entities have no causal relationships—at least none of the kind that are relevant here: non-epistemic efficient causal relationships to non-mathematical entities. But it's only among mathematical entities that we seem to be able to find well-recognized cases of an entity that 'exists through its own essential nature'. The nature *even prime number*, for instance, is a nature that is necessarily instantiated, and everybody who fully knows that nature knows on that basis alone that it must be instantiated, and that there must be exactly one instantiation of it. Judging from what we've been seeing so far, then, it may look as if eliminating predicate K amounts to claiming that Alpha exists through its own nature the way the even prime number does: its essential nature entails its being. This interpretation of the relationship between Alpha's essential nature and its being as *entailment* is what I mean by the cautious interpretation of the claim that Alpha's being is not other than its essential nature.

However, Aquinas more often (and more characteristically) offers a bolder interpretation in chapter 22 and in his other discussions of this issue. His bold interpretation is incompatible with the cautious entailment interpretation. We can see this when, in advancing the bold interpretation, he argues that we must *avoid* (cautiously) interpreting the claim that Alpha's nature is not other than its being as meaning that it exists '*through* something that belongs to that thing's essential nature or *through* the essential nature itself (*per aliquid quod est de essentia illius rei sive per essentiam ipsam*)' (22.207).[12] Instead, he insists, in this one case a thing's essential nature and its being are *identical*, just as 'not other

---

[12] ST Ia.3.4c contains a fuller argument against the entailment interpretation than can be found in SCG I.22.

than' would seem to require. This bold identity interpretation isn't easy to understand or to accept, but I think it can be understood and should be accepted. We can begin to understand it by looking at two different routes by which he tries to reach it.

b. Basing the identity interpretation on the elimination of compositeness

The first route goes through the elimination of predicate G, compositeness. We can see Aquinas taking this route in the two premisses of one of his arguments in chapter 22 for eliminating predicate K: '[1] Every thing that cannot be without the concurrence of more than one is composite. But [2] no thing in which the essential nature is other than the being (*in qua est aliud essentia et aliud esse*) can be without the concurrence of more than one—namely, essential nature and being. Therefore, every thing in which the essential nature is other than the being is composite' (22.209). Premiss [1] is unsurprising, but premiss [2] shows Aquinas taking a thing's being or existing as a *component* of it. No doubt a thing whose existing is other than its nature is conceptually more complex than one of which that isn't true, but conceptual distinctions don't entail real components. Not all complexity is compositeness (nor does susceptibility to conceptual analysis entail any passive potentiality). So the fact that a thing's nature is other than its being can't by itself show that thing to be composite in a respect in which it seems right to say that Alpha can't be composite, just because it's conceivable that the thing's nature may simply *entail* its being. The nature *even prime number* is other than, conceptually distinct from, mathematical being; but the even prime number is not composed of even-prime-numberhood *plus* mathematical being as it is composed of two units.

Again, another argument for the elimination of predicate K begins by observing that since the first entity has no components (in virtue of the elimination of predicate G), it can't be true that its being is a *part* of its nature (*non autem pars eius esse potest*) (22.207). So, Aquinas infers, either its being simply *is* its nature—the identity interpretation—or 'this kind of existing must be something over and above its essential nature' (ibid.). But to suppose that the only way existing could belong to the essential nature of a thing is as a *part* of its nature is simply to leave out of account the possibility that it could belong to it in the sense of being entailed by it. Aquinas continues the argument in this way: 'Now everything that is associated with something but does not belong to its essential nature is associated with it through some cause' (ibid.). The cause in this case could not be the thing's own nature, Aquinas says, because then something would be 'the cause of its own existing', and so 'it would be understood as existing before it had existence, which is impossible' (ibid.). But the entailment interpretation is the only serious rival to the identity interpretation, and to say that Alpha's existence belongs to its essential nature in the sense of being entailed by it certainly does not commit one to holding that its existence is one *component* of its nature, or to the absurdity that its nature must be instantiated *before* it is instantiated. It seems to me, then, that Aquinas's attempt to arrive at the identity interpretation via the elimination of compositeness does not succeed. Eliminating compositeness does not destroy the viability of the entailment interpretation, which is more cautious and, in just that respect, more appealing.

c. Basing the identity interpretation on argument G6

The first and longest of Aquinas's arguments for the elimination of predicate K begins by claiming that 'it was shown above that there is something the existing of which is necessary through itself (*aliquid esse quod per se necesse est esse*)' (22.203). The earlier passage in which this was shown is the portion of 15.124 that I've picked out as argument G6. Having drawn its first premiss from the results of G6, this argument in chapter 22 for the elimination of predicate K goes on to reject, in an elaborate destructive dilemma, any case in which 'this existing that is necessary belongs to an essential nature that is not what this existing itself is (*Hoc igitur esse quod necesse est, si alicui quidditati quae non est quod ipsum est*)'. The case in which 'this kind of existing *depends on* the [thing's] essential nature (*esse huiusmodi dependeat ab essentia*)' is then ruled out as 'contrary to the very idea of that which is, through itself, necessary being (*contra rationem eius quod est per se necesse esse*)', just because 'if it depends on anything else, it is for that reason alone not necessary being (*si ab alio dependet, iam non est necesse esse*)' (ibid.). So Aquinas, in developing this argument, seems to be supposing that G6's entity 'the existing of which is necessary through itself' can, simply on that basis, also be characterized as 'that which is, through itself, necessary being [or existing]'. But the claim that X *is*, in virtue of itself, necessary being is surely much stronger and more mysterious than the claim that X's existing is necessary in virtue of X itself.

Arguing for the elimination of predicate K seems to provide a context in which sliding from the weaker to the stronger of those claims might be especially tempting; but Aquinas also helps himself to the stronger claim earlier in the application of the eliminative method, in the quite different, cooler context of eliminating predicate D, passive potentiality: 'Again, that which is, through itself, necessary being (*est per se necesse esse*) is not in any way possible being (*nullo modo est possibile esse*). For what is, through itself, necessary being does not have a cause, as was shown above.' (Here again the reference is unquestionably to the G6 portion of 15.124.) 'But God is, through himself, necessary being. Therefore, he is not in any way possible being. And so no potentiality at all is found in his substance' (16.130).[13]

The worries raised by these passages can be allayed, I think, by reflecting on the way argument G6 works. Viewed very broadly, G6 infers the existence of Alpha from the existence of ordinary things. On that initial broad view there is every reason to consider the two existences to be on a par metaphysically, as in inferring the existence of a certain amount of oxygen in the atmosphere of a room from the existence of a person in the room. But, of course, the way G6 works requires the recognition that Alpha must exist necessarily through itself in a way that explains all existing. That means, among other things, that Alpha's existing is absolutely independent, and thus *radically* different from all the contingent existence it explains. Moreover, the way G6 works requires Alpha's own necessary existence to be explained through Alpha itself—that is, through Alpha's essential nature. And so the upshot of G6 (as

---

[13] Explaining that God can't in any way be possible being (or even just exist possibly) by pointing out that he can't have a cause draws on the first part of G6, where a cause is required for the existing of any *contingently* existing thing. In modern talk about modalities, things whose existence is possible include things existing necessarily. But Aquinas's possibles here are existent things 'that can exist and can also not exist (*sunt possibilia esse et non esse*)', as he puts it in G6—i.e. contingently existing things, things that exist but not necessarily. (Note that the *sunt possibilia esse* of that phrase, which I translate rather blandly as part of G6, is just the plural of the *est possibile esse* that shows up in 16.130.)

distinct from its conclusion) is that Alpha—that is, Alpha's nature—is, somehow, what explains the existing of everything that exists.

Now it can't be the case that what explains the existing of everything that exists is itself just another thing that exists, even just something that uniquely exists necessarily through itself. As Aquinas says elsewhere in the chapter on the elimination of predicate K, '[The word] "existing" names a kind of actualization (*actum quendam*), since something is said to exist not because it is potentially but because it is actually' (22.208). That is the way 'existing' is used, all right, but for just that reason it can't be quite right to say regarding whatever is at the basis of all existing simply that it exists. That standard way of talking suggests an instantiated nature, even if it should be a nature that entails its own instantiation. If the essential nature we're concerned with here isn't *identical* with its own unique, necessary, ultimately explanatory being, then, as Aquinas points out, 'it follows that [that] essential nature and being are related to each other as potentiality and actuality' (ibid.). If all existing, including its own, is to be explained through Alpha, then Alpha—that is, its essential nature—has to be uniquely necessary, ultimately explanatory being itself. Alpha = Alpha's nature = Alpha's being = uniquely necessary, ultimately explanatory being. The absolute independence argued for in G6 excludes even the sort of conceptual distinction between essence and existence that is compatible with entailment.

If I'm right in maintaining that Aquinas can get to the identity interpretation via this route that begins in G6, we now have good reason for accepting the identity interpretation. But exactly which identity is at issue? It may seem more elegant for Alpha's nature to be finally identified simply with being. Aquinas himself sometimes puts the identification that way in these chapters and elsewhere: God, or God's nature, is 'being itself (*ipsum esse*)'.[14] However, that way of putting it suggests that God is nothing but existence, and, as one recent critic puts it, 'nothing subsistent could be just existence: a merely existent substance is too thin to be possible' (Hughes 1989: 21).[15] The identification Aquinas seems to prefer is this: God, or God's nature, is 'his own being (*suum esse*)'[16]—that is, the

[14] See e.g. 23.214, 24.223, 25.229 (twice), 25.232, 27.252.
[15] See also Kretzmann and O'Connor 1992 (review of Hughes 1989).
[16] See e.g. 24.224, 25.231, 25.236, 26.240, 28.259, 28.260 (three times), 28.266.

uniquely necessary being of the kind that ultimately explains all existing. What kind is that? We do have some grasp of different kinds of being—corporeal and mathematical, for instance. But, having grasped the full import of eliminating predicate K from Alpha (or God), we have to admit, as Aquinas observes elsewhere in this connection, that its 'being is itself also unknown to us, just as its essential nature (*substantia*) is' (QDP 7.2, obj. 2). But that admission is compatible with our knowing *that Alpha exists*. G6 justifies the belief that Alpha exists, but the way it does so leaves us having to admit that Alpha's 'existing is cognized not through itself but [only] through a likeness to a creature'—to something dependent on Alpha for its existing (ibid., obj. 3).[17] We can know that Alpha must exist without really knowing what its existing is like.

5. The metaphysics of Exodus

In chapter 22, as in all of Aquinas's applications of the eliminative method, he draws his conclusions not regarding Alpha but, of course, regarding God, taking the existence of God to have been shown in chapter 13. Eliminating predicate K provides him with new and different grounds for identifying the first cause as God, however. After providing his arguments to show that the essential

---

[17] QDP 7.2 is roughly parallel to SCG I.22. Although this passage and the one quoted just above are found among the objections, they are actually preliminary rejoinders to previous objections—a sort of thing often found in disputed questions—and they generate further objections. Thus the first passage immediately follows obj. 1, and is introduced with *Sed diceretur quod*. It is immediately followed by an objection to it (obj. 2), introduced with *Sed contra*. The second passage immediately follows that objection, and is introduced with *Sed dicendum quod*. It, too, is immediately followed by a *Sed contra*, which constitutes obj. 3.

See also ST Ia.3.4, another parallel to SCG I.22, esp. obj. 2: 'Regarding God, we can know *whether* he is (as was said above), but we cannot know *what* he is. Therefore, God's existing and his essential nature (*esse Dei, et quod quid est eius, sive quidditas vel natura*) are not the same', and Aquinas's rejoinder to it: ' "existing" is used in two ways. In one way it signifies the actuality of being (*actus essendi*). In the other way it signifies a proposition's composition, which the soul encounters whenever it joins a predicate to a subject. Taking "existing" in the *first* way, we cannot know God's existing any more than we can know his nature. Instead, [we can know it] only in the *second* way, since we know that the proposition we frame when we say "God exists" is true; and we know *that* [only] on the basis of his effects' (ad 2).

nature of the entity that 'is, through itself, necessary being' must be identical with its being, he steps outside the confines of natural theology to observe that 'Moses was taught this sublime truth by the Lord' when (in Exod. 3: 13–14) Moses asked what he should tell the Israelites if they asked for God's name and the Lord answered 'I am Who Am (*Ego sum qui sum*). Say to the children of Israel, "Who Is (*Qui est*) has sent me to you"'. Aquinas interprets the oracular reply, not implausibly, as the Lord's revealing 'that God's very being is his essential nature (*quod ipsum divinum esse est sua essentia vel natura*)' (22.211). No doubt biblical scholarship would dismiss Aquinas's interpretation, even as applied to the Latin text of the passage. I'm in no position to defend it as an interpretation, though I can imagine, and perhaps even share, the intellectual satisfaction he seems to have felt on seeing this connection between the abstrusest sort of metaphysical thesis and the epiphany at the burning bush. In any case, whether or not Aquinas's reading of *Ego sum qui sum* is warranted as biblical interpretation, the argumentation of chapter 22, leading to the identification of the first cause with its own necessary being, picks out the first point in Aquinas's natural theology at which I think we might be said to have some warrant to begin replacing the non-committal designation 'Alpha' with the name 'God'. Very many unmistakably divine attributes have yet to emerge, and what has emerged so far, taken all together, doesn't constitute a condition indisputably sufficient for deity. But the fact that Aquinas aptly draws on the theistic tradition in recognizing the metaphysical thesis of SCG chapter 22 in 'the sublime truth' of Exodus 3 marks a noteworthy advance in that direction.

6. *Alpha's separateness, God's transcendence*

Of the four remaining predicates, three—F, Q, and R—are eliminated in ways that clarify the nature of the first cause's causality. For Aquinas, the kinds of causality exercised by God are clear from the existence arguments of chapter 13: G1 and (especially) G2 are supposed to show that the absolutely immovable first mover must somehow be a final cause, and G3 argues for a first efficient cause. Aquinas's ideas of causality are of course shaped by the Aristotelian doctrine to which he subscribes, according to which final and efficient are the two kinds of causes that are *extrinsic* to the things, events, or states of affairs of which they are the explanations. So it's clear that he's thinking of the first cause of contingent things and events as extrinsic to them, as it must be if the first cause is to emerge as transcendent God. But he knows that some who accept the notion of a first cause may be inclined to think of it as *intrinsic* to what it explains. And so he is concerned to argue that the first cause cannot be intrinsic either as the universal material cause (F) or as a universal formal cause (Q).

Even if we're disinclined to consider causes in quite the way Aristotle and Aquinas did, we can certainly recognize, and probably sympathize with, the tendency to suppose that anything that might count as an ultimate explanatory entity would be likely to be something like the pre-Socratics' sort of world-stuff—hylozoic in the manner of Thalean Water or Heraclitean Fire—more like twentieth-century matter-energy than like transcendent God.[18] But whatever else might have to be true of that sort of inherent explanatory entity, it would clearly have to be mutable, spatio-temporal, imbued with passive potentiality, and subject to accidental characteristics—in short, not in itself *ultimately* explanatory, and thus not Alpha. The same objections rule out attempts to present the ultimate explanatory entity as 'the soul of the world', attempts Aquinas deals with in eliminating predicate R.[19]

The least that is to be said about Alpha on the basis of argument G6 is that it exists necessarily through itself as a first sustaining cause, by which is meant at least the ultimate explanation of the natural laws and all the other conditions necessary for the presently continuing existence of contingent things. And perhaps a sustaining cause seems especially likely to be understood as intrinsic to the things whose present existing it ultimately explains, so that G6 may seem to present Alpha as intrinsic to the natural world. But, as Aquinas points out, when we say of such an ultimately explanatory entity that 'it is in all things', we don't mean that 'it is in things as something that *belongs* to a thing, but rather as a cause that is in no way lacking to its effect' (26.249), as a cause whose efficacy is all-pervasive.

[18] Aquinas briefly discusses and rejects the theories of these 'first natural philosophers' in 20.189–92.
[19] See esp. 27.258.

7. Perfection

Imperfection, predicate S, is the last to be ruled out in an application of the eliminative method. Chapter 28, in which imperfection's elimination is argued for, also marks the beginning of a new stage of Aquinas's project, as we'll see. His arguments in the chapter approach their conclusion via the eliminative method, using previous eliminations as bases on which to rule out as impossible any kind of imperfection in Alpha. But throughout chapter 28, beginning with its title, 'On Divine Perfection',[20] Aquinas emphasizes the affirmative version of the conclusion over the denial of imperfection. I'll follow his lead in focusing directly on perfection.

As might be expected, the familiar use of 'perfect' to express the highest possible evaluation is at the centre of Aquinas's concern in the chapter. But in addition to its evaluative aspect, perfection has a metaphysical aspect that is crucial to his account of it, a metaphysical aspect that no writer of Latin could fail to recognize. Aquinas knows that his word *perfectum* is just an adjectival use of the perfect passive participle of a Latin verb meaning to do thoroughly—to fulfil, finish, achieve, complete, accomplish. The fact that the word's fundamental sense has to do with the culmination of a process leads him to warn that 'perfection (*perfectio*) cannot appropriately be attributed to God if one pays attention to the signification of the noun from the standpoint of its derivation, for what is not *done* (*factum*) [at all] cannot be called *thoroughly done* (*per-fectum*). But everything that gets done (*fit*) is brought from potentiality to actuality, and from not-being to being, when it has been done (*factum est*); and so it is correctly said to be *perfectum*—as if to say "totally done" (*totaliter factum*)—when the potentiality has been totally brought down to actuality so that it retains no not-being but has complete being' (28.268). So immutability and pure actuality in God make the attribution of perfection to him misleading etymologically. But, as Aquinas observes, 'through a kind of extension of the [adjectival] name, not only that which *achieves* complete actuality *through* getting done (*fiendo*) but also that which *is in* complete actuality *without* any doing or

[20] SCG is one of very few of Aquinas's works to survive in a manuscript written in his own hand, and ch. 28 is one of only a few chapters of SCG I for which Aquinas himself supplied titles.

bringing about (*factione*) is called *per-fectum*. And it is in *this* way that we say that God is perfect' (ibid.).

Focusing on this metaphysical sense of 'perfect' makes it easy for Aquinas to argue for perfection by the eliminative method based on earlier eliminations, and he does provide arguments of that sort. For instance, 'anything is perfect in so far as it is actualized [and] imperfect in so far as it is in a state of potentiality, lacking actuality. Therefore, that which is in no way in a state of potentiality but is pure actuality must be most perfect. But that is what God is. Therefore, he is most perfect' (28.264).[21]

The abstractness of such considerations may make the metaphysical aspect of perfection seem remote from its familiar evaluative aspect, but everything Aquinas says about the metaphysical aspect—being fully actualized, in no respect incomplete—helps to show how it provides the basis for the ordinary use of 'perfect' as the term of highest praise. A thing is perfect of its kind in the laudatory sense to the extent to which it is a whole, complete specimen, free from relevant defect, to the extent to which it is fully realized or developed, to the extent to which the potentialities definitive of its kind—its specifying potentialities—are actualized. And so, as Aquinas puts it elsewhere, a thing is perfect and hence desirable (good of its kind) to the extent to which it is in being.[22] The degree of excellence in a particular daisy is the same as the degree to which that flower has actualized the potentialities that specify a daisy; the degree of excellence in a child's memorization of a poem is the same as the degree to which the child has actualized the potentialities that specify a memorization of that poem.

These considerations clarify the conception of perfection *in a certain respect*—perfect daisy, perfect memorization. But the results of the eliminative method so far have shown that Alpha (or God) can't be specified, and so if perfection can be attributed to it, it can't be merely perfection in some respect or other. Aquinas is, of course, fully aware that nothing less than absolute perfection will do, and in most of chapter 28 he argues that God must be '*most* perfect (*perfectissimus*)', as in the short, purely metaphysical argument I quoted just above. But in his first, main argument in the

---

[21] See also nn. 24 and 25 below.

[22] ST Ia.5.1. For a fuller discussion of the connection between metaphysical and evaluative considerations in Aquinas's thought, see Stump and Kretzmann 1988.

chapter he gives an account of absolute perfection that makes the argument worth a closer look: he argues that God must be *'universally* perfect', and explains 'universally perfect' in terms that commit him to arguing for perfection in the *evaluative* sense,[23] basing his argument directly on chapter 22's identification of God's essential nature as his being.[24]

The perfection argument

God, who is not other than his being (*esse*), is the universally perfect being (*ens*). I call that universally perfect which does not lack the excellence (*nobilitas*) belonging to any genus. For every excellence of any thing whatever belongs to it in keeping with its being. For no excellence would belong to a human being from his wisdom if it were   5
not the case that through it he *is* wise—and so on as regards other [excellences and kinds]. Therefore, a thing's mode of excellence is in keeping with the mode in which it has being; for a thing is said to be more or less excellent in so far as its being conforms to (*contrahitur ad*) some greater or lesser specific mode of excellence. Therefore, if   10
there is anything to which the whole capacity (*virtus*) of being pertains (*competit*), it can lack no [specific] excellence that is associated with any thing. But being in keeping with the whole capacity of being (*esse secundum totam essendi potestatem*) pertains to the thing that is its own being. (Similarly, if there were a separated whiteness, it could not   15
lack any of the capacity (*virtus*) of whiteness; for any white thing lacks some of the capacity (*virtus*) of whiteness because of a defect in whiteness's recipient, which receives it in keeping with its own mode [of being] and probably not in keeping with the whole capacity (*posse*) of whiteness.) Therefore, God, who is his own being (as was proved   20
above), has being in keeping with the whole capacity of being. There-

---

[23] Eliminating predicate S in this way, then, marks the first systematic introduction of an evaluation into the emergent series of affirmative counterparts to the eliminated predicates, although Aquinas does seem to have anticipated it at least twice, in 20.159 ('Therefore, a body is not that than which nothing is more excellent [*nobilius*]; but that is what God is') and 27.254 ('Therefore, since God is the most excellent [*nobilissimum*] being, as the first cause of existing, he cannot be the form of anything'). See also 18.146.

[24] In presenting this argument I'm omitting Aquinas's introductory allusion to the Porphyrian–Augustinian hierarchy: being → life → understanding—viz. 'Now even though things that both are and live are more perfect than those that only are, God, who is not other than his being . . .' (28.259). The allusion plays no part in the body of the argument, which is all that concerns me here, but it does set the stage for an appendix to the argument (28.262).

fore, he cannot lack any excellence that is associated with any thing. (28.259–60)[25]

In lines 1–3 Aquinas provides a preliminary version of the conclusion along with an explanation of universal perfection. The machinery of the eliminative method is still plainly at work here in the denials that God is other than his being or lacks the excellence of any genus, although denials of a distinction and a lack are perhaps more naturally construed as affirmations of identity and possession. Merely introducing God as not other than his being doesn't yet show that the argument depends on that identification, but it does suggest the importance of the identification here, and the argument bears out the suggestion (in lines 13–15 and 20–1). The combination of the strictly metaphysical identification of God with the plainly evaluative sense given to 'universally perfect' provides a special challenge for this perfection argument, because, as we've seen, Aquinas does have purely metaphysical arguments for perfection, and presumably could more easily have used one of those here. What makes the explanation of 'universally perfect' plainly evaluative, of course, is the word 'excellence', the unmistakably evaluative force of which is fully warranted here by Aquinas's Latin word *nobilitas*. But what's meant by 'the excellence belonging to any genus' (lines 2–3)?

One intended effect of associating excellence with genus in this way is to show that the focus here is *not* on intra-specific, individual excellences, such as great speed in one horse as compared with others. Also, 'genus' here is pretty clearly not being used in the technical sense in which it is distinguished from 'species', but means, instead, something like natural kind. A natural kind is picked out by specifying potentialities—for example, rationality or the capacity for thought and deliberated action in the natural kind *human being*. The excellence belonging to any natural kind will be the fullest possible realization of the potentialities that specify that kind—for example, wisdom for the natural kind *human being*.

---

[25] Aquinas doesn't end this perfection argument at this point, but extends it with a more purely metaphysical segment that strikes me as important in its own right but inessential to the main argument: 'But just as every excellence and perfection is in a thing in so far as it *is*, so every defect is in it in so far as it *is not*. Now just as God has being wholly, so is non-being wholly absent from him; for in the way any thing has being it lacks non-being. Therefore, every defect is absent from God. Therefore, he is universally perfect' (28.261).

Aquinas's explanation of the relevant sense of 'perfect' in terms of not lacking the excellence belonging to *any* genus makes the designation '*universally* perfect' perfectly apt. But how, exactly, is God (or Alpha) supposed not to lack any such excellence?

The argument begins its development of an answer to that question by pointing out a special connection between a thing's excellence and its being, taking as its paradigm wisdom, the excellence specific to rationality (lines 4–7). I don't think Aquinas means to suggest that someone might *have* wisdom but not *be* wise (as someone might have a fine library without being well-read). A person can't really have that excellence without really being excellent in the relevant respect. This distinction must be purely conceptual. None the less, it is wisdom's being truly predicable of the person that marks the excellence's belonging to him, and wisdom (or any other excellence) is predicable of its subject by means of the verb 'to be'. And so the predication 'Socrates is wise' is in theory more fundamentally revealing than the apparently equivalent 'Socrates has wisdom', because the 'is wise' formulation tells us something about the kind of *being* Socrates has. I've been told, more than once, that it is a mere accident of certain languages that they use the same verb to express being and to effect predication. If that's so, it's a happy accident. The point Aquinas wants to make here is that for a thing really to have a certain excellence is for it to be excellent in that certain way, which is for it to be in a certain way; and that seems unproblematic. The point is a good one, illustrated by, but not dependent on, the way predication is carried out in Latin and in English (for instance).

Aquinas continues the argument by introducing a ranking principle (lines 8–10). Again, the ranking of things here can't be intraspecific, as is shown by the explicit reference to modes of excellence that are associated with *species*. Instead, this ranking of things is solely in terms of the natural kinds they represent—for example, the ranking of a human being *qua* human relative to a cat *qua* feline.

The ranking of natural kinds has acquired a bad name—'speciesism'—and, considering the evils people have tried to justify on grounds of human supremacy among natural kinds, this sort of ranking deserves at least a cautious scrutiny. Aquinas's metaphysics provides a systematic basis on which to rank natural kinds, a basis that is summarized handily in the Porphyrian Tree, a standard device of medieval metaphysics inherited from late Greek philosophy. (It doesn't have to be accepted as universally applicable or utterly trustworthy in order to assess Aquinas's use of it as a basis for ranking kinds, but I wouldn't introduce it now if I thought it had only antiquarian interest.) A Porphyrian Tree begins with an Aristotelian category—*substance* is the standard example and the one that suits this discussion—and moves via a series of dichotomies from that most general genus through at least some of its species. The dichotomies produce progressively more specific species by the application of a pair of complementary characteristics (differentiae) to a less specific species (a genus) that is already in the tree. In this way, for example, *substance* is made to branch into *corporeal substance* and *incorporeal substance* to begin the tree. Corporeal substances can in turn be divided into those with and those without capacities for growth, reproduction, and other biological processes; and corporeal substances with capacities for biological processes can be divided into those that have and those that lack a capacity for perception—animals and plants, roughly speaking. Finally, those with a capacity for perception can be divided into those with and those without the capacity for rational processes—human beings and other animals. And so one of the two species (or genera) encountered in any pair after the first is picked out by a type of capacity that is over and above the capacities of its counterpart. In a clear, uncontroversial sense, then, a specific excellence that is constituted by the full actualization of more types of capacities than specify another species is for just that reason and in just that sense 'greater' than the excellence specific to the other one.[26]

The *being* of a cat conforms to the feline *essential nature*: what it is to exist as a cat, the mode in which a cat has being, the mode in keeping with which there is a specific mode of excellence (feline). And that is a lesser mode of excellence than one constituted by the full realization of a larger set of types of capacities. Individual things can be ranked in this way as more or less excellent considered *only* as representatives of different species, *not* as individuals within a single species.

The perfection argument next spells out the way in which something might count as universally perfect, and picks out 'the thing that is its own being' as filling that bill (lines 10–15). We are to

---

[26] For further development of this material see Stump and Kretzmann 1988.

consider the possibility of something 'to which the whole capacity of being pertains'. The notion of the whole capacity of being (*tota virtus essendi*) enters the argument for the first time at this point, but we're offered two kinds of help in understanding it. In the first place, the sentence in lines 10–13 is presented as following from what has gone before it, and so the course of the argument so far should show us how to read it.

Here's my attempt to weave the claims in lines 10–15 into the argument, drawing on my discussion of its development up to this point. The greatness of a thing's specific mode of excellence is determined by how many types of capacities are included within its essential nature, since the excellence specific to a thing consists in the realizing of the capacities essential to it. Relative greatness among specific modes of excellence will be determined, then, by the relative range of the capacities whose realization constitutes excellence. For instance, the human mode of excellence will be greater than the feline mode of excellence in this respect. And so if there is anything the essential nature of which includes the *whole* range of such capacities, whether or not they are instantiated in nature, its excellence will include all specific modes of excellence. The only thing whose essential nature includes this whole capacity of being is the thing whose essential nature is uniquely necessary, ultimately explanatory being itself.

Aquinas's analogy based on an imaginary Platonic Form (lines 15–20) provides a second kind of help in understanding the notion of the whole capacity of being. The relevance of the analogy can be clarified by recasting it in this form. The whiteness of china cups is different from the whiteness of linen table-cloths because of differences between the natures of glazed clay and of woven threads, and neither of those whitenesses is all there is to whiteness. Analogously, the being of cats is different from the being of people because of differences between the natures of cats and of people, and neither of those kinds of being is all there is to being. Any ordinary white thing lacks some of the capacities intrinsic to whiteness just because of limitations in its nature (apart from whiteness), which determines its receptivity to whiteness. Analogously, any ordinary existent thing lacks some of the capacities intrinsic to being just because of limitations in its nature, which determines its receptivity to being. But if there were any thing that could be identified as whiteness, in the sense of a single entity that would have to figure in the ultimate, metaphysical explanation of any white thing's having whiteness, then that entity couldn't lack any of the capacities intrinsic to whiteness. It would have to be identified as the full reality corresponding to, and explanatory of, all those capacities, as perfect whiteness. Analogously, if there is any thing that can be identified as being itself, in the sense of a single entity that must figure in the ultimate, metaphysical explanation of any existent thing's having being, it can't lack any of the capacities intrinsic to being; it has to be identified as the full reality corresponding to, and explanatory of, all those capacities, as universally perfect being. And, as was shown in chapter 22, there is such a thing. So, it seems to me, the entity whose essential nature has been shown to be identical with its uniquely necessary, ultimately explanatory being has also been shown to be universally perfect.

8. Concluding observations

Is universal perfection as spelled out in this perfection argument a sufficient condition for deity? Maybe not. At any rate, even this culminating application of the eliminative method hasn't yet turned up any explicit indications of personhood or even, strictly speaking, of goodness, knowledge, and power. But, as Aquinas's use of the concept of universal perfection will show, all four of those traditional divine attributes are implicit in perfection. And so the elimination of predicate S, imperfect, marks another notable advance in the direction of identifying Alpha as God.

Once S has been eliminated, especially in the way the perfection argument eliminates it, we may be able, retrospectively, to view all the previously eliminated predicates as general metaphysical imperfections the elimination of which is particularly important on the way to establishing universal perfection.

And establishing universal perfection provides the basis for introducing a new sort of method with which to pursue this project, as we'll see in Chapter Five.

FIVE

FROM PERFECTION TO INFINITY

1. Methodology

Aquinas is methodologically conscientious about his project in the first three books of SCG, as anyone engaging in natural theology should be. As we saw in Chapter One, his introduction to all of SCG in chapters 1–9 of Book I is devoted almost entirely to considering methods appropriate to theology generally, and to justifying the purely philosophical approach he means to take in Books I–III. Then, having argued in chapter 13 for the *existence* of a first source of being, he undertakes a detailed presentation of its *nature*, prefacing that new undertaking with a second discussion of methods, in chapter 14. There he explains the eliminative method and the need to adopt it (at least to begin with), and he shows how its negative results contribute to carving out the concept of 'God considered in himself'.

But in that same chapter he also promises to introduce another approach as soon as applications of the eliminative method have achieved a certain cumulative effect. 'In this way, through negations of that sort, [derived] in order, [God] will be distinguished from everything that is other than himself. And then, when there is cognition of him as distinct from all [other] things, there will be a consideration focused on his substance. It will not be complete (*perfecta*), however, because there will not be cognition of what he is in himself' (14.118). That consideration, focused on God's substance, or nature, turns out to be a systematic derivation of some *affirmative* predications on the basis of the eliminative method's distinctions between God and everything else. (But, as he carefully points out, even all those affirmative predications taken together cannot give us 'cognition of *what he is in himself*', cannot enable us to provide a full account of God's essence.) The transition to the new, less indirect consideration takes place in chapter 28, with Aquinas's linked arguments *against* every *imperfection* in the first source of being and *for* its *universal perfection*, the topic with which my Chapter Four ended. In recognition of this transition, Aquinas presents a third methodological discussion, devoting the next eight chapters (29–36) to providing a systematic basis for developing the consideration of God's 'substance'.[1]

As a consequence of chapter 28's arguments for the necessary elimination of all imperfection from God, Aquinas can now refer to divine attributes generally as perfections. Within the limits of natural theology there are, he observes, only two sorts of bases on which we can justifiably ascribe perfections to God: either '[1] through *negation*, as when we call God eternal [i.e. beginningless, endless, timeless], or infinite [i.e. limitless]; or also [2] through a *relation* he has to other things, as when he is called the *first* cause, or the *highest* good. For as regards God we cannot grasp what he is, but rather [1] what he is not, and [2] how other things are disposed relative to him' (30.278). Having used the first of these two bases for the eliminative method, he now develops the second as the basis for the more elaborately justified of his two specific methods for natural theology. This 'relational method', as I'll call it, governs most of Aquinas's philosophical account of God's nature.[2] And since any philosophical account of God's nature must be based on inferences from the natures of things other than God, something more or less like Aquinas's relational method will have to be used by anyone undertaking natural theology.

2. The extensive aspect of absolute perfection

In my Chapter Four I treated Aquinas's chapter 28 as the culmination of the account developed by means of the exclusive application

---

[1] In the light of Ch. Four there are two reasons for changing the designation of the subject from 'Alpha' to 'God' at this point in our investigation: (1) the special importance of 'the metaphysics of Exodus' (Ch. Four, sect. 5) in conjunction with the philosophical identification of the first cause with its own necessary being (sect. 4); (2) the fact that the introduction of absolute, universal perfection (sect. 7) entails further attributes of which some, to be made explicit later, are unmistakably personifying. So switching from 'Alpha' to 'God' here in Ch. Five is to some extent justified retrospectively. But the move also anticipates the results of unpacking 'universal perfection'.

[2] The relational method is essential also in Aquinas's systematic development of revealed theology. See e.g. ST Ia.13.2. For a very helpful survey of Aquinas's methods in theology generally, see Wippel 1992.

of the eliminative method. In chapter 28, as we've seen, he more than once argues for perfection as a divine attribute (or meta-attribute) by showing the impossibility of any imperfection in the first source (28.260–2 and 264). Those eliminative arguments for God's absolute perfection bring out its purity, or what might be thought of as its intensive aspect. But absolute perfection also has an extensive aspect, reflected in his designating it *'universal* perfection': 'I call universally perfect that which does not lack the excellence associated with any natural kind (*alicuius generis*)' (28.259); 'none of the perfections that are associated with any things are lacking to God' (28.266).[3]

The extensive aspect of absolute perfection, its universality, is what lies behind Aquinas's beginning chapter 28 with the announcement of a *tour de force* for the eliminative method. The ranking of specific perfections is naturally concomitant with the wider or narrower ranges of potentiality essential to various species of being. An *in*animate being perfect of its kind has less perfection extensively than a perfect *living* being of some kind, and so on. *Absolute* perfection, then, must be extensively *universal*—inclusive, somehow, of all specific perfections. *None the less*, he says, in chapter 28 divine universal perfection will be established (in what I've called the 'perfection argument') on the basis of the elegantly meagre claim that God 'is *not other than his being*', the central result of the eliminative method (derived in chapters 21 and 22): 'Now although things that both are and are alive are more perfect than those that merely are [and so on], God, who is not other than his being, is, none the less, the *universally* perfect being' (28.259). Aquinas accomplishes this *tour de force* in the perfection argument when he concludes on that meagre basis that God 'cannot lack any excellence that is associated with any thing' (28.260). All the specific perfections associated with all kinds of inanimate things, and of living things, and of things that have minds—and, indeed, of natural things of *any* kind—must be found in God somehow.[4]

This universality of absolute perfection helps give chapter 28 its uniquely transitional function among the chapters in which the

[3] See also 'every excellence of any thing whatever belongs to it'; 'it can lack no excellence that is associated with any thing'; 'he cannot lack any excellence that is associated with any thing' (28.260).

[4] So he needn't postpone arguing for perfection until he has introduced separately such positive divine attributes as *life* and *intellect* as increments contributing to a cumulative concept of universal perfection. (The attribution of life to God is established in I.97–9, divine intellect in I.44–71. On the latter, see Ch. Six.)

eliminative method is applied. Most of the metaphysical concerns of chapters 15–27 are peculiarly formal, with an arid look about them. It takes some doing to show the fecundity of such results as that there is no passive potentiality in God, and that God is not other than his being. By contrast, that God is universally perfect, chapter 28's result, is expressly overflowing with further implications for God's nature.[5] So the first indication of a need for a methodological supplement is the fact that the project is no longer concerned merely with relationships that give rise to the differences uncovered by the eliminative method, relationships almost all of which obtain between God and everything else considered globally.[6] The introduction of universal perfection appears to provide an opportunity for investigating specific relationships between God and one or another *kind* of thing, an opportunity the new relational method will be designed to exploit. And so chapter 28 marks an expansion in the sort of content to be expected in the propositions that will be uncovered in this project as the consideration of God's substance develops.[7]

3. The introduction of terminological sameness

The introduction of the attribute of perfection signals a change not only in the content, but also in the form of those propositions. The results of chapters 15–27 are typically achieved by showing the inapplicability of such positive attributes as corporeality or definability to God, and so chapter 28's elimination of purely negative imperfections marks an important shift in the direction of more unmistakably positive results. As if in recognition of this shift, Aquinas ends chapter 28 with a section designed to ward off a misinterpretation of the chapter's use of the word 'perfect', as we

---

[5] The unmistakable fecundity of universal perfection accounts for Aquinas's devoting a whole chapter to showing that not only the plurality of divine attributes but also the single attribute of perfection is compatible with absolute simplicity: ch. 31, 'divine perfection and the plurality of the divine names are not incompatible with divine simplicity'. The elegant way in which universal perfection is argued for in the perfection argument certainly contributes to dispelling the appearance of incompatibility.

[6] Some of the eliminations—of materiality, e.g.—do not distinguish God from *everything* else.

[7] For an excellent critical discussion relevant to many aspects of this chapter, see Alston 1993.

saw in Chapter Four. No such cautionary appendix would have been appropriate at the end of a chapter establishing, for instance, that God is not a member of any genus, or that God is devoid of any sort of composition, since those paradigmatic results of the eliminative method simply establish differences between God and everything we're familiar with. Even without supposing that God's existence has been established, such propositions of essential difference are strictly true as they stand, and introduce no problems of interpretation. Whether the results of the eliminative method before chapter 28 are negative propositions employing only terms we apply to ordinary things or affirmative propositions employing negatively defined technical terms, such as 'eternal' or 'simple', those results are hardly liable to any kind of misinterpretation. But questions of interpretation arise as soon as God is called perfect. For we can, and sometimes do, correctly use the word 'perfect' in talking about daisies or memorizations, having learned the meaning of the word in such ordinary usage, and the cumulative effect of the eliminative method has been to show us how deeply different God is from any ordinary thing we talk about. And so the result of chapter 28, which for the first time uses a term with *familiar* applications to *affirm* something about God, moves us on from an exclusive concern with straightforwardly interpretable propositions founded on differences between God and other things to the broader, more intricate realm of propositions in which predicates affirmed of other things are affirmed of God as well.

The elaborate methodological discussion in chapters 29–36, providing the basis for the relational method, is called for, then, by the two transitional developments in chapter 28: the shift to positive results affirmatively expressed and the newly acquired opportunity to somehow trace specific relationships between God and various sorts of other things.[8] Because those two developments work together to provide apparent occasions for extending to God the

---

[8] When the 'consideration focused on God's substance' begins in earnest after those eight methodological chapters, the shift to positive results is evident at once in the chapters arguing for God's goodness (37–41) and uniqueness (42), while the attention to specific relationships between God and this or that kind of things first emerges unmistakably in the detailed account of God as intellective (44–71). From the look of its title, ch. 43, devoted to arguing that 'God is infinite', seems to constitute another application of the eliminative method. But, as we'll see, the methodological status of chs. 42 and 43 isn't quite so simple as the chapters' titles make it look.

application of terms that apply ordinarily to other things, much of the discussion in chapters 29–36 is concerned with this terminological sameness. It is greeted with suspicion, as it should be. Unless we're provided with some special theoretical justification for talking otherwise, we know what we're talking about only when we're using ordinary terms in ordinary ways. And since in natural theology 'all our cognition of God is drawn from [our cognition of] created things', if this terminological sameness were 'agreement only as regards names, we would know nothing of God other than empty names under which there would be no reality' (QDP 7.7c).[9] That is, in the absence of some special theoretical justification for applying ordinary terms to the most extraordinary being, the results of doing so would be strictly uninterpretable—and in a particularly pernicious way, since the uninterpretability would be masked by the familiarity of the words. So, if this project in natural theology is to remain viable, the terminological sameness that makes its first clear appearance with the attribution of perfection to God calls for special justification: semantic backing in the form of some sort of real sameness between God and ordinary things. The development in chapters 29–36 of a basis for the relational method is intended to support the expansion of philosophically justified language about God to include not only negative propositions or fundamentally negative technical terms, but also affirmations involving terms we apply primarily to ordinary things—adjectives such as 'living' and 'good', nouns such as 'intellect' and 'will'.

4. Likeness and agent causation generally

That's why Aquinas starts chapter 29's methodological development by tying it to the introduction of perfection in chapter 28— 'Now *on that basis* one can consider how likeness to God can or cannot be found among things' (28.269)—and, more precisely, to his warning about the easy misinterpretation of the word 'perfect' as applied to God. It provides the immediate occasion for considering the possibility of likenesses between God and other things despite the eliminative method's establishment of so many unlikenesses.

[9] See also e.g. SCG I.33.295.

In several places Aquinas develops a general account of kinds of likenesses,[10] beginning with the basic observation that if X can literally and truly be said to be like Y in any way at all, then X has some form that Y also has.[11] Fundamentally, then, likeness is con-formity, sameness in respect of sharing at least one form.

Likeness shows up in many different contexts, of course. But our present concern is solely with likeness between God and ordinary things, and its context is the metaphysically primary relationship of anything else to God, the relationship of causal dependence— which is of course also the relationship on the basis of which our cognition of God is drawn inductively from our cognition of things. And so an understanding of the relationship of causal dependence is indispensable to natural theology not only theoretically but also practically, since it serves as the basis for the project of deriving truths about the ultimate explanatory principle from observations about the things the principle is meant to explain. For purposes of investigating the possibility of genuine likeness between God and ordinary things with a view to justifying the application of ordinary terms to God, we can, then, focus exclusively on Aquinas's analysis of the kinds of likeness obtaining between an effect and its cause. And although his agenda for the eight methodological chapters is oriented toward drawing practical conclusions regarding the use of language about God,[12] my present interest in this material is focused on the metaphysical underpinnings of those linguistic con-clusions, the basis for the relational method.

Aquinas, of course, thinks of ordinary efficient causation not as a mere regular concatenation of events but, instead, as either the natural generation or the artificial production of effects. He under-stands this in terms of an agent's (or active subject's) initiating the sharing with a patient (or passive object) of some form the agent

[10] Besides SCG I.29, see e.g. QDP 7.7c; QDV 23.7, ad 11; ST Ia.4.3c.

[11] See e.g. 29.273: '[W]hat is called like something is what possesses a quality or form of it'; ST Ia.4.3c: '[L]ikeness is associated with agreeing in or sharing a form.'

[12] The titles of the chapters give a pretty accurate impression of Aquinas's aims: 'The likeness of created things [to God]' (29); 'Names that can be predicated of God' (30); 'Divine perfection and the plurality of the divine names are not incom-patible with divine simplicity' (31); 'Nothing is predicated univocally of God and of other things' (32); 'Not all names are said purely equivocally of God and of created things' (33); 'Things that are said of God and of created things are said analogically' (34); 'The several names said of God are not synonyms' (35); 'How our intellect frames a proposition about God' (36). (With the exception of ch. 34, which he left untitled, all these chapters were titled by Aquinas himself; see Ch. Four, n. 20.)

possesses antecedently, often in some way quite different from the way in which the patient comes to possess the shared form. For present purposes I'm adopting Aquinas's understanding of efficient causation, and so, as a reminder, I'll write in terms of 'agent causation'.[13] Some sort of likeness between an effect and its cause is an immediate consequence of this notion of agent causation, since agent causation shares a necessary condition with likeness: if A is the agent and P is the patient, then A antecedently somehow has some form, f, that P also somehow has, consequently. In agent causation the effect that is brought about by the actualizing of some potentiality in A or by A's exercise of some power is the informing of P with f.[14]

Agent causation, then, entails a con-formity between cause and effect: 'Since every agent does something like itself in so far as it is an agent, but each thing acts in keeping with a form belonging to it, it is necessary that there be in the effect a [consequent] likeness of a form belonging to the agent' (ST Ia.4.3c).[15] Clearly, 'likeness' (*similitudo*) is a technical term in this context, closer to 'correspondence' than to 'resemblance' in the ordinary sense, even if in some cases the correspondence may be detailed enough to count as resemblance. The only immediately relevant con-formity between an agent cause and its effect is the presence in the effect of characteristics that could serve to identify, or at least to type, the agent— physical or metaphysical fingerprints providing the basis for an inductive argument to the agent's existence and some aspects of its nature.

Agent causation does not include the generation of *accidental*

---

[13] My use of this term here is broader than, but includes, its standard contemporary use, especially in discussions of free will, where 'agent causation' is regularly contrasted with 'event causation'.

[14] Herbert McCabe observes that the notion that effects are like their causes is one 'that the modern reader is likely to find most puzzling', but the puzzlement should be reduced if not eliminated by limiting the application of the notion to agent causation. As McCabe observes, Aquinas's 'typical causal proposition . . . is not concerned with two events but with a thing, a form, and a subject into which the form is introduced by the thing. His general causal proposition would be something like "A brings it about that F is in B", where A is a thing, the efficient cause, F is a form and B is the "material cause", the subject upon which A's causality is exerted. According to St Thomas what F is depends on the nature of A, so that if "A" is a name expressing the nature of A, the meaning of "F" will be related to the meaning of "A". What the effect will look like will depend not only on F but also on B' (McCabe 1964: 101).

[15] See also SCG I.29.270, quoted on pp. 149–50 and 151 below.

effects: 'what is generated by something *accidentally* is not generated by it in so far as it is of such-and-such a sort, and so in what
generates something there *need not* be a likeness of what is generated', just because in cases of accidental generation there is no
antecedent likeness of the effect, which is at least often what we
would call a chance effect. 'For example, the discovery of a treasure
has no [antecedent] likeness in the person who finds the treasure
accidentally while digging in order to plant something' (In Met.
VII: L8.1443). On the other hand, the person's deliberately digging
in order to plant something does have an antecedent likeness in his
ideas and intentions, and is an instance of (artificial) agent causation. And if the treasure had been uncovered, instead, by a storm's
uprooting a tree, (natural) agent causation would account only for
features of the cause that could be inferred from the effect, such as
the direction and force of the wind, forms belonging to A that
constitute in it an antecedent likeness of the effect in P.

5. Univocal and equivocal causation

The strongest sort of likeness possible between an effect and its
cause considered just as such is the kind occurring in connection
with the sort of agent causation that requires the inclusion of the
agent cause and its effect within the same species. Biological reproduction is the paradigm, but not the only instance: 'if the agent is
included in the same species along with its effect, then between the
maker and what is made there will be a likeness in form that is in
keeping with the same *ratio* as is associated with the species—for
instance, [when] a human being generates a human being' (ST
Ia.4.3c), or 'when the form of what is generated is antecedently in
the generator in the same mode of being and in similar matter—for
instance, when a fire generates a fire' (In Met. VII: L8.1444), or
when 'heat produces heat' (In Sent. I.8.1.2c).

Aquinas uses the word *ratio* often and importantly in these discussions, and I haven't found a single fully satisfactory translation
for it here, mainly because in its various occurrences it conveys a
variously proportioned blend of *meaning, definition, concept,
model,* and *essential nature.* 'Theoretical account' or 'intelligible
nature' may come close to being acceptable as a single equivalent,
but I'm going to leave *ratio* in Latin, commenting on what I take to

be its sense when it seems problematic. In the example of human reproduction in these passages the form is evidently humanity, and the *ratio* associated with the species is pretty clearly the definition *rational animal*, which is necessarily suited to both the agent and its effect, because they're both members of the human species.[16]

'Mode' is another term used importantly in these passages on same-species agent causation and elsewhere in Aquinas's account of likeness, causal and otherwise. Sometimes, as here, it picks out the *way in which* the shared form is realized in the cause and in the effect: flesh and bone in the example of human reproduction. But, as we'll see, Aquinas uses 'mode' in this context also to indicate the *degree to which* the shared form is realized in the cause and in the effect. In the example of human reproduction the mode in this second sense is essentially just the same, since humanity is realized completely, perfectly, in both cause and effect.[17]

This strongest sort of causal likeness supports an altogether univocal application of the same species-term both to the agent cause (which is more conveniently designated 'C' here) and to its effect, E (where the effect is P's having been informed with f). For that reason Aquinas calls this sort of agent causation *univocal* (or even *entirely univocal*[18]). The detailed essential likeness of E to its univocal agent cause C and the fact that 'human being', 'fire', or 'heat' is predicable univocally of both C and E in such cases is founded on three (or four) samenesses: (1) the same form, f, is antecedently in C and consequently in E; (2) f is associated with

---

[16] See e.g. ST Ia.13.5, obj. 1: '[U]nivocal agents . . . agree with their effects in name and definition', and esp. Ia.13.1c: '[T]he name "human being" by its significa-tion expresses the essence of a human being as it really is (*secundum quod est*), for it signifies its definition declaring its essence, since the *ratio* that a name signifies is its definition.' In notes to this passage the editors of the Marietti edn. say: 'The *ratio* here is the objective concept (or that which we understand of any thing formally—*per se*, primarily), since it is what is cognitively primary about a thing (*principium cognoscitivum rei*).' They also cite Ia.15.3c and Aristotle's *Metaphysics* III 7, 1012a21–4 with In Met. III: L16.733.

[17] ST Ia.4.3c provides a helpful introduction to the use of *ratio* and 'mode' in connection with likeness outside the context of causality: '[S]ome things are said to be like each other that share in the same form both as regards the *ratio* and as regards the same mode. They are called not only alike, but equal in their likeness. For instance, two things that are equally white are called alike in whiteness. And this is the most perfect likeness. Things that share in a form as regards the same *ratio* although *not* as regards the same mode but, rather, to a greater or lesser degree (*secundum magis et minus*) are said to be alike in another way—as what is less white is said to be like what is whiter. And this is an imperfect likeness.'

[18] See e.g. In Met. VII: L8.1444.

the same *ratio* in both C and E;[19] (3a) *f* is essentially realized in the same way in both C and E; and (3b) *f* is essentially realized to the same degree in both C and E.[20]

But, for several reasons, univocal causation can't be a relationship that provides a basis for likeness between God and any of his effects. Among the more interesting and less obvious of those reasons is the fact that, as we saw in Chapter Three, Aquinas acknowledges that in a series of the sort of causes and effects that are here identified as univocal it's theoretically possible for there to be an infinite regress. Furthermore, the fact that in univocal causation the form shared by C and E is realized in the same way and to the same degree is guaranteed by the fact that the relationship between C and E must be the natural generation of one member of a species by another member of the same species. But if C and E aren't included in a single species, 'it is possible that the effect's actualization be [essentially] more imperfect than the actuality of the agent cause, since an action can be weakened as a consequence (*ex parte*) of that in which it terminates' (28.265). And since God belongs to no species or genus at all (I.25), God as agent cause and God's effects can't be included in any single species. Finally, 'every effect of a univocal agent is on a par with the agent's power; but no created thing, since it is finite, can be on a par with the first agent's power, since it is infinite.[21] And so it is impossible that a likeness of God be received univocally in a created thing' (QDP 7.7c).

So God's effects, even those that are perfect of their kind, are in some essential respect essentially less than their cause, and, according to chapter 29, 'effects that are [essentially] less than their causes (*a suis causis deficientes*) do not agree with them in name and *ratio*. None the less, it is necessary that *some* likeness be found between them, for it is part of the nature of action that an agent does what is like itself, since each thing acts in keeping with its being in actuality (*secundum quod actu est*) [not in a state of mere potentiality]. That is why the form of the effect is indeed found *somehow* in a cause that [essentially] surpasses its effect, but in another mode, and in connection with another *ratio*. And for that reason

---

[19] See Aristotle, *Categories* 1, 1a6; translated from the Latin version Aquinas would have read: 'But those that have a name in common and the same *ratio* of substance corresponding to the name are called univocal—e.g. animal: a human being and a cow.'

[20] By 'essentially' here, I mean to exclude individuating distinctions.

[21] As Aquinas will argue in SCG I.43.

[such a cause] is called an *equivocal* cause' (29.270). So if C is an equivocal cause of E, then (1) the same form, *f*, is antecedently in C and consequently in E; but (2′) it is not the case that *f* is associated with the same *ratio* in C and in E;[22] (3a′) it is not the case that *f* is essentially realized in the same way in C and in E; and (3b′) it is not the case that *f* is essentially realized to the same degree in C and in E.

Since univocal causation supports a univocal application of the same term to both the effect and the cause, it might be supposed that equivocal causation could support only an equivocal application—in which case it would look as if any terminological sameness in this connection would be 'agreement only as regards names'. And if that's so, it might then look as if we can 'know nothing of God other than empty names under which there would be no reality' when we try to move beyond the negations of the eliminative method. But only the already discounted *accidental* efficient causation could be *purely* equivocal (as biological reproduction is purely univocal). Only of that sort of case would it be true also that (1′) it is not the case that the same form is antecedently in C and consequently in E. Purely equivocal causation is efficient causation by chance, as pure equivocation is terminological sameness by chance.[23] And in the systematically justifiable propositions of natural theology, 'nothing is predicated of God and of other things in accordance with pure equivocation' (33.291).

6. *The sun as an equivocal cause*

Well, then, is it equivocal causation, despite its off-putting label, that obtains between universally perfect God and God's necessarily less than universally perfect effects? Aquinas's model of

---

[22] See Aristotle, *Categories* 1, 1a1; translated from the Latin version Aquinas would have read: 'Things that have only a name in common but a different *ratio* of substance corresponding to the name are called equivocal—e.g. animal: a human being and a picture [of a human being].'

[23] e.g. 'ball' for a round object and for a formal dancing party. What we have in this case, considered etymologically, is two words that just happen to be spelled and pronounced the same. See e.g. 33.290: '[N]ot everything predicated of God and of other things is said in accordance with pure equivocation, like those [terms] that are equivocal by chance.'

equivocal agent causation in chapter 29 does seem to provide some of what we'd expect to find in an account of divine causation.

The sun causes heat in terrestrial bodies (*corporibus inferioribus*) by acting in keeping with its state of actuality. That is why the heat generated by the sun must hold some sort of *likeness* to the sun's active power, through which heat is caused in terrestrial things. For that reason the sun [also] is called hot, even though not in connection with one [and the same] *ratio* [as applies to terrestrial things that are called hot]. And in this respect the sun is said to be somehow *like* all the things in which it produces its effects in the manner of an agent cause (*efficaciter*). But, on the other hand, it is *unlike* all of them in so far as such effects do not possess heat (and [other forms] of that sort) in the same mode in which it is found in the sun. (29.270)

'Heat is in the sun in a mode that exceeds the mode in which it is in a fire' (ST Ia.6.2c); and so 'the sun and fire generated by the sun are not called hot univocally' (32.284).

The sand is hot and dry, and so is the sun. It's quite all right to talk that way, but our interest now is in acquiring knowledge about the remote sun on the basis of our familiarity with some of its local effects, not in making conversation on the beach. If we understand the natures of the effected heat and dryness in the sand, then perhaps the first step toward learning about the nature of their agent cause on that basis is to understand that simply in virtue of the structure of agent causation those effects must somehow be fundamentally *like* their cause, in the sense that there must be some theoretically discoverable way in which the forms of heat and dry-ness are also in the sun. But then, surely, the very next step toward learning in this way about the nature of the sun as a heating and drying agent is to recognize that since the sun and the sand are not in the same species and so do not share the same *ratio*, the forms of heat and of dryness must be realized differently in the cause and in its effects: '[S]uch effects do not possess heat (and [other forms] of that sort) in the same mode in which it is found in the sun.'

The forms familiar to us in the effects, Aquinas says, are not *realized* in familiar ways in their equivocal agent cause, but are in the cause

in respect of power, the way heat is in the sun. Now if that sort of power did not belong to the genus of heat somehow, the sun acting through it would not generate anything like itself. It is on the basis of this power, then, that the sun is called hot—not only because it produces heat, but also because the power through which it does this is something in con-formity with heat (*aliquid conforme calori*). However, through the same power through which the sun produces heat it also produces many other effects in terrestrial bodies—dryness, for instance. And in this way heat and dryness, which are different qualities in [a terrestrial body[24]], are attributed to the sun on the basis of its single power. (31.280)

'Every effect that is inadequate to the power of its agent cause receives a likeness of the agent not in accordance with the same *ratio* but in an [essentially] lesser way (*deficienter*), so that what is in the effects in many different ways is in the cause simply and in [one and] the same mode—as the sun in keeping with its one power produces in terrestrial things many different sorts of forms' (ST Ia.13.5c). Solar power, understood as nuclear fusion or otherwise, of course produces tremendous heat, but, strictly speaking, that power is not itself hot. Still, this equivocal agent cause of heat is itself appropriately, though non-univocally, *called* hot for two reasons: first, because solar power produces heat (in the sun as well as in the sand); second, because solar power is 'something in conformity with heat', something that shares a form with the heat it produces in the sand.[25] It is for these two reasons that it is said to 'belong to the genus of heat somehow'.

The example of heat may make these reasons look clearer than they are, since we know that the sun really is hot,[26] albeit in a mode different from anything terrestrial, short of the explosion of a hydrogen bomb. Solar power really does belong to the genus of heat, even though the way the form of heat is in the power of this agent cause is specifically different from the way it's realized in its terrestrial effects. 'Since every agent does something like itself in so far as it is an agent, but each thing acts in keeping with its form, it is necessary that there be a likeness of the agent's form in the effect. . . . However, if the agent is not included in the same species' with the effect, as in equivocal causation it is not, 'there will be a

---

[24] I'm introducing 'a terrestrial body' here as a replacement for Aquinas's 'fire', which strikes me as accidentally misleading because of antiquated natural science.

[25] The first is the solar power's *agent* causation; the second is what Aquinas sometimes calls *exemplar* causation. See e.g. In Sent. IV.43.1.2.1c, where the distinction is drawn regarding a univocal cause.

[26] Aquinas believed the contrary. See ST Ia.13.5, obj. 1: '[T]he sun causes heat even though it is not hot, except equivocally'; and In Sent. I.8.1.2c: '[T]he sun, which is not hot, produces heat.'

likeness, even though not in keeping with the same *ratio* as is associated with the species. For example, things that are generated by the sun [e.g. heat] do indeed approach a likeness to the sun— not, however, so as to receive a form belonging to the sun in accordance with a *specific* likeness but [only] in accordance with a *generic* likeness' (ST Ia.4.3c).

But dryness, like most other effects of solar power, requires an account different from the one provided for heat. Of course solar power involves no water at all, and the sun must be perfectly dry, in the sense that it could not contain even a single water molecule; but those facts are utterly irrelevant to solar power's generating perfect dryness in a grain of sand. It should be clearer regarding dryness than it is regarding heat that Aquinas's second reason in support of calling the sun hot or dry is fundamentally the con-formity that is essential to his analysis of agent causation, whether or not the equivocal cause and its effect can be correctly called by the same name. If solar power causes hardening of clay and softening of wax, bleaching of cloth and tanning of skin, then solar power has in it hardening and softening, bleaching and tanning. If objects with various passive potentialities are exposed to the sun, solar power will actualize those passive potentialities differently, which makes it appropriate for us to talk as if solar power included various active potentialities: hardening power, tanning power, and so on. But those conveniently discriminated active potentialities don't support calling the sun hard or tan, even generically, because hardening and tanning are effects much more specific than heating or drying, effects that depend on solar power's affecting passive potentialities that we know cannot characterize the sun itself, although they are quite familiar in terrestrial bodies.[27]

[27] ST IaIIae.60.1c: 'It is important to consider that the patient's matter'—i.e. its set of passive potentialities—'is related to the agent in two ways. For [1] sometimes it receives a form belonging to the agent in accordance with the same *ratio* as is in the agent, as happens in connection with all univocal agents. And in that case it is necessary that the matter receive the form of one species if the agent is one in species (*unum specie*). For instance, only something that is in the species of fire is generated univocally from fire. But [2] at other times the matter receives a form from the agent not in accordance with the same *ratio* as is in the agent. This is clear in connection with non-univocal generating causes, as [when] an animal is generated by the sun. And in that case the forms received in the matter from the same agent are not of one species but are varied according to the varying proportion of the matter relative to receiving the agent's input (*influxum*). For instance, we see that by the one activity of the sun animals of various species are generated through putre-faction in accordance with the varying proportion of the matter.'

7. *God as partly univocal, partly equivocal cause*

Considerations of just this sort apply also to sorting out the ways in which other things are really like God, as Aquinas observes when he concludes some of those passages about the sun's equivocal causation with observations associating it with God's causation: 'So, too, God also confers all perfections on things and on that basis has likeness and unlikeness at once with all of them' (29.270); 'So, too, the perfections of all things, which go together with those other things in accordance with various forms, must be attributed to God in accordance with his one power' (31.280). Does this mean that God's causation is equivocal in just the way the sun's is? No, not in *just* that way, although an understanding of the sun's equivocal causation is obviously a step toward properly understanding God's causation: '[A]ll perfections found in other things are attributed to God the way effects are found in their equivocal causes' (31.280).

Simply in virtue of God's being the ultimate agent cause of other things, there is con-formity between them and God: (*1) every thing caused by God has a form, *f*, that God shares with it. In this case the appropriate paradigm of *f* is the thing's species, or the *ratio* associated with that species, since 'each species must have its own mode of perfection and of being', Aquinas says, and, consequently, 'every name imposed to designate a species of created thing' expresses a perfection (30.276).[28] And the concept of universal perfection entails that every such species-specific *f* must be in God *somehow*.

Because God's causation of other things can't be univocal, there must be unlikeness between God and other things as regards the *ratio* associated with *f* in cases of divine causation. It isn't only that in non-univocal causation the agent cause and its effects can't belong to the same species: God can't be located in any species or genus or category at all (I.25). And 'if there is an agent that is not included in a genus, its effects will approach even more remotely to a likeness of a form belonging to the agent' (ST Ia.4.3c).[29] There-

---

[28] An imperfection is properly attributable only to an individual and only in so far as the individual falls short of the perfection appropriate to its species.

[29] '[P]erfections flow from [God] as from their first cause. They do not flow from him, however, as from a univocal agent, . . . but as from an agent that does not agree with its effects either in the *ratio* of a species or in the *ratio* of a genus' (ST Ia.6.2c).

fore, (*2') it cannot be the case that the form of any of God's effects is associated with the same *ratio* in the effect and in God.

Furthermore, as we've already seen in connection with universal perfection, no other thing's form can be realized in the same way or to the same degree in God: 'every perfection associated with a creature must be found in God, but in a different, superior (*eminentiorem*) mode' (30.276); 'that in virtue of which the likeness is observed of course belongs to God absolutely, but not to the creature' (29.273). 'Things other [than God], even if they did come to possess a form altogether like [a form of God's], would not come to possess it in accordance with the same mode of being' (32.285).[30] Therefore, (*3a') no form can be realized in the same way in God and in any other thing, and (*3b') no form can be realized to the same degree in God and in any other thing.

So, when God is the agent cause under consideration, the unlikeness between cause and effects may seem overwhelming, especially after having been established in depth by the results of the eliminative method and then reinforced by these observations growing out of the analysis of equivocal agent causation. In these circumstances is there really any way to make good on the claim that the perfections specific to topaz, tulips, and tapeworms must be found in God *somehow*?

The perfections associated specifically with topaz, tulips, and tapeworms essentially involve corporeality, 'a mode [of realization] that is proper to creatures' (30.276). And so, if we stay with the sun as the model of non-univocal agent causation, those perfections can be in God, their non-univocal agent cause, only 'in respect of power', as hardness is in the sun. Just as the sun could be called hard only metaphorically, so any such terms designating specific perfections 'can be said of God only on the basis of simile and metaphor, through which characteristics that belong to one thing are *conventionally* adapted to another' (30.276).[31] Still, some terms

---

[30] The continuation of this passage is also worth noting: 'For nothing is in God that is not the divine being itself (as is clear from things said above [I.21–2]), as does not happen in connection with other things. Therefore, it is impossible that anything be predicated univocally of God and of other things.'

[31] Explaining a sort of terminological sameness on the basis of convention is tantamount to acknowledging that that sort is justified solely on the basis of a more or less artificial conceptual relation, and so the *metaphorical* applicability of predicates to God, which is undeniably important in religious literature, is of no further interest in an investigation of the metaphysical basis of some sorts of terminological sameness.

'designate a perfection absolutely, without any [implied essential] lessening (*defectu*)' or mode of realization proper to creatures, and such terms 'are predicated of God and of other things' literally, even though not univocally[32]—'for instance, "goodness", "wisdom", "being" (*esse*), and others of that sort' (ibid.).

What I've said so far about the way specific perfections are in God stays within the confines of the sun model, as does Aquinas's account in these methodological chapters of SCG. But there's more to be said, and Aquinas is postponing saying it because he hasn't yet argued for ascribing to God intellect and will, the crucial ingredients for the fuller, apter account he means to give. For that reason I won't go far in that direction now, but I want just to look ahead.

Regardless of considerations of likeness, the sun's causal relationship with terrestrial things, events, and states of affairs obviously can't be quite right as a model for God's. For one thing, the results of the eliminative method distinguish God from the sun just as sharply as from any other thing and in respects that are clearly relevant to these considerations. The reasons that eventually ruled out our taking Alpha to be any sort of natural entity, subject to natural laws, would apply all the more obviously to any already identifiable particular natural entity.

More importantly, and more directly to the point, there are two kinds of non-univocal agent causation: natural—the kind of which the sun's causation is Aquinas's paradigm—and artificial—the kind that involves ideas and volitions, the artisan's kind of non-univocal agent causation.

In some agents a likeness of the form of what is to be brought about exists antecedently in keeping with *natural* being, as in those agents that act *through nature*—the way a human being generates a human being and a fire generates a fire. But in others [a likeness of the form of what is to be brought about exists antecedently] in keeping with *intelligible* being, as in those agents that act *through intellect*—the way a likeness of the house exists antecedently in the builder's mind. And [that likeness] can be called an *idea* of the house, because the artisan intends to assimilate the house to the form he has conceived in his mind. Therefore, because the world was brought about not by chance but by God acting through intellect (as will

---

[32] 'Therefore, even if—*per impossibile*—goodness in God and in a creature is of the same *ratio*, "good" would nevertheless not be predicated univocally of God [and of the creature], because what is in God immaterially and simply is in a creature materially and variously' (QDP 7.7c).

appear hereafter), it is necessary that there be a form in the divine mind, a form in the likeness of which the world was made. (ST Ia.15.1c)[33]

Looking ahead, then, we can see that Aquinas's fuller answer to the question of *how* 'every perfection associated with a creature must be found in God' will be that a specific perfection must be found in God as the form of a house is found in the architect's mind, roughly speaking. This preferred artisan model brings with it a kind of causation midway between the univocal and equivocal kinds that have been dealt with up to this point in SCG. Since the status of entirely univocal causation depends on the sameness in C and E of both the *ratio* associated with the shared form and the way in which the form is realized or exists, an artisan producing pots or poems is obviously not a univocal cause. For 'even if the *ratio* of the form occurring in the agent and in its effect is one [and the same], a different mode of existence blocks univocal predication' of the same term as applied to the shared form in both the effect and its cause. 'For although the *ratio* of a house that exists in matter and of the house that is in the artisan's mind is the same (since the latter *is* the *ratio* of the former[34]), "house" is not predicated univocally of both of them because the form (*species*) of the house has material being in the matter but immaterial being in the builder's mind' (QDP 7.7c).[35] And so Aquinas sometimes calls this artificial, intellective-volitional sort of agent causation *partly univocal and partly equivocal*.[36] (In later chapters I'll consider some details of this account of God's causation and some arguments in support of adopting it.)

---

[33] See also e.g. ST IaIIae.79.3c: 'God is the universal cause of the illumination of souls ... as the sun is the universal cause of the illumination of bodies, but in different ways. For God [unlike the sun] acts voluntarily, through the ordering of his wisdom'; ST Ia.19.4: 'God's will is the cause of things, and God acts through will, not through a necessity of nature.'

[34] I'm interpolating 'the latter' and 'the former' for the sake of clarity. The Latin is merely *quia unum est ratio alterius*.

[35] Aquinas's recognition of the importance of the shared form's mode of realization seems to have come after his early commentary on the *Sentences*. See e.g. the discussion of three kinds of agent cause in In Sent. I.8.1.2c, where there is no mention of *modus* and where an agent cause is said to be univocal 'when the effect agrees in both name and *ratio* with the cause'. See also In Sent. IV.43.1.2.1c on univocal agent causes.

[36] See e.g. In Met. VII: L8.1445. He also calls this sort of causation *analogical*; see e.g. In Sent. I.8.1.2c. On analogical causation see esp. McInerny 1961*b*. For a helpful, critical, up-to-date account of the logical side of Aquinas's concept of analogy, see Ashworth 1991 and 1992.

8. Goodness, uniqueness, and infinity

The investigation of likeness and causation I've been focusing on in this chapter evidently sets the stage for the immediate introduction of divine attributes that are, first, known to us primarily as characteristics of other things and, second, needed as components of Aquinas's fuller account of God's causation of other things. Both those expectations are fully met by Aquinas's arguing in support of attributing intellect to God. And in his *Summa theologiae* and *Compendium theologiae* Aquinas does begin his consideration of the mind of God immediately after considering how creaturely predicates may be ascribed to God.[37] In SCG, however, this natural sequence is interrupted. The eight methodological chapters devoted to considering the basis on which other things can be assimilated to God are followed by chapters arguing for God's goodness, uniqueness, and infinity before Aquinas tries to justify attributing intellect to God. From the viewpoint of broad-scale topical organization, it plainly makes sense to take up those three last metaphysical attributes before turning to the personifying attributes of intellect and will, the detailed investigation of which occupies almost all the rest of SCG's Book I. But is there a good reason for postponing their consideration until after perfection has been introduced?

Of course, the order in which topics get considered has some general methodological importance in natural theology developed along the lines Aquinas establishes in SCG I–III, where new claims are typically justified on the basis of propositions already established. That consideration alone might well explain his taking up goodness right after perfection, since Aquinas's analyses of goodness and perfection make God's being good an obvious corollary of God's being perfect.[38] The same consideration has some bearing

[37] ST Ia.13, 'Names of God'; Ia.14, 'God's Knowledge'. In CT I, chs. 24–7 deal with names of God, chs. 28–31 with the mind of God. The ordering of these topics in In Sent. simply follows their ordering in Lombard's *Sentences*—i.e. immediately after the consideration of the procession of the persons of the Trinity in Book I there are seven 'distinctions' devoted to God's knowledge (35–41), followed by considerations of God's power and will.

[38] Goodness is taken up immediately after perfection in ST as well. The closeness of the connection is apparent in his one scriptural citation in SCG's chapter on perfection (I.28). It doesn't mention perfection at all, but shows that he takes universal perfection to be equivalent to 'the fullness of all goodness': 'That is why when Moses asked to see the divine face or glory, he was answered by the Lord in

(though not as much) on his including the treatments of divine uniqueness and infinity among these intermediate chapters, even though many of his arguments in support of either of those attributes draw not on perfection or goodness but on results achieved earlier, in applications of the eliminative method.

As we've been seeing, the introduction of universal perfection brings with it a shift to positive results affirmatively expressed and the novel opportunity to trace specific relationships between God and various sorts of other things. But the three intermediate topics don't seem to suit those novel conditions nearly so well as does the topic of the mind of God. There's no specific creaturely perfection associated with any of them, as there is with intellect. As for positive results, I suppose God's goodness is as distinctively positive as any result could be. God's uniqueness, however, could readily be construed as the impossibility of there being more than one entity that fits the emerging conception of God, and for logical purposes it is more conveniently construed in that way, as we'll see. What's more, infinity, the third of these three intermediate topics, doesn't merely seem unmistakably negative; it was also expressly identified in the preceding methodological chapters as involving the ascription of a perfection to God 'through negation, as when we call God . . . infinite' (30.278). None the less, in the chapter on God's infinity Aquinas associates it intimately with universal perfection, arguing that it makes sense to ascribe infinity to non-quantitative God in only two ways: as regards his power and as regards the goodness or completeness of his nature (43.357)—'but not in such a way that "infinite" is taken privatively, as it is in connection with extensional or numerical quantity' (43.358). Not *privatively*, yet 'in connection with God "infinite" is understood only *negatively*, since there is no limit or end to his perfection; instead, he is supremely perfect. And it is in this way that "infinite" must be attributed to God' (ibid.).

On balance, then, I'd say that God's goodness couldn't have

this way: "I will show you all good" [Exod. 33: 13 and 19], meaning by this that the fullness of all goodness is in himself' (28.267). See also the first of the five chapters on God's goodness, where his opening argument concludes this way: 'On this basis, then, anything that is perfect is good, which is why everything seeks its perfection as the good that is appropriate to it. But it has been shown that God is perfect. He is, therefore, good' (37.304). Furthermore, 'the *ratio* of the good is perfection' (39.320), and 'the goodness of anything is its perfection' (40.325).

been introduced more appropriately at any other point in the structure of SCG I, that treating God's infinity here makes more sense than it might at first seem to do, and that of these three, only God's uniqueness could have been introduced before perfection at least as well as after it.

I won't say more about God's goodness here.[39] I've said nothing at all yet about specifically moral goodness in God, but it can't be specifically at issue in this systematic account until intellect and will, necessary conditions of *moral* goodness, have been introduced. What's essential in Aquinas's conception of metaphysical goodness in God has already been brought out, especially in what I've had to say about perfection in this chapter and in the previous one, and Aquinas's five chapters on the topic develop those essentials in predictable ways.[40]

9. God's uniqueness

As for God's uniqueness, the claim that there can't be more than one first source of being, it strikes me as not obviously entailed by any claim about God's nature we've already considered. In particular, it seems not to be validly derivable directly from claims about God's goodness or perfection, although the first two of Aquinas's sixteen arguments for uniqueness constitute unconvincing attempts at such derivations. One of them depends on the implication of uniqueness in the superlative 'highest good', an implication that strikes me as specious.[41] The other depends on the implicit assumption that every characteristic must count either as a perfection or as an imperfection, an assumption that strikes me as false.[42]

---

[39] See Stump and Kretzmann 1988.

[40] The titles of the five chapters: 'God is good' (37); 'God is goodness itself' (38); 'In God there can be nothing bad' (39); 'God is the good of everything good' (40); 'God is the highest good' (41).

[41] 'It is not possible that there be two highest goods, for what is said [of anything] on the basis of superabundance is found in only one. But God is the highest good (as has been shown [I.41]). Therefore, God is one' (42.336).

[42] 'It has been shown that God is altogether perfect, to whom no perfection is lacking [I.28]. Therefore, if there is more than one God, there must be more than one perfect being of that sort. But that is impossible. For if none of them lacks any perfection and is not mixed with any imperfection—which is required for anything's being absolutely perfect—there will be nothing by which they are distinguished from one another. Therefore, it is impossible to posit more than one God' (42.337).

The most powerful and interesting of his arguments against the possibility of more than one God are those that reach all the way back to Aquinas's argument G6 for their basis in the identification of God as the entity that is necessary being through itself. There are three of those arguments in chapter 42. I want to consider the most elaborate of them, which I'm calling the 'uniqueness argument'.[43]

The uniqueness argument

[If there are two entities each of which is necessary being through itself, then,] given that they are supposed to be alike in necessity of being, [they must differ in something other than necessity of being. Therefore,] either [a] that in which they differ is required in some way to complete necessity of being, or [b] it isn't.   5

If [b] it isn't required, then it is something accidental, since whatever comes to a thing without effecting anything for its being is accidental [to it]. Therefore, this accidental characteristic has a cause. Therefore, either [c] it has as a cause the essence of that which is necessary being, or [d] [the cause of that accidental characteristic is]   10
something else.

If [c] the accidental characteristic has the essence of it as a cause, then, since necessity of being is its essence (as is clear from things said above[44]), necessity of being will be the cause of that accidental charac-

---

[43] The uniqueness argument is in 42.343. Here are the other two. 42.342: 'If there are two entities, each of which is necessary being, they must be alike under the concept (*conveniant in intentione*) of necessity of being. Therefore, they must be distinguished from each other through something that is added either to only one or to both of them, and so one or both of them must be composite. But nothing composite is necessary being through itself (as was shown above [18.143]). Therefore, it is impossible that there be more than one entity each of which is necessary being. And so neither can there be more than one God.'
42.345: 'It is not possible for anything that belongs to this individuated thing (*signato*) in so far as it is this individuated thing to go together with something else. For what is singular about any thing belongs to nothing other than that single thing. But, as for that which is necessary being, its necessity of being goes together with it in so far as it is this individuated thing. Therefore, it is impossible that [that necessity of being] go together with anything else. And so it is impossible that there be more than one thing each of which is necessary being. Consequently, it is impossible that there be more than one God. (Proof of the middle premiss: For if that which is necessary being is not this individuated thing in so far as it is necessary being, then the individuation (*designatio*) of its being is not necessary in itself but depends on something else. But anything is distinct from all others in so far as it is in actuality, which is to be this individuated thing. Therefore, that which is necessary being depends on something else in so far as its being in actuality is concerned, which is contrary to the *ratio* of that which is necessary being. Therefore, that which is necessary being must be necessary being in so far as it is this individuated thing.)'
[44] In Aquinas's ch. 22, discussed in my Ch. Four.

teristic. But necessity of being is found in each of the two entities, and   15
so each of them will have that accidental characteristic, and so they
will not be distinguished on the basis of it. [Therefore, not [c].]

But if [d] the cause of that accidental characteristic is something
else, then if there were not that other thing, there would not be that
accidental characteristic. And if there were not that accidental charac-   20
teristic, there would not be the distinction we are talking about.
Therefore, if there were not that other thing, these two entities that
are supposed to be necessary being would be not two but one. Therefore, the being proper to each of them is dependent on something else,
and so neither of them is necessary being through itself. [Therefore,   25
not [d]. And, therefore, not [b].]

On the other hand, if [a] that on the basis of which they are distinguished is necessary for completing necessity of being, that will be
either because [e] it is included in the *ratio* of necessity of being as
animate is included in the definition of *animal*, or it will be because [f]   30
necessity of being is specified through it as *animal* is completed by
rational.

If [e], then wherever there is necessity of being there must be that
which is included in its *ratio* as *animate* goes with whatever *animal*
goes with. And so, since necessity of being is attributed to both the   35
entities we are talking about, they could not be distinguished on this
basis. [Therefore, not [e].]

But if [f], then, again, it cannot be. For the differentia specifying a
genus does not complete the *ratio* of the genus; instead, the genus's
being in actuality is acquired through it. For the *ratio* of *animal* is   40
complete before the addition of *rational*, but *animal* cannot be in
actuality unless it is either *rational* or *non-rational*. In this way, therefore, something completes necessity of being as regards its being in
actuality and not as regards the concept of necessity of being.

[However,] this is impossible, for two reasons. In the first place,   45
because the quiddity of that which is necessary being [through itself]
is its being (as was proved above[45]). In the second place, because in
that case necessary being [through itself] would acquire being through
something else, which is impossible. [Therefore, not [f]. And, therefore, not [a].]   50

Therefore, it is not possible to posit more than one entity each of
which is necessary being through itself.

Formally, the uniqueness argument is a chain of destructive dilem-
mas designed to reduce to an absurdity the assumption that there is

---

[45] In ch. 22. (The Leonine edn. offers a mistaken reference to ch. 18, which is
repeated in the Marietti edn. and in Pegis's trans., which is based on the Leonine
edn.)

more than one God, where God is understood as that which is necessary being through itself. So, if it succeeds, it indirectly establishes the thesis that there can't be more than one God. In chapter 42 the uniqueness argument immediately follows another of the arguments based on identifying God as that which is necessary being through itself, and so it can rely on its predecessor for some background. In lines 1–4 I've supplied in brackets the relevant bits available in the argument's original setting.[46]

The argument supposes that there are two entities, E_1 and E_2, each of which is necessary being through itself. The argument's strategy for reducing that supposition to an absurdity consists in exhausting all possible bases on which E_1 and E_2 might be distinguished from each other. Exhaustiveness of possibilities is guaranteed in the first dilemma because its members, lemmas [a] and [b] (lines 4–5), are mutually contradictory. Since it's likely to seem quite implausible offhand that what *distinguishes* E_1 from E_2 could be any sort of component of their necessity of being, in which they are exactly alike, lemma [b] looks like the livelier alternative.

Taking up lemma [b] means considering the apparent possibility that what distinguishes E_1 from E_2 is some characteristic(s) *accidental* to either one or to both of them. In claiming that the existence of any such distinguishing characteristic, D^*, must have a cause (lines 6–8), Aquinas is, of course, applying the principle of sufficient reason. His application of it here strikes me as unexceptionable, particularly since it leaves open lemma [c], the apparent possibility that the explanation for the occurrence of such an accidental D^* might lie in E_1 or E_2 itself (lines 9–10). It may seem odd to consider it even apparently possible that an accidental characteristic of a thing might be causally connected with the thing's essence rather than with something extrinisic to it, but Aquinas is no doubt thinking of a proprium, an accidental characteristic of just that sort.[47] A proprium is a characteristic that is symptomatic of the essence of the thing that has it without being itself a component of the essence: the paradigm of a proprium is a rational animal's capacity for laughter. And so lemma [c] may be thought of as the apparent possibility that D^* is a proprium. But Aquinas quickly

---

[46] See the beginning of the argument in 42.342, quoted in n. 43 above.

[47] See e.g. 32.286: '[A] proprium belongs to the genus of accidents'; and ST Ia.77.1, ad 5: 'A proprium does not belong to a thing's essence but is caused by principles essential to the [thing's] species, and so, spoken of in that way, it is midway between essence and accident.'

shows that this possibility is only apparent, since any proprium of E_1 would have to be E_2's proprium as well, and so could not be D^*, the distinguishing characteristic (lines 12–17).

This brings us to [c]'s contradictory, lemma [d], the apparent possibility that the cause of the accidental characteristic D^* is something other than the essence shared by E_1 and E_2 (lines 10–11 and 17). Suppose we designate that extraneous cause E_x. Then E_1 and E_2 are two distinct entities only if E_x causes what distinguishes them (lines 18–21). Suppose, then, that D^* is a property that E_x causes only in E_2. Without that property D^* in E_2, E_1 and E_2 'would be not two but one' (line 23). So, if E_x didn't exist and cause D^* in E_2, there would be only one entity that is necessary being through itself. And in that case the existence of 'these two entities that are supposed to be necessary being' (lines 22–3) 'is dependent on something else, and so neither of them is necessary being through itself' (lines 24–5), since even E_1's separate existence would depend on E_x's causing D^* in E_2. And since lemmas [c] and [d] exhaust the possible explanations of a D^* conceived of as *not* 'required in some way to complete necessity of being' in E_1 and E_2, the only remaining apparent possibility is lemma [a] (expressed in lines 4–5 and 27–8).

The simplest interpretation of lemma [a], that D^* 'is necessary for completing necessity of being', is in terms of [e], the apparent possibility that D^* is a component of 'the *ratio* of necessity of being as *animate* is included in the definition of *animal*' (lines 29–30), which Aquinas understands to be *sensitive animate body*. But, of course, no such essential component of E_1 and of E_2 could serve as D^* any more than *sensitive*, *animate*, or *corporeal* could serve as a characteristic distinguishing a tapeworm from a tiger, and so lemma [e] is easily dismissed (lines 33–7).

That leaves only lemma [f], that D^* 'is necessary for completing necessity of being' in that 'necessity of being is specified through it as *animal* is completed by *rational*' (lines 31–2). In other words, perhaps E_1 and E_2 represent two species of that which is necessary being through itself, carved out of that genus by two differentiae. Suppose, then, that D^* is E_1's differentia, carving the E_1 species out of the genus *necessary being through itself* (and D^{**} is E_2's differentia).[48] But in that case nothing could be necessary being through

---

[48] Aquinas writes here as if he were considering only one such species, and so needed to consider only one differentia, D^*.

itself any more than anything could be just an animal rather than a tiger or a tapeworm or some other sort of animal: '*animal* cannot be in actuality unless it is either *rational* or *non-rational*' (lines 41–2).[49] And, to follow just one of Aquinas's two routes to the rejection of lemma [f], if necessary being through itself required D* as a differentia, then 'necessary being [through itself] would acquire being through something else, which is impossible' (lines 48–9).

Therefore, not [f]. And, therefore, not [a]. And, therefore, 'it is not possible to posit more than one entity each of which is necessary being through itself' (lines 51–2). I think the uniqueness argument succeeds.[50]

10. God's infinity

Calling God infinite seems, offhand, at least odd because, as Aquinas acknowledges, infinity is associated with quantity (43.356). So he begins his attempt to justify attributing infinity to God by sorting out types of quantity. God could not be infinite in virtue of *plurality* as regards infinitely many individual gods, infinitely many parts, or infinitely many accidental characteristics. On the contrary, God has already been shown to be unique (I.42), simple (I.18), and utterly without accidental characteristics (I.23). Nor, he says, could God be infinite in virtue of *extent*, since God has already been shown to be necessarily incorporeal (I.20).[51]

Plurality and extent are clearly not the only kinds of quantity, however. Qualities and powers such as colour, heat, and force also vary quantitatively, in ways that provide the bases for our measure-

---

[49] It's important to see that he's presenting no more than a *necessary* condition of being in actuality: 'cannot be in actuality unless . . .'. As he would emphatically agree, neither can *non-rational* animal be in actuality unless it is either *Felis tigris mongolica* (a tiger), *Amphilina foliacea* (a tapeworm), or some other most specific species of non-rational animal. And, of course, he wouldn't stop there, either, since it's not *Felis tigris mongolica* that is in actuality, but only this Siberian tiger or that one.

[50] I didn't want to present and examine more than one argument for the uniqueness of the entity that is necessary being through itself, but I think that at least the argument in 42.345, the second one quoted in n. 43 above, also deserves attention.

[51] But since Aquinas recognizes the possibility of beginningless time, as we've seen, incorporeality seems an insufficient basis on which to rule out infinity of extent. In order to rule out infinity for time as well as for space, he would have to invoke details of his Boethian concept of divine atemporality, on which see e.g. Stump and Kretzmann 1981, 1987, 1991, and 1992.

ments of them. Aquinas labels this remaining kind of quantity 'spiritual magnitude', a designation that seems misleading in at least two respects. In the first place, it's certainly not obvious that only material entities can be more than one, or extended; both plurality and extent seem applicable to immaterial (or spiritual) entities, too. In the second place, there's nothing spiritual about, say, degrees of whiteness, one of his own examples (43.357). I think he might have done better to have focused on intensive quantity rather than on 'spiritual magnitude', but I'll stay with his terminology.

'Spiritual magnitude is recognized in two respects: as regards power, and as regards the goodness or completeness of [a thing's] own nature' (43.357). But Aquinas shows that these two reduce to one: 'The magnitude of a power is weighed on the basis of the magnitude of the [corresponding] action or the things brought about, since one of those magnitudes[52] follows the other. For anything is active in virtue of its being actualized, and so the mode of the magnitude of its power is in keeping with the mode in which it is completed in its actuality. Therefore, we are left with the conclusion that things are called spiritually great[53] on the basis of the mode of their completeness' (ibid.). 'Mode' here clearly means the same as 'degree'. The upshot is that if God is properly to be called infinite at all, then, as we've seen, the attribution must be based on the degree of his actualization, which is the universal perfection already argued for: 'there is no limit or end to his perfection . . . And it is in this respect that "infinite" must be attributed to God' (43.358).

Although the infinity of power can be reduced to the more fundamental concept of infinity of being, there are contexts in which it is more natural and convenient to conceive of divine infinity in terms of power. In fact, since the inductive reasoning indispensable to natural theology begins with reasoning from effects to the existence and nature of their cause, divine power is conceptually intermediate between other things and God conceived of as universally, infinitely perfect. An ingenious argument

[52] Following the variant *magnitudinum* rather than the Leonine and Marietti edns.' *magnitudinem*.

[53] What Aquinas actually says here is: '[S]piritual things are called great.' To preserve what I think he meant, and what is better supported by the context, I'm reading *spiritualiter* for *spirituales*.

in Aquinas's chapter on God's infinity approaches it through a consideration of power. He begins by observing that 'there cannot be infinite power in a finite essence, because everything acts through a form belonging to it, either its essence or a part of its essence, and "power" names a source of action' (43.367). Moreover, 'any agent is more powerful in acting to the extent to which it brings into actuality a [passive] potentiality that is further removed from actuality; for instance, it takes more power to heat water than to heat air' (43.368). On that basis he develops a two-part argument to accommodate, first, the idea that God's effect is a world that began to exist: 'that which is altogether non-existent is infinitely far from actuality and is not in any way in potentiality. Therefore, if the world was made after it was altogether non-existent, its maker's power must be infinite' (ibid.).

'But', he points out, 'this argument works as a proof of the infinity of divine power even for those who posit' a beginningless world.

They[54] say that eternal God is the cause of the sempiternal world as a foot would from eternity have been the cause of a footprint if from eternity it had been pressed into some dust. Once that assumption has been made, it nevertheless follows according to the argument we are discussing that God's power is infinite. For whether he produced in time (*ex tempore*) (according to us) or from eternity (according to them), there can be nothing in reality that he did not produce, since he is the universal source of being. And he produced in a way that presupposes no matter or potentiality. . . . We are, therefore, left with the conclusion that since a finite power produces an effect when the potentiality of matter has been presupposed, God's power, which presupposes no potentiality, is not finite but infinite; and so is his essence infinite. (43.368)[55]

The basis on which active power is measured in both parts of this argument as I've presented it may be summarized along these lines. In producing a given effect, any agent of course *actualizes* a certain amount of passive potentiality, and almost every agent also *utilizes*

[54] Certain Platonists, according to Augustine, *De civitate Dei* X.31; see the editors' note to this passage in the Marietti edn.

[55] My quotation of this extension of the argument omits a passage (at the ellipsis dots) that strikes me as introducing a quite different basis on which to measure active power: 'Now one must arrive at the proportion of active power on the basis of the proportion of passive potentiality. For the greater the passive potentiality that pre-exists or is preconceived, the greater the active power by which it is completely actualized' (43.268).

a certain amount of passive potentiality—the amount that the exercise of the agent's power 'presupposes'. Making a drawing on blank paper *actualizes* more passive potentiality than does tracing an already made drawing. But tracing *utilizes* more, because in that case the material cause contributes more to the production of the effect, and (so) the efficient cause contributes less. The degree of active power, then, varies inversely with the amount of passive potentiality utilized by an agent.

So far, so good: if Alice produces a drawing of a house and Kate produces a drawing of the same house by tracing Alice's drawing, then on this occasion Alice exhibits a greater degree of active power than Kate does. And if Alice also manufactures her own paper and pencil before producing her drawing, then she exhibits still more active power, and so on.

But can we extrapolate along this line to an *infinity* of active power? Aquinas's principle of measurement for active power seems to lend itself to a graphic and perhaps not altogether artificial demonstration of such a result. Suppose that in my example we represent the active power in fractions, letting the numerator represent the effect—a drawing of a house—and the denominator represent the amount of passive potentiality the agent utilizes in producing the effect. Then the degree of active power exhibited in Alice's producing the drawing in the first instance might be represented as 1/10, in Kate's tracing it as 1/25, in Alice's producing the drawing after first having manufactured paper and a pencil for that purpose as 1/3. And so, on this model, the degree of active power exhibited in an agent's producing an effect utilizing no passive potentiality at all would be represented as 1/0 ($= \infty$). Q.E.D.

SIX

INTELLECT

1. Simplicity and other attributes

The natural theology we've been investigating has undertaken to show that there must be a necessarily unique, absolutely simple being that constitutes the ultimate explanation of everything. It has also undertaken to show that this being, despite its absolute simplicity, can and should be characterized from our point of view in various ways. 'Perfectly good' and 'infinitely powerful' are among the various 'names of God' whose correctness has been argued for so far. I think most philosophers would agree that if this natural theology has succeeded in showing everything I've just mentioned, it has shown that there is a god.

Traditional theists, on the other hand, whether or not they are also philosophers, have to require more than that of any natural theology before they can agree that it has shown that God exists. What has emerged in this investigation so far is a being that only a metaphysician could love, a being whose perfect goodness hasn't yet been clearly seen to include moral goodness, a being that as yet shows no unmistakable signs of being able to know, to will, or to love anything itself—no unmistakable signs of being a person. A natural theology like Aquinas's, which aims at providing a philosophical presentation of as much of Christian theology's subject-matter as can be presented philosophically, without recourse to revelation, must of course undertake to derive not only such *metaphysical* divine attributes as we've been considering, but also as many of the traditional *personifying* attributes as can be derived by that means. In Book I of SCG Aquinas begins this new task in chapter 44, which he devotes to arguing that mind must be ascribed to God. And since mind is the fundamental personifying attribute, the one without which any outward sign of personhood would be spurious, it's the right one with which to begin. But before trying to establish not merely more attributes, but more attributes of a new sort, it seems only prudent to look more closely at the grounds for tolerating this apparent complexity in simplicity.

The multiplication of attributes for a simple God is motivated practically by natural theology's need to construct an a posteriori, analogical, piecemeal account of the being whose simple essence couldn't be known to us as such. The principal reason why the resultant proliferation of attributes doesn't simply constitute a fiction regarding perfectly simple God is that in virtue of what I've been calling the 'extensive aspect' of his universal perfection God is supposed to possess, somehow, all specific perfections: 'none of the perfections that are associated with any things are lacking to him' (28.266). So the complexity of natural theology's theory of a simple God is expressly linked with the extensive aspect of universal perfection. Because of our cognitive limitations, 'we need to give God more than one name. For since we can cognize him naturally only by inferring (*deveniendo*) to him on the basis of effects, the names by which we signify his perfection must be various, just as the perfections in things are found to be various' (31.282). We've seen Aquinas using universal perfection's inclusion of all specific perfections as the basis for supplementing the eliminative method of doing natural theology with the relational method, which is intended to provide good grounds for adding attributes to this account of God's nature.[1] But we haven't yet seen what sort of affirmative propositions are warranted by the new method, or how we are to understand the extensive aspect of universal perfection, which underlies the method, or even just what those included specific perfections are supposed to be. I'll try to answer those questions in the course of this chapter on attributing mind to God.

The wide scope of the Christian philosopher-theologian's programme is by no means the only motivation which Aquinas's project provides for moving at this point from metaphysical attributes to mind. If it were, traditional revealed theology would be setting the agenda for his project in natural theology. That's not a bad thing in itself, and, as I've remarked more than once before, at some junctures in the development of a natural theology the established pattern of a dogmatic theology does provide the most sensible basis on which to decide what to take up next. But, as it

---

[1] See e.g. 14.118; 30.278; also Ch. Five, esp. sects. 1–3.

happens, this particular transition from metaphysical attributes to the foundational personifying attribute is motivated also by considerations of formal aspects of this theory of God's nature as it has been developed so far.

One of those formal aspects is associated with the relational method itself. Whatever the details of the method turn out to be, by its means some likenesses between a perfection natural to one or another kind of creatures and a conceptually distinguishable aspect of God's absolute perfection are supposed to justify predicating of God, somehow, some of what we ordinarily predicate of certain creatures. Now, since the meanings of the words we use in natural theology to predicate things of God 'are known to us only in so far as they are used of creatures' (33.295),[2] and since for any creature who is actively engaging in natural theology the most intimately known of all creaturely characteristics must be mind, any reflective practitioner of the relational method has another good reason for choosing mind as the first specific perfection to be used along those lines: it provides the epistemologically securest bridgehead from which to try to extend a creaturely predicate to God.

More significantly, the accounts that Aquinas has provided of certain crucially important metaphysical attributes themselves seem to anticipate the attribution of mind to God. The anticipation is only implicit in connection with some attributes, but it emerges explicitly in his account of divine causation. Aquinas's general conception of agent causation involves the cause's informing the effect with a form that is antecedently in the agent cause one way or another (see Ch. Five, sect. 4). And it's the extensive aspect of God's universal perfection whereby God perfectly possesses, one way or another, *all* the forms bestowed on other things, including the uncountably many forms that could not be directly *predicated* of God, even analogically. So it's only natural that Aquinas links the extensive aspect of universal perfection to God's agent causation of all things:

[I]t is impossible that an effect that is brought about through action occur in [any] actuality more excellent (*nobiliori*) than the agent's actuality. (It is, however, possible that the effect's actuality be more imperfect than the actuality of the agent cause, because an action can be weakened as a consequence of the nature (*ex parte*) of that in which it terminates.) Now

---

[2] See also e.g. QDP 7.7c.

in the genus of efficient cause we trace things back (*fit reductio*) to one cause that is called God (as is clear from things that have been said) by whom all things exist (as will be shown in discussions to follow [II.15]). Therefore, whatever is actual in any other thing must be found in God much more outstandingly (*multo eminentius*) than in that thing, not vice versa. (28.265)[3]

So the extensive aspect of universal perfection underlies divine causation, and the rest of what we've seen so far of Aquinas's account of divine causation strongly suggests that the way God perfectly possesses all those forms must turn out to be in some recognizable sense mental.

Aquinas first compares God's agent causation of all things with the impersonal sun's equivocally causing many different kinds of terrestrial effects naturally by its single, mindless power (see Ch. Five, sect. 6). But he then compares it more precisely with a human artisan's deliberately, extra-mentally, materially instantiating mental forms, or ideas: 'God is the cause of things through intellect' (50.420, 51, 52.433); 'God's knowledge is related to all created things as an artisan's knowledge is related to the things he makes by his art, but an artisan's knowledge is a cause of the things he makes by his art' (ST Ia.14.8c).[4] So a fuller account of the fundamental divine attribute of universal causality depends on showing that mind must be ascribed to God, and on explaining what it means to ascribe mind to God. And in view of the special relationship between causality and perfection, understanding the extensive aspect

---

[3] See also e.g. ST Ia.4.2c: '[S]ince God is the first efficient cause of things, the perfections of all things must exist antecedently in God in a more outstanding way.'

[4] See Ch. Five, sect. 7. See also e.g. In PH I: L3.30: '[A]ll natural things are related to the divine intellect as artificial things are related to their art'; ST Ia.15.1c: 'In some agents a likeness of the form of what is to be brought about exists antecedently in keeping with *natural* being, as in those agents that act *through nature*—the way a human being generates a human being and a fire generates a fire. But in others [a likeness of the form of what is to be brought about exists antecedently] in keeping with *intelligible* being, as in those agents that act *through intellect*—the way a likeness of the house exists antecedently in the builder's mind. And [that likeness] can be called an *idea* of the house, because the artisan intends to assimilate the house to the form he has conceived in his mind. Therefore, because the world was brought about not by chance but by God acting through intellect (as will appear hereafter [ST Ia.47.1]), it is necessary that there be a form in the divine mind, a form in whose likeness the world was made.' For a thorough review of Aquinas's use of the notion of divine ideas, both as media of cognition and as instruments of causation, see Wippel 1993*b*.

of universal perfection seems likewise to depend on establishing and understanding the attribution of mind to God.

Aquinas doesn't ordinarily put it in just those terms, however. Although he does occasionally talk about 'the divine *mind*',[5] investigating his systematic treatment of the topic calls for some terminological adjustment. He doesn't make much use of the Latin word for 'mind' (*mens*) even in discussing human beings. In his developed adaptation of Aristotelian philosophical psychology, what corresponds most closely to the broad notion ordinarily conveyed by our use of 'mind' is the notion of the rational part of the human soul (*anima rationalis*)—the rational as distinguished from the nutritive and sensory parts of the soul. But in his theology, natural and otherwise, Aquinas typically uses the narrower term *intellectus* for what I've been calling 'mind' as an attribute of God. In its primary, ordinary application (to human beings) *intellectus* has a precise sense, picking out just the cognitive faculty of the rational part of the human soul (and not also its appetitive faculty, will).[6] Of course, Aquinas means a good deal more than that when he uses the word to describe, or even simply to designate, God, as can clearly be seen, for instance, in a passage from very near the beginning of SCG: 'The first originator and mover of the universe is *intellectus*, as will be shown below' (1.4). He does have reason to prefer that terminology, as we'll see, and so in this investigation of mind as an aspect of God's essence I'm going to use various forms of the word 'intellect' and words plainly related to it, roughly corresponding to members of the family of Latin words that Aquinas uses in this connection.

2. Intellect's place in the extensive aspect of universal perfection

The crucial importance of divine intellectivity in the scheme of this natural theology is borne out by the fact that in Book I of SCG

---

[5] See e.g. ST Ia.15.1c, quoted in n. 4 above.

[6] However, like most other philosophers, Aquinas sometimes also uses such terms broadly—e.g. when he says that the human faculty of rational cognition 'is called mind, or intellect', and even very broadly, as when he refers to 'the human soul, which is called intellect, or mind' (ST Ia.75.2c). For recent general discussions of Aquinas's philosophy of mind, see e.g. Kenny 1993; Kretzmann 1993.

Aquinas develops his presentation of the single attribute of intellect in twenty-eight chapters (44–71), more than twice as many as he used for his entire application of the eliminative method in chapters 15–28, in which many attributes were argued for. After chapter 44, where he shows that God must be characterized by something analogous to human intellect, he devotes the remaining twenty-seven of those chapters to clarifying the characterization and establishing the range of the objects of God's intellect. In this chapter I'll focus almost exclusively on the primary task of showing that intellectivity must be a divine attribute.[7] The answers to the questions I raised earlier will emerge in that investigation.

As we've seen in Chapter Five, when Aquinas draws out the implications of universal perfection, he observes that '*every* name imposed to designate a species of created thing' implies a specific perfection, and that '*each* species must have its own mode of perfection and of being' (30.276). This doctrine of universally distributed specific perfections looks harder to grant than it turns out to be, once we see how he's understanding it. When he refers to 'the perfection' associated with any natural kind, it really is 'its own *mode* of perfection and of being' that he has in mind: 'each thing is classified under a genus or a species in virtue of its *form*, which *is* the thing's perfection' (CT I.21.43). So far, then, the specific perfections seem to be the forms that differentiate natural kinds. But it turns out that a creaturely perfection need not be even species-specific. '*Every* form, proper as well as common, is a kind of perfection as regards its positing something (*secundum id quod aliquid ponit*); but it includes no imperfection, except in so far as it falls short of the true being' posited by that form (54.451)—that is, in so far as the thing whose form it is may fail to actualize all that the form provides in potentiality.

The *paradigms* of specific perfections are the differentiae of species, but the notion clearly includes all natural forms considered just as such, apart from any individual shortcomings, even apart from any particular instantiations: 'forms occurring in particular real things are incomplete (*imperfectae*) because they occur in them as particularized (*partialiter*) and not in accordance with the generality that is a feature of their essential nature' (44.379). It's just

---

[7] In doing so, I will, naturally, be drawing on chs. 45–71 as well. For a critical exposition of Aquinas's account of the operations and objects of God's intellect, see Stump and Kretzmann 1995.

because the exigencies of their occurrence in creatures are excluded from consideration that these forms can be reasonably called 'perfections', and, of course, it's only as perfections that they can be included within God's universal perfection. But, on Aquinas's Aristotelian theory of forms, 'forms that are complete (*perfectis*) and not particularized (*particulatis*) . . . cannot occur except as intellected, since no form is found in its universality except in intellect' (ibid.). In this way, too, then, God's universal perfection entails God's intellectivity.

As they occur in creatures, however, creaturely perfections need not be even *completely realized* forms, though that's certainly suggested by their being called perfections.[8] A specific perfection may well be an open-ended *potentiality*, a *capacity* that is perhaps never fully developed in the course of creaturely existence, but one such that the development of it to any degree is a natural good for any thing that has it. And again, the paradigms of such forms may be the *specifying* potentialities, the *species-specific* capacities. So the fact that human intellectivity is a capacity that is never fully developed is no obstacle to its counting as a paradigmatic specific perfection, as the perfection that specifies our species: 'The activity proper to a human being considered just as a human being is intellective activity (*intelligere*), for it is in this respect that a human being differs from all others' (In Met. I: L1.3).

3. Intellectivity, reason, and wisdom

But can intellectivity legitimately be counted as the perfection that specifies our species? What about rationality, the differentia of the species? After all, in Aquinas's view human beings are defined not as intellective but as *rational* animals, and we've seen (sect. 1 above) that 'rational' and 'intellective' are not synonymous in his usage. So might we just as well, or even better, be asking how to construe the specific perfection *rationality* as a divine attribute?

In introducing and using the relational method, Aquinas indicates more than once that applying a creaturely predicate to God in

---

[8] In this connection it's worth noting that in SCG I.28, the chapter devoted to showing that God must be universally perfect, the word used most often to designate a specific perfection is not *perfectio* but *nobilitas*. See e.g. the perfection argument in Ch. Four.

the way prescribed by the method is rarely, if ever, a matter of simply extending the use of a familiar term. The method requires two kinds of adjustment to the meaning of ordinary predicates when applied to God. First, one's understanding of the familiar term must be stripped of any ordinary implications that cannot be associated with God, in view of the results of the eliminative method. The outcome of this first adjustment alone may well be the exclusion of the term from any further consideration for use in predicating an attribute. Second, one's understanding of the extended application of any term that survives the first adjustment must be subjected to an incompletely specified extension beyond experience, since it has been shown that no term in its application to God can be univocal with its primary, creaturely application: 'whatever is actual in any other thing must be found in God *much more outstandingly*' (28.265). Both these adjustments are designed to filter out imperfections associated with creaturely predicates, either essentially or at least in our experience of them. As Aquinas puts it, in deriving divine attributes from creaturely predicates, 'things said of God must always be understood superlatively (*per eminentiam*), after everything that can be associated with imperfection has been eliminated' from them (In Sent. I.35.1.1, ad 5).

Now, what happens when rationality is subjected to the first sort of adjustment? Rationality implies *knowing*, which implies *being right*, which implies no obvious imperfection. So far, so good. But rationality also implies *acquiring* knowledge by means of *discursive reasoning*, which does imply imperfections that have already been eliminated—ignorance, temporality, and dependence, for example. 'That's why', Aquinas says, 'in so far as knowledge (*scientia*) is in God, one must remove from knowledge the discursive process of inquiring reason and retain being right (*rectitudinem*) about the known thing' (ibid.).[9]

---

[9] See also e.g. QDV 2.1, ad 4: 'Because that which is in God without any imperfection is found in creatures together with some defect, if anything found in creatures is attributed to God, we have to separate [from it] all that pertains to the imperfection so that what remains is only what belongs to the perfection; for it is only in that respect that a creature imitates God. I maintain, then, that the knowledge that is found in us has something associated with perfection and something associated with imperfection. What pertains to its perfection is its certainty; for what is known (*scitur*) is cognized (*cognoscitur*) with certainty. What pertains to its imperfection, on the other hand, is intellect's discursive process from principles to the conclusions organized knowledge (*scientia*) is concerned with. For that discursive process occurs only in so far as an intellect that has cognition of the principles

Intellective cognition is Aquinas's paradigm of knowing, and so of course involves being right. In our experience of it, intellective cognition is often also a result arrived at through reasoning; but, unlike reasoning itself, intellective cognition has no *essential* connection with a learning process. The fact that we do learn everything we know is a consequence of *our* nature, not of the nature of knowledge. What's more, 'intellective cognizing (*intelligere*) is, strictly speaking, the cognizing of the quiddity [or essence] of a thing'—which again entails no obvious imperfection—and since the primary object of God's cognition is his own essence, 'he is called *intellective* (*intelligens*) in so far as he cognizes his own nature' (ibid.), which, of course, he cognizes perfectly.

So, even though rationality is the differentia of the species from which this application of the relational method gets the material for its extended predication, uncovering essential imperfections built into the meaning of 'rational' leads one to look for other terminology in which to ascribe this specific perfection to God. A consideration of human intellect—which is *also* implied by rationality—leads to saying of God not that he is rational, but that he is intellective, perfectly. This extended predication of intellectivity is all the more appropriate because, although rationality is the differentia of our species, 'what is *supreme* as regards our cognition is not reason, but intellect, which is the *source* of reason' (57.480).[10] And, of course, in saying of God that he is intellective, one does make at least a tacit extension of the term, recognizing that in 'Human beings are intellective' and 'God is intellective', 'intellective' is not univocal because, for one thing, as applied to God it designates an eternal aspect of absolute perfection rather than a capacity that develops and gets exercised over time.

But, even so, is intellectivity really the best choice in these circumstances? If what's wanted is a plausible candidate for a divine attribute stemming from a mode of perfection specific to the human creature, what about wisdom (in the sense in which Aristotle and Aquinas recognize it as a virtue of intellect)? The trouble with

cognizes the conclusions in potentiality only, since if it cognized [them] in actuality, no discursive process would take place. (There is no movement except a going from potentiality to actuality.) Therefore, knowledge is said to be in God because of certainty regarding things cognized, but not because of the discursive process just described.'

[10] On the inappropriateness of attributing rationality to God, see ch. 57, 'God's cognition is not discursive', generally.

'wisdom' is the contrary of the trouble with 'reason' in this connection. Unlike 'reason', 'wisdom' implies no essential shortcomings of
any kind, which is why its paradigmatic application is not to anything creaturely but to God directly. 'The only knowledge that is
wisdom is the sort that considers the supreme causes, those on the
basis of which all consequent things are ordered, and [thus] cognized. That's why God is properly called wise in so far as he
cognizes himself, and properly called intellective and knowing in so
far as he cognizes himself *and* other things' (In Sent. I.35.1.1, ad 5).
Human beings can't help being intellective, but they can only as-
pire to be wise: 'a human being . . . is said to have . . . wisdom *to the
extent to which* it has cognition of the supreme cause' (ST Ia.14.1,
ad 2). And no human being aspiring to wisdom, as Aquinas is
expressly doing in SCG,[11] can fail to recognize the glaring deficien-
cies in his or her cognition of the deepest explanations. 'Wisdom',
like 'goodness' or 'being', is one of a few terms that 'designate a
perfection *absolutely*, without any [implied essential] deficiency' or
mode of being proper to creatures (30.276). So, for the purposes of
the relational method, intellectivity is the best choice of a perfection specific to humans (although knowledge, too, has something to
be said for it in this connection[12]). But because Aquinas describes
the cognitive aspect of wisdom as having ultimate explanatory
principles as its objects, it has a role of its own in his account of
God's intellective causation.

  The idea behind using the relational method to attribute intellect
to God is sketched by Aquinas in this way: 'the perfections of all
things, which fit things other than God in keeping with various
forms, must be attributed to God in keeping with his one power.
And, again, that power is not other than his essence, since nothing
can be his accidentally (as has been proved [I.23]). In this way,
then, "intellective" is said of God not only in that he effects

---

  [11] See SCG I.2.9, considered in Ch. One, sect. 7.
  [12] Knowledge (*scientia*), a species of cognition (*cognitio*) accessible only to intellective beings, is apparently used by Aquinas in this connection more often than
intellectivity, perhaps because Aristotle often speaks of knowledge when he might
just as well or even more naturally have referred to intellect (see e.g. *De anima* III
8, discussed below), and probably because Scripture speaks of God's knowledge
more often than of God's mind. See e.g. In Sent. I.35.1.1 ('Is Knowledge Suitably
Attributed to God?'), QDV 2.1 ('Is There Knowledge in God?'), and ST Ia.14.1 ('Is
There Knowledge in God?'). CT I.28 ('God Must Be Intellective') is like SCG I.44
('God is intellective').

intellectivity [in us] but also because in our being intellective we are
to some extent imitating his power, by which he makes us intellective' (31.280).[13] 'God is intellective', the proposition that results
from an observation of that sort, is an instance of non-univocal,
non-equivocal, analogical predication. As we've seen (Ch. Five,
sect. 7), the connection between the subject and the predicate in an
affirmative predication about God can't be any stronger than that,
though it can be weaker. 'God is intellective' is meant as one
characterization of God's infinite power, which is God's *essence*:
'God's being intellective is the divine essence, the divine being, and
God himself' (45.383). 'God is intellective' isn't a characterization
of God relative to human needs and feelings, as is 'The Lord is my
shepherd' or 'The Lord is my light'. And, unlike such propositions,
'God is intellective' is intended *literally*, as it can be, since
intellectivity is not associated essentially with corporeality, temporality, or any other creaturely mode of being.

Obviously, almost all forms of creatures do entail corporeality,
temporality, dependence, finiteness, or other modes of being that
preclude one's predicating them of God's essence, extending them
into divine attributes. Except for terms such as 'being', 'goodness',
and 'wisdom', which designate perfections 'absolutely' (30.276),
'intellectivity' and 'knowledge' are the only terms we've considered
so far that designate a form that is not disqualified on such grounds
from achieving the status of a divine attribute.[14] And yet, God's
universal perfection is presented as involving God's possession of
all specific perfections, which turn out to be all creaturely forms,
considered just as such. Moreover, Aquinas's account of God's
universal causation depends on that utterly complete possession of
creaturely forms, of which very, very few—so far, only two—can be

---

[13] I'm rewording this passage, which actually discusses being wise rather than
being intellective. As I read it, the passage involves no considerations that distinguish wisdom from intellectivity. In fact, what's said in the passage strikes me as
better suited to intellectivity than to wisdom.

[14] Even in this case, of course, extending the meaning of a term applied primarily
to created things must be carefully circumscribed. 'Intellectivity' is one of a handful
of terms that 'convey a perfection without any [implied essential] deficiency' or
mode of being proper to created things, but only 'as regards *that which the name was
imposed to signify*. For as regards *the mode of signifying*, every name is associated
with [such a] deficiency. . . . [I]n connection with every name said by us we find an
imperfection that is not suited to God as regards its mode of signifying, even though
the thing signified applies to God in a superlative mode (*aliquo eminenti modo*)'
(30.277). On this distinction in Aquinas's usage, see Alston 1993: esp. 161 ff.

literally (albeit analogically) predicated of God. Since God's universal causation is to be explained in terms of his antecedently possessing all specific perfections, he must of course somehow possess, perfectly, the form of stone. Still, except metaphorically, God 'is not called stone, even though he made stones, [just] because in the name "stone" we understand a determinate mode of being [e.g. corporeality] in accordance with which stone is [essentially] distinguished from God' (31.280);[15] and 'any name that expresses perfections of that sort together with a mode [of being] that is proper to creatures can be said of God only on the basis of simile and metaphor' (30.276). In the names 'intellective' or 'knowing' we understand no such essentially creaturely mode of being. And so God's possession of intellectivity or knowledge as a specific perfection supports literal predications regarding his essence, such as 'God is intellective' or 'God knows'. Predications of this sort couldn't be supported on the basis of his possessing, perfectly, such specific perfections as the diamond's hardness, the rose's perfume, the eagle's vision, the nettle's sting, or the skunk's stink. And yet, of course, the developing theory of God's nature maintains that he must possess all those forms, too: '*all* perfections found in other things are attributed to God in the way effects are found in their equivocal causes, and, of course, those effects are in their causes in respect of *a power*', a power that is 'something in con-formity with' the effects (31.280). Judging on the basis of all that's been seen so far, the nature of that divine power must be intellective: 'in our being intellective we are to some extent imitating his power, by which he makes us intellective' (31.280).[16]

So if, as seems obvious, universal perfection does supply the basis for an argument showing that God must perfectly possess the specific perfection intellectivity in a way that supports the affirmative proposition 'God is intellective', it might thereby also supply the basis for an explanation of his perfectly possessing such other, non-predicable specific perfections *intellectively*, as ideas comprehended perfectly, in the way ideas are comprehended by the perfect mind that conceives them.[17] And perfect intellective possession

---

[15] The passage concludes with this sentence, which immediately follows the part I'm quoting: 'All the same, a stone does imitate God as its cause—in being, in goodness, and in other such respects—as do other creatures.'

[16] In my modified version; see n. 13 above.

[17] See e.g. QDV 3.1: '[T]he definitive nature *(ratio)* of an idea is that an idea is a form that something imitates in virtue of the intention of an agent who determines an end for the thing.' See also Wippel 1993*b*.

by itself of course does not support literally predicating the possession of the possessor. Except figuratively, it's just not true that
Mozart is music.

4. The argument from perfection

The simple, short argument from perfection I just alluded to is, I
think, the most effective and important of Aquinas's several sorts
of arguments for intellect in God,[18] and certainly the most natural
one to use at this stage in the development of his theory of God's
nature, so soon after the introduction of universal perfection and
its associated relational method. In chapter 44 the argument from
perfection is the shortest of the seven arguments to show that God
must be intellective. Even so, it's the fullest version of this argument I've found anywhere in Aquinas, and the one I will focus on
here, after glancing at two even shorter, simpler versions of it.

In his early commentary on the *Sentences* the following argument
is introduced as a *sed contra* following a series of objections to the
thesis that knowledge is correctly ascribed to God: 'No perfection
is absent from that which is most perfect. But knowledge is the
noblest (*nobilissima*) perfection. Therefore, knowledge cannot be
absent from God, in whom the perfections of all natural kinds
(*generum*) are united (as is said in *Metaphysics* V [16, 1021b30–2])'
(In Sent. I.35.1.1, sc 2). This version of the argument from perfection draws dialectical strength from the fact that it requires predicating of God not just any perfection that may be predicable of him
but only what is called the 'noblest' one, thereby making it at least
psychologically easier to carry out an appropriate extension of the
term 'knowledge', which implies intellect. No support is offered
here for this superlative ranking of that perfection, but it may well
be based on the familiar Porphyrian–Augustinian hierarchy, which
gives the first (noblest) rank to things that are intellective as well as
living and existent, above things that live without mind or exist
without life.[19] Ordinarily, I would translate *nobilissima* as 'most

---

[18] For present purposes I'm including his arguments for knowledge in God among
his arguments for intellect in God.

[19] Aquinas often alludes to the hierarchy in this connection. See e.g. QDV 2.1c; In
Sent. I.35.1.1, obj. 2 and ad 2. See also In DA II: L6.301: 'In mortal beings possessed
of intellect, however, it is necessary that all the other [faculties] exist before it, as
instruments of and pre-conditions for *intellect*, which is *the ultimate perfection aimed
at in the operation of nature.*'

excellent', but I've left it as 'noblest' here because I wonder whether it isn't meant to allude to the fact that 'knowledge', unlike almost all other creaturely perfections, is free from the usual creaturely impediments to divine attribution. *That* sort of nobility, as we've seen, would make a substantive contribution to the argument.

On the other hand, the extensive aspect of universal perfection, which Aquinas has already elaborately argued for when he infers on this basis in SCG that God must be intellective, is supported in this early version of the argument from perfection simply on Aristotle's authority. It's not at all clear to me that universal perfection is what Aristotle has in mind in the cited passage,[20] but Aquinas in his commentary on the *Metaphysics* interprets the passage in a way that does make it at least a prefiguring of his own notion of universal perfection.[21] However, when he argues for universal perfection in SCG I.28 (between writing his commentaries on the *Sentences* and on the *Metaphysics*), he doesn't cite Aristotle at all.[22]

A little later, in his *Compendium theologiae*, Aquinas offers the following, slightly more forthcoming version of the argument from perfection as the first of three arguments intended to show that God must be intellective: 'It has been shown [I.21] that all perfections of any beings whatever are antecedently in him superabundantly. But among all perfections of beings the one that evidently ranks first is being intellective (*ipsum intelligere praecellere videtur*), since intellective things have more power (*sunt potiores*) than all others. Therefore, God must be intellective' (CT

---

[20] Translated from the medieval Latin text the passage reads this way: 'Things called perfect in themselves, then, are of course said to be so in all these ways (*toties*): some, indeed, because they lack nothing in respect of their goodness (*secundum bene*), they have no higher degree [of goodness], and they do not acquire anything extraneously; others universally (*omnino*), in that they have no higher degree in any natural kind (*unoquoque genere*), and they have nothing extraneous to them.'

[21] In Met. V: L18.1040: '[In this passage Aristotle] shows how some things are variously related to the kinds of perfection that have been discussed. And he says that certain things are called perfect in themselves, in two ways. Some are indeed universally perfect in that nothing at all is lacking to them absolutely, nor do they have any higher degree—i.e. further excellence—because by nothing are they intrinsically (*penitus*) excelled in goodness, nor do they acquire anything extraneously, because they need no extraneous goodness. And this is the condition of the first principle—viz. of God, in whom is the most perfect goodness, *to whom is lacking none of all the perfections found in the various natural kinds (singulis generibus)*.'

[22] The same is true of CT I.21, where he argues specifically for the extensive aspect of universal perfection.

I.27.56).[23] Notice that this time the thesis of the extensive aspect of universal perfection is formulated in a way that implicitly associates it with divine causation: 'all perfections of any beings whatever are antecedently in him'. But the most significant difference between the earlier version of the argument from perfection and this CT version is the fact that this one does offer support for the premiss that being intellective ranks first among specific perfections: 'intellective things have more power than all others'. I intend my translation 'have more power' to be broad enough to convey both 'are more powerful' and 'are richer in potentiality'. 'Richer in potentiality' enhances the plausibility of supposing that this version, too, ultimately relies on the Porphyrian–Augustinian hierarchy. Since the hierarchy's ranking principle is purely additive, things in its first rank have the generic potentialities that things in the lower two ranks have, and then some. On the other hand, it might not be so readily granted that an intellective being is simply more powerful than a hurricane, say, or a horse.[24] In fact, it seems clear that the only basis on which an intellective being can rightly be said to have more power than any and every sort of non-intellective being is its possession of an immeasurably wider range of powers or potentialities, reflected in the nature of human intellective causation. It's that aspect of intellect on which this version of the argument seems to depend.

[23] Here are the other two of the three arguments in CT I.27: '57. Again, it was shown above [I.10] that God is pure actuality, without any admixture of potentiality. Matter, however, is being in potentiality. Therefore, God must be altogether free (*immunem*) from matter. Now freedom from matter is the cause of intellectivity. The fact that material forms are made actually intelligible by being abstracted from matter and material conditions is a sign of this. Therefore, God is intellective.

'58. Again, it has been shown [I.3] that God is the first mover. Now that is evidently a proprium of intellect, for intellect evidently uses all other things as instruments with which to bring about movement. Thus even a human being by its intellect uses animals, plants, and inanimate things as instruments. Therefore, God, who is the first mover, must be intellective.'

For the sort of argument in sect. 57 see also e.g. In Sent. I.35.1.1c, ST Ia.14.1c, and SCG I.44.376. Various arguments based, like the one in sect. 58, on aspects of God's status as first mover may be found in e.g. SCG I.44.373–5 and 378. The first and longest of these is developed in two stages in 44.373–4, and is based on argument G2 in SCG I.13 (see Ch. Two); the one in 44.378 is of the same sort as another in In Sent. I.35.1.1c.

[24] But see CT I.27.58 (quoted in n. 23), which can be read as offering a basis on which to rank an intellective being as generally more powerful than 'animals, plants, and inanimate things': it can use any of them as instruments, but none of them can use it.

5. The intellectivity argument

The fullest version of the argument from perfection to intellectivity I've found in Aquinas, and the one I want to examine, occurs in 44.377:

No perfection that may be found in any natural kind (*genere*) of beings is absent from God (as was shown above). Nor is there any complexity in him as a consequence of this (as is also clear from things said above). Now among the perfections of things the one with the most power (*potissima*[25]) is something's being intellective, for on this   5 basis it 'is in a certain way all things', having within itself the perfection of all things. God, therefore, is intellective.

I think it will be easier to investigate this argument in the following form, which stays very close to the text.

  1 No perfection that may be found in any natural kind of beings is absent from God.
  2 There is no complexity in God as a consequence of the presence of all those perfections.
  3 On the basis of being intellective something is in a certain way all things.
  4 Something's being in a certain way all things on the basis of being intellective is its having within itself the perfection of all things.
∴5 Among the perfections of things the one with the most power is something's being intellective.
∴6 God is intellective.

Since step 5 is the first derived step in the intellectivity argument, it looks as if at least one advantage this argument has over the more primitive versions we've glanced at must lie in the nature of the support supplied for the claim of greatest power for intellect. What constitutes that support?

---

[25] Although *potissima* is the superlative form of *potis* (= 'able', 'capable', 'possible'), in classical Latin it would ordinarily (though not always) mean simply principal, chief, most important. But I think that in Aquinas's use of it here the superlative *potissima* retains the special sense of the positive and comparative forms, and so I'm translating it as 'the one with the most power'. The CT version of this argument (quoted in sect. 4) tends to confirm this interpretation, since it bases its broad claim that being intellective 'ranks first' (*praecellere*) on its narrower claim that 'intellective things have more power (*sunt potiores*) than all others'.

a. Steps 1 and 2

Step 1 supplies an ingredient that is obviously indispensable to
any of these versions of the argument from perfection, the thesis
of the extensive aspect of universal perfection. And, as Aquinas
points out in line 2 of the passage, the extensive aspect of
God's perfection has already been argued for—in chapter 28,
as we've seen. But step 1, indispensable to the argument and explicitly supported as it is, contributes nothing at all to the support of
step 5.

Step 2, Aquinas claims, 'is also clear from things said above'
(lines 3–4). In this case the reference is clearly to chapter 31, which
was devoted to arguing in detail that the plurality of divine attributes derivable from universal perfection is not incompatible
with God's absolute simplicity. So step 2, like step 1, is explicitly
supported. Its contribution to the argument generally or to the
support of step 5, however, is at best obscure. In fact, a careful
reading of the argument shows that, formally, step 2 is an idle
premiss.

I want to keep open the possibility that the sentence in lines 2–4
is intended as more than a parenthetical remark that ought not to
be represented at all as a step in my extracted version of the
argument. I think there are reasons to take it seriously—besides
the principle of charity—and I think that the strongest of those
reasons are implicit in this argument itself. But perhaps a feature
shared by other SCG arguments that are particularly relevant to
this one can make us more receptive to the idea that that sentence
is meant to make a contribution to this argument. After chapter 28,
where Aquinas argues for the extensive aspect of universal perfection, he bases three other arguments on it in SCG before he
presents this intellectivity argument in chapter 44. There is one
such argument for each of the attributes introduced between perfection and intellectivity: for goodness (40.325), for uniqueness
(42.337), and for infinity (43.359). In each of those arguments
Aquinas is just as explicit about the inclusion of all specific
perfections in divine perfection as he is here in the intellectivity
argument, but in none of them does he bother to point out, as he
does here, that that inclusion in no way compromises divine simplicity. So we have some grounds for supposing that, even if this

argument has no formal need for step 2, there is some special reason for alluding here to simplicity's compatibility with universal perfection.

b. Step 3 and thesis EQO

Whatever may be the case regarding step 2's role in the argument, the structure of the sentence in lines 4–7 leaves no doubt that the next two steps, which I've extracted from that sentence, are intended as support for step 5. The sentence in lines 4–7 contains a phrase in quotation marks, which are meant to indicate that Aquinas would have expected his readers to associate the phrase with a famous thesis of Aristotle's: 'In a certain way the soul is all the things there are' (*De anima* III 8, 431b21). And because step 3 incorporates that phrase, it, like steps 1 and 2, may be considered to be explicitly supported by another argument—in this case, one of Aristotle's. The Aristotelian thesis Aquinas alludes to here concerns *both* the cognitive parts of the soul, sense as well as intellect. And so Aquinas's thesis in step 3 consists in just half of Aristotle's thesis, the half concerning intellect. I'll call Aquinas's restricted thesis EQO (from the Latin words in which he states it: *est quodammodo omnia*).

All that can save this EQO thesis from being dismissed out of hand is an interpretation of the modifying phrase 'in a certain way' that will tame the wild implausibility of its two implicit, interrelated claims: (A) that an intellective being *is* things other than itself, and (B) that an intellective being is *all* things.

As for claim A, Aquinas, following Aristotle, reduces its implausibility enormously by including within his interpretation of 'in a certain way' what I'll call the forms-only condition: 'if the soul *is* all things, it must be either the sense-perceptible and knowable things *themselves* [as Aristotle says some pre-Socratic philosophers claimed] . . . or *their forms* (*species*). Now the soul is *not* the things themselves, as they supposed, because [when a stone is sensed, or cognized intellectively] the *stone* is not in the soul but, rather, a *form* of the stone' (In DA III: L13.789). So the forms-only condition blocks one obviously unacceptable reading of the EQO thesis. Of course your intellect is not identical with the extra-mental things it cognizes; it *is* its objects only in virtue of being intellectively informed by forms of those things. Even though the form of stone is precisely what makes the extra-mental stone *stone* rather than wood or mud, the *mental* form of that cognized extra-mental thing is prevented from petrifying your intellect by the radically different mode of its instantiation—conceptual rather than corporeal. For you to cognize the extra-mental thing as shale is for you to have acquired its nature, quiddity, or form *intellectively*—a process radically unlike that mindless ancient mud's acquiring of the form shale. 'Cognizers are distinguished from non-cognizing things in this respect, that non-cognizing things have only their own form, while a cognizer is naturally suited to have a form of something else as well, for a form of what is cognized is in the cognizer' (ST Ia.14.1c). More needs to be said about this forms-only condition, but I'll postpone saying more in order to see, first, how Aquinas handles the implausible implied claim B.

In his commentary on the relevant passage in Aristotle's *De anima*, Aquinas naturally deals with the full Aristotelian thesis, which he presents in this form: 'the soul is in a certain way both the sense-perceptible and the intelligible things. For in the soul are sense and intellect, . . . but sense is in a certain way those that are sense-perceptible, and intellect those that are intelligible' (In DA III: L13.787). The full Aristotelian thesis, covering both cognitive parts of the soul, depends on a principle of universal cognizability: in theory, absolutely everything there is *can* be cognized, either sense-perceptively or intellectively. Aristotle puts it this way: 'The things there are are either sense-perceptible or intelligible' (*De anima* III 8, 431b21–2). Bold as it may sound, this principle of universal cognizability strikes me as truistic, or at least irrefutable, especially when, as in Aquinas's use of it, 'intelligible' need not mean susceptible of being perfectly understood by a human being: 'the human intellect does not immediately, in its first apprehension of a thing, acquire a complete cognition of it. Instead, the intellect first apprehends *something* about it—namely, its quiddity, which is the first and proper object of intellect; and *then* it acquires intellective cognition of the properties, accidents, and dispositions associated with the thing's essence' (ST Ia.85.5c). Moreover, that intellective cognition of the quiddities of creatures is itself always very far from complete, even in the most advanced instances of human intellection, now as well as in the thirteenth century: 'our cognition is so feeble that no philosopher has ever been able to investigate *completely* the nature of *a fly*' (*Collationes super Credo in Deum*, preface). And since knowledge, full-fledged cognition, involves intellection even when its objects are individuated forms cognized initially through the senses,[26] the principle of universal cognizability can, without relevant loss, be reduced to a principle of universal intelligibility: in theory, absolutely everything there is *can* be cognized intellectively—just the principle for Aquinas's restricted EQO thesis to depend on.

Such a principle of universal intelligibility is readily abstracted from Aquinas's interpretation of 'in a certain way' in his *De anima* commentary: 'that which can know—i.e. the intellective power—*is* not . . . the knowable thing itself, but is, rather, *in potentiality to it'* (L13.788). To be intellective as we are is to have a certain power or capacity for conceptually taking on a form of any and, in theory, every intelligible object—which is every thing. An intellective being need not be *all* things other than *potentially*. And so, once a principle of universal intelligibility is in place, the universality in it is fully ascribed to intellect even on the creaturely level: 'the result is that a human being is in a certain way the totality of being (*totum ens*), to the extent to which [the human being] as regards the soul is in a certain way all things, in so far as its soul is *receptive* of all forms. For intellect is a power receptive of all intelligible forms, and sense is a power receptive of all sense-perceptible forms' (L13.790).[27]

So Aquinas's interpretation of 'in a certain way' combines the forms-only condition with a principle of universal intelligibility, providing the materials for this fuller and, I think, not at all implausible version of the EQO thesis in step 3 of the intelligibility argument:

---

[26] See e.g. In DA III: L7.680: '[O]ur intellect is naturally suited to have intellective cognition of all sense objects . . . it is capable of cognizing not only one kind of sense objects (as sight or hearing is), or only one kind of common or proper accidental sensible qualities, but, instead, universally, of [cognizing] sensible nature entirely.' Also SCG I.31.281: '[W]ith a single power, intellect cognizes all the things that the sensory part of the soul apprehends with various powers, and many more things as well.'

[27] See also e.g. '[A] human being can by means of intellect acquire cognition of the natures of all bodies' (ST Ia.75.3c); 'If the human intellect comprehends the substance of any thing—a stone, say, or a triangle—none of the intelligible aspects of that thing exceeds the capacity of human reason' (SCG I.3.16). For a more detailed discussion of Aquinas's principle of universal intelligibility, see Kretzmann 1991c.

3′ On the basis of being intellective something is in a certain way all things in the sense that it is potentially informed intellectively by a form of any and every thing.

However, in working at dispelling the initial implausibility of EQO, I don't want to have left the impression that there's nothing brave about it. Even if it's only in potentiality that intellect is all things, and even if it's only forms of them and not the things themselves that can be attributed to intellect on any instance of that potentiality's actualization, Aquinas takes each such instance to warrant a kind of identity claim: 'In virtue of [the soul's being all things in] *this* way'—that is, in the way prescribed by Aquinas's interpretation of 'in a certain way'—'intellect actualized is said to be the actualized object of intellective cognition itself, to the extent to which a form of the object of intellective cognition is the form of the actualized intellect' (L13.789); 'something is actually cognized intellectively in that the actualized intellect and what is actually cognized intellectively are one' (SCG I.47.398). Every instance of intellective cognition is an instance of the actualization of an intellect's potentiality for taking on a form of some thing, an instance of intellect actualized.

It is necessarily also, and equally, an instance of the actualization of that extra-mental thing's intelligibility, an instance of that thing's becoming an object of actual intellection. The stone in the quarry wall is, like anything anywhere, always intelligible whether or not any intellect is actively cognizing it; and what is *per se* intelligible about it is its forms—medium hard, dark grey, brittle, Palaeozoic, Devonian shale. But its intelligibility is actualized when and only when a form of that stone is also informing some intellect, whose potentiality for intellective cognition is thereby actualized. When you consciously recognize the stone in the quarry wall as Palaeozoic, or even as dark grey, your intellect takes on a form that is also a form of the stuff in the wall. Your intellect doesn't thereby become the stone as such, but it does thereby become the stone as an intelligible object whose intelligibility is being actualized. Partly in order to distinguish between the extra-mental and the mental forms of intellectively cognized extra-mental things, Aquinas often calls the *mental* forms 'likenesses' (*similitudines*) of the things: 'By means of its likeness, what is cognized intellectively is in the one who is doing the intellective cognizing. And it is in this sense that we say that what is actually cognized intellectively *is* the intellect actualized, to the extent to which a likeness of the thing that is being cognized is [on such an occasion] the form of the intellect' (ST Ia.85.2, ad 1).[28] Intellect actualized, intellect actually cognizing, is intellect in touch with its real object, which is typically not the cognizing intellect itself. A form of the thing is taken on intellectively, and that *ensouled* form (as distinct from its *enmattered* counterpart) is a likeness of the thing. That likeness serves as the means whereby intellect's real object, the stone out there in the quarry wall, is cognized intellectively: 'the intelligible forms by which the possible intellect is actualized are not intellect's object, for they are related to intellect not as *what* is cognized intellectively but, rather, as *that by which* it cognizes' (In DA III: L8.718).[29]

c. *Step 4 and having within itself the perfection of all things*

In my presentation of the intellectivity argument, step 4 is more nearly reconstructed than extracted from Aquinas's text. His phrase in lines 6–7, 'having within itself the perfection of all things (*habens in se omnium perfectionem*)', seems clearly to be intended as an exposition of the EQO thesis, and so I've written step 4 to bring out that intention.

Step 4 seems to be a strong claim, especially because although whatever is said in or about the EQO thesis at this point in the argument must apply to intellective beings generally, it must still apply particularly to humans, the only beings whose known intellective nature can provide a basis for this argument that God's nature must be intellective. Even after the implausibility of the EQO thesis itself has been dispelled, can it be plausibly said of any human being that its 'being in a certain way all things on the basis of being intellective is its having within itself *the perfection* of all things'? It would be utterly implausible if the claim concerned the

[28] See the helpful account of this in Geach 1961: 95 ff.

[29] See also e.g. QDV 10.4: '[E]very cognition is in keeping with some form that is the source of the cognition in the cognizer. But this sort of form can be considered in two ways. In one way, as regards the being that it has in the cognizer; in the other way, as regards the relation it bears to the thing whose likeness it is. Considered in connection with the first relationship, it makes the cognizer actually cognizant. Considered in connection with the second relationship, however, it determines the cognition to some determinate cognizable thing'; and QDV 3.1.

innumerable perfection*s* of all things, but step 4 isn't talking about perfections.

To say instead, as step 4 does say, that merely on the basis of being intellective a being has within itself the perfection of all things is, I think, only to say differently what the EQO thesis already says—namely, that merely on the basis of being intellective a being has within itself, formally and potentially, absolutely all there is, 'the perfection of all things'. Or, as we've already seen Aquinas putting it, 'a human being is in a certain way *the totality of being* (*totum ens*), to the extent to which [the human being] as regards the soul is in a certain way all things' (In DA III: L13.790). In this context step 4 might have been expressed more clearly, and might have been easier to grant at once, if it had read this way:

4′ Something's being in a certain way all things on the basis of being intellective is its intellectively having within itself the perfection—that is, the totality—of all things.

But once we see that that's what step 4 comes to, we can, I think, grant it in the form in which Aquinas gives it.

Still, if that is what step 4 comes to, is it any more than a rewording of step 3? I don't think it is more than that, but the rewording is helpful, especially as regards intellectivity's role in reconciling divine simplicity and perfection. I think step 4's phrase 'having within itself the perfection of all things' is a highly compressed version of Aquinas's interpretation of the EQO thesis adapted to purposes of this argument. To say that an intellective being *is all things*, as step 3 says, can seem to inject an irreducible plurality into any being that is characterized by intellect. Step 4's glossing of 'is all things' as 'has within itself the perfection of all things' reminds the attentive reader that the EQO thesis, properly interpreted, doesn't identify an intellective being essentially with an exhaustive *plurality*, but rather ascribes to it an intellective identity—a formal, potential identity—with the universal *totality*, 'the totality of being'.[30] Construing the EQO thesis in this way helps to remove an apparent obstacle in the way of ascribing perfection to God along with the perfect intellectivity it entails.

---

[30] The same sort of unifying of the extensive aspect of universal perfection seems to be under way in the final clause of the earliest version of the argument from perfection: 'in whom the perfections of all natural kinds are united'. See sect. 4 above.

The obstacle is, of course, the apparent strain put on divine simplicity by the extensive aspect of universal perfection. But the introduction of the EQO thesis and the way it's construed in this argument are designed to show that since God's *intellective* possession of every 'perfection that may be found in any natural kind of beings' is his *being* in a certain way all those perfections interpreted as 'the totality of being', there isn't 'any complexity in him as a consequence of this'.

Of course, *human* intellectivity *does* involve complexity, not least because it involves an actualizing process. In its primary, creaturely instance, intellectivity is a power that is *not always* actualized and, even on occasions when it is actualized, is *never fully* actualized, especially (but not only) because of its universal range. It's for those reasons that the principle of universal intelli*gibility* is crucial to the interpretation of the EQO thesis in its original application, to intellective beings that are also human.

Still, as we've seen, every instance of an intellect's actualizing its universal potentiality constitutes a union of the intellect and the intelligible object whose intelligibility is actualized in that instance. As Aquinas puts it in another passage, 'In a human intellect [that is actively cognizing something] . . . the likeness of the intellectively cognized thing is other than the intellect's substance and occurs as its form. That's why the intellect and the thing's likeness make up one complete thing, which is the intellect intellectively cognizing in actuality' (In Sent. II.3.3.1c). So, if eternal, universally perfect God is, as such, intellective; if, as Aquinas puts it, 'his being is his being intellective' (SCG I.51&52.432); then God as intellective must be the eternal, perfect actualizing of the universal intellective potentiality. Since 'God's being intellective is his essence, his being intellective must be simple, eternal, invariable, purely actual, and all the [other] things that have been proved about the divine being' (45.388). It is God's *being* intellective that provides the basis for the fuller account of his *having* all specific perfections: intellectivity is the characterization of God's essence in terms of which the extensive aspect of universal perfection has to be understood. The real difference between thesis EQO's general claim about any intellective being and the extensive aspect of God's universal perfection understood as an aspect of God's intellectivity is not in the scope, which is exhaustive in both cases, or in the relationship between actualized intellect and intelligibles, which is in both cases formal identity, but simply in the fact that the totality of specific perfections included within universal perfection must be possessed by the divine intellect *perfectly*, as it couldn't be possessed by the temporal, dependent, finite human intellect.

So it seems to me that the point of step 2 in the intellectivity argument is to advertise God's intellectivity as the aspect of God's nature that best explains the compatibility of simplicity with universal perfection. Aquinas couldn't explain it in those terms in chapter 31, his first attempt to square perfection with simplicity, because he hadn't yet argued for intellect in God. And this argument introducing intellectivity in chapter 44 is perhaps not yet the best place for a full disclosure. But he does offer such explanations in later chapters—for example:

> [T]he divine essence comprehends within itself the excellences (*nobilitates*) of all things—not, of course, by way of having them [all] added together (*per modum compositionis*), but by way of perfection [itself] (*per modum perfectionis*). . . . [T]he divine intellect can comprehend in its own essence that which is proper to each thing by having intellective cognition of [the respects] in which anything imitates its essence and in which the thing falls short of its own perfection. For instance, in having intellective cognition of its own essence as imitable by way of life without cognition, it takes up the form proper to *plant*; while if [it has intellective cognition of its own essence] as imitable by way of cognition without intellect, [it takes up] the form proper to [non-human] *animal*; and so on as regards other things. (54.451)[31]

d. *Step 5 and* potissima

Although steps 3 and 4 present all that Aquinas explicitly provides by way of support for step 5 in this argument, he must be taking an additional bit of support for granted, since there's still nothing explicit in steps 3 and 4 to warrant step 5's characterization of intellectivity as the perfection that carries with it the most power. As I see it, the assumed premiss can be made explicit in a supplementary step that reads like this:

4a A perfection the possession of which involves the possessor's intellectively having within itself the perfection of all things is the one that has the most power.

---

[31] See also e.g. ST Ia.15.2c.

Step 4a also needs support. Aquinas's perfection argument, which we examined in Chapter Four, can be read as setting the stage for such a claim when it moves toward concluding God's universal perfection through derived characterizations of God as something 'to which the whole power (*virtus*) of being pertains', something that is 'in keeping with the whole power (*potestatem*) of being' (28.260). But step 4's crucial element is the phrase 'having within itself the perfection of all things', which I've already identified as an exposition of the EQO thesis. And so all the support step 4a really needs is available, I think, in the already developed analysis of EQO. And from steps 3', 4', and 4a we can validly infer

∴5 Among the perfections of things the one with the most power is being intellective.
∴6 God is intellective.

6. Behind the scenes of the intellectivity argument

Although this outcome looks like success for the intellectivity argument, it might disappoint someone who has been following the argument carefully, for of course this derivation of step 6 really uses only steps 1 and 5. If we take step 1 as our first premiss and consider an underived instance of step 5 as our second premiss for the conclusion, step 6, we have the same sort of argument from perfection as the ones we glanced at from the commentary on the *Sentences* and the *Compendium theologiae*. For although steps 3 and 4 do indeed support step 5, the only piece of it they support is the claim that among specific perfections intellectivity is 'the one with the most power'; and that piece isn't needed in this derivation of step 6. The other component of step 5, the one that is needed here, is the claim that being intellective is one of the perfections of things. And although we've seen good reasons to accept that claim, nothing in the intellectivity argument itself expressly supports it. So, for purposes of this derivation of step 6, not only step 2 but also steps 3 and 4 (not to mention step 4a) and the part of step 5 that is supported by them seem superfluous. If this derivation of step 6 is, as I think it is, an acceptable way of showing that universally perfect God must be intellective, then the intellectivity argument that contains it looks like an extravagance half the components of which are merely ornamental.

However, as my discussion of the argument should have shown, I'm unwilling to accept that appraisal of it. While I have no explanation of Aquinas's uncharacteristically allowing the stronger, more interesting features of this argument to remain partially behind the scenes and logically superfluous, I think none of those pieces of the argument are irrelevant to providing a preliminary sketch of the importance of God's intellectivity to the theory of God's nature, even though they aren't really needed for the derivation of the conclusion 'God is intellective'. Since I've been bringing out that relevance of theirs in my discussion of Aquinas's intellectivity argument, I think I can provide a summary conclusion to this chapter by simply offering a radical but recognizable recasting of his argument.

The intellectivity argument recast

1 {1} No perfection that may be found in any natural kind of beings is absent from God.

2 Of perfections that may be found in any natural kind of beings, all and only those that do not entail any mode of being that is peculiar to creatures are predicated of God literally (albeit analogically).

3 Of perfections that may be found in any natural kind of beings, intellectivity is one that does not entail any mode of being that is peculiar to creatures.

∴ 4 {6} God is (perfectly) intellective.

5 {3'} On the basis of being intellective something is in a certain way all things in the sense that it is potentially informed intellectively by a form of any and every thing.

6 {4'} Something's being in a certain way all things on the basis of being intellective is its intellectively having within itself the perfection of all things.

∴ 7 God intellectively has within himself the perfection of all things.

8 God's being (perfectly) intellective is God's essence.

∴ 9 {2} There is no complexity in God as a consequence of the presence of all those perfections (that is, his intellectively having within himself the perfection of all things).

10 {4a} A perfection the possession of which involves the possessor's intellectively having within itself the perfection of all things is the one that has the most power.

∴11 {5} Among the perfections of things the one with the most
     power is being intellective.

The conclusion of this recast argument is obviously well suited to
some important results noted in Chapter Five: namely, that among
the perfections of things, being intellective is most like God's
causal power (sect. 7) and that God's causal power is infinite
(sect. 10).

SEVEN

WILL

1. Will and personhood

Any being we could consider to be a person would, of course, have to be characterized by mind. But mind or, more precisely, intellect—especially as conceived of along the lines traced in Chapter Six—seems not to be enough for personhood. When intellect is conceived of as primarily a faculty of cognition, and intellective cognition is conceived of as primarily the acquisition of intelligible forms, the concept of intellect may fall short even of the concept of mind. For mind involves at least occasional states of full consciousness, which involve attention. And attention, at least in finite minds, involves selection and direction, which are not essential to cognition generally. Nobody would be tempted to consider an electronic traffic-counting device a person, even though it provides a close analogue to abstractive intellective cognition by interpreting the electrical impulses it receives as the passing of vehicles with various numbers of axles and recording its results in those terms.

The standard view of persons requires that beings that count as persons be quite a lot like the being who takes that standard view—that they be entities that are typically if not always fully conscious, self-directed, responsible, free agents that are capable of certain attitudes toward and relationships with other beings of this sort: personifying relationships and attitudes, such as wronging or loving. Every component of the standard view, from full consciousness to loving, involves not only intellect but also will. Moreover, intellect and will do, I think, constitute jointly sufficient conditions of personhood.

What about emotion? Intellect and will don't include emotion, and it may seem that emotion counts as a third necessary condition, especially in connection with the attitudes and relationships that help to specify a person. An essentially emotionless person would quite rightly be called *inhuman*, but nothing in the standard view of the nature of persons restricts the application of the concept of a person to human beings, or even to corporeal beings. If our concept were restricted in that way, we wouldn't create or be able to understand fairy-tales, ghost stories, or the kind of science fiction in which extra-terrestrials play a part. And leaving emotion out of the mix leaves out less than might at first be supposed. Whether or not only persons can be wronged, certainly only a person can do the wronging, and certainly emotion is not a prerequisite for immoral action.[1] On the contrary, unemotional human wrongdoing is at least prima facie worse than the kind that stems from rage or jealousy. Human loving, even when being in love is left out of account, is of course typically emotional. But, as we'll see in Chapter Eight, loving as an essentially personifying relationship needn't be emotional. Love's association with emotion diminishes as its association with will grows stronger.

Since intellect and will are conceptually distinct, and since intellect without will would not constitute a person, showing that personhood must be attributed to reality's ultimate principle, a process that began in arguing that it must be intellective, remains incomplete until it can be shown to be characterized essentially by will as well.

Now, showing that God must be characterized by will may seem to be absurdly easy, given Aquinas's relational method, founded on the extensive aspect of universal perfection. For, as we saw in Chapter Six, he uses that method in establishing intellectivity as a divine attribute on the basis of its occurring as a perfection specific to human beings; and, as we'll see in this chapter, he takes will to be essentially associated with intellect. None the less, will's status as a specific human perfection is not a basis on which he ever argues for will in God, as far as I know. I suspect that this apparently easy line of reasoning is left out of the array of argumentation he offers in support of attributing will to God just because our will's relationship to our intellect leaves will as we know it looking far less like a

---

[1] Wronging of course includes permitting bad things to happen as well as perpetrating them. If a natural disaster is one whose central event involves only natural forces and no personal agent at all, then its victims are not wronged. Victims of a natural disaster may be said to have been wronged only if some person or persons, human or otherwise, perpetrated the 'natural' disaster; or knowingly permitted it to occur when he, she, or they could have prevented it; or knowingly permitted the victims to be in harm's way when he, she, or they could have warned, removed, or protected them.

specific perfection than human intellect does. What weakens will's claim to the status of a specific perfection has nothing to do with its role as the source of moral imperfection. It stems, rather, from the fact that Aquinas's account of will leaves it looking like an append-age to intellect, not a specific perfection in its own right.[2] So, before considering ways Aquinas does argue for will in God, I want to say a few things about his conception of will generally, at least about those aspects of it that strike me as most relevant to my concerns here.

2. The universal appetite for good

The genus under which Aquinas locates will as a species is what he identifies as an *appetitus* for what is good, an absolutely universal *appetitus*, associated with all being. *Appetitus* can't be given an accurate, illuminating, one-word English translation in this con-text.[3] 'Wanting' comes closest to getting it right for instances of *appetitus* in rational and non-rational animals, where it is associ-ated with cognition, but even then only in case *wanting* X is under-stood as compatible with *having* X.[4] But since Aquinas would

---

[2] There may be a hint of this status in the transitional passage with which Aquinas begins his investigation of will in SCG I.72.617: 'Having dealt with matters that pertain to the divine intellect's *cognition*, it now remains for us to consider God's *will*.' He does observe, at least once, that 'among other perfections of things, intellect and will stand out' (CT I.33.66); but I'm inclined to read this as if the outstanding perfection had been identified as intellect-and-will, the personifying perfection. Of course, if he had actually given that composite the status of a speci-fying perfection in his theory, he clearly would have provided himself with a very short argumentative route to the establishing of will as a divine attribute.

[3] See Stump and Kretzmann 1982: n. 18. Sects. 5 ('Will') and 6 ('God's Will') of that article are especially relevant to this chapter.

[4] See e.g. SCG I.77.659: *Appetitus* occurs 'in so far as *appetitus* is directed toward an appetible thing—either a thing pursued by whatever has the *appetitus* or a thing in which it [whatever has the *appetitus*] is at rest'; ST Ia.19, ad 2: 'In our case will pertains to the appetitive part [of the rational soul] which, even though it gets its name from "*appetendo*" (seeking), has not only the activity of seeking what it does not have but also that of loving what it has and delighting in it.' It seems that Aquinas may sometimes have recognized a strict sense of *appetitus* that was not to be understood in that way. Obj. 1 in In Sent. I.45.1.1 ('Is There Will in God?') argues against attributing will to God just because 'will is a kind of *appetitus*, but every *appetitus* belongs to what is incomplete' in so far as it lacks that for which it has the *appetitus*. In his rejoinder (ad 1) Aquinas claims that 'although will is said to be in God, it is not granted that there is *appetitus* in him, because, according to Augustine, *appetitus*, *strictly* speaking, is for a thing one does not have. God, however, has all his

include the heliotropism of (non-cognitive) plants and even the weight of (inanimate) stones among clear instances of this universal *appetitus*, 'wanting' obviously won't do in general. In the expectation that misleading connotations can be set aside, I'll simply use 'appetite' as a rough English equivalent for *appetitus*.

In one of Aquinas's SCG arguments for God's goodness he begins by quoting and offering an explanation of Aristotle's famous citation of a principle of universal appetite:

The good is what all things have an appetite for—which the Philosopher introduces in *Ethics* I [1, 1094a2–3] as having been very well said. But all things have an appetite for (*appetunt*) being actualized in their own way, as is clear from the fact that each thing in keeping with its own nature resists harm to itself (*repugnat corruptioni*). Therefore, being actualized constitutes the essential nature of what is good. And that is why a potentiality's being deprived of its actualization leads directly to the bad that is opposed to the good [associated with the actualization of that potentiality], as is clear from what the Philosopher says in *Metaphysics* IX [9, 1051a4–17]. (I.37.306)

This interpretation of the universal appetite for good grows naturally out of Aquinas's thesis that the terms 'being' (*ens*) and 'goodness' (*bonum*) are the same in reference and differ only in sense.[5] Part of what this means, as we saw in Chapter Four, is that any thing is good of its kind to the extent to which it is a whole, complete specimen of that kind, free from relevant defect, to the extent to which it is fully realized or developed, to the extent to which its specifying potentialities are actualized. And so a thing is good of its kind to the extent to which it is in being as a thing of that kind.

Now every appetite is only for what is good. The reason for this is that appetite is nothing other than some sort of inclination for something on the part of whatever has the appetite. But a thing is inclined only to something like [it] and suitable [for it] (*aliquid simile et conveniens*). Therefore, since every thing is some sort of good to the extent to which it is a being and a substance, it is necessary that every inclination be toward what is good.

good in himself. That is why even in our case will is not *appetitus*, *strictly* speaking, when it is joined together with that which is willed.' See also QDV 23.1, ad 8, quoted on p. 214 below.

    [5] See ST Ia.5.1. On this thesis and some of its consequences see Stump and Kretzmann 1988; also MacDonald 1991*b*.

And it is for this reason that the Philosopher says (in *Ethics* I) that the good is what all things have an appetite for. (ST IaIIae.8.1c)

So, the single referent shared by the terms 'X's being' and 'X's goodness' is X's nature to the extent to which it has been realized in X. The difference in sense between those terms shows up plainly in the fact that 'X is a good φ' explicitly commends X, as 'X is a φ' does not. A thing's goodness is its capacity to elicit appetite, to operate as a final cause.[6] And in a being that has cognition— instinctual, sensory, or intellective—the being's cognition of some- thing as good for itself (whether or not that has already been attained) will elicit appetite for that, activating the being's innate inclination toward and approval of its own preservation and fulfil- ment. As Aquinas reads the Aristotelian principle of universal appetite as applied to imperfect, temporal beings, then, it looks like a not implausible principle of developmental inertia: a thing tends to actualize its specifying potentialities unless adversely acted upon.

3. *Will as intellective appetite for what is good*

'An appetite for good is in *all* things,' Aquinas says in SCG II, 'since, as philosophers teach, the good is what all things have an appetite for. Now in things that lack cognition this sort of appetite is of course called *natural* appetite; a stone, for example, is said to have an appetite for being farther down [than it is]. But in things that have sensory cognition it is called *animal* [instinctual or sen- sory] appetite, which is divided into the concupiscible and the irascible [e.g. the instincts to seek food or to avoid pain, and to struggle for survival]. In those that have intellective cognition, however, it is called *intellective* or *rational* appetite, which is *will*' (II.47.1237).

---

[6] As at least a *subsidiary* final cause, since it may elicit appetite because of its perceived utility as something directed toward an end the agent is already inclined to, rather than as an end in its own right: 'Now the essential nature of what is good, which is the object of the will's power, is found not only in an end but also in things that are directed toward the end. . . . However, things that are directed toward an end are not good or willed for their own sakes, but rather in virtue of their ordered relationship to the end. And so will is drawn to them only in so far as it is drawn to the end' (ST IaIIae.8.2c).

As physical objects, as animals, and as rational, human beings are characterized by all three species of the universal appetite for good, but by will distinctively. And what differentiates will from other appetites is will's essential association with intellect, parallel-ing the essential association of our instinctual drives with sense-perception. In the passage I just quoted, however, the nature of will's association with intellect is left unspecified. For all that's said there, 'will' might designate no more than a special instantiation of the universal appetite found in beings that have intellect, somewhat as 'heliotropism' designates one of its instantiations found in beings that have roots. But, naturally, Aquinas thinks that the occurrence of the universal appetite in the absence of all cognition, or associ-ated essentially with one or the other sort of cognition, produces relationships that distinctively link the appetite with the good it's oriented toward:

All things are inclined by appetite in their own way toward what is good, but variously. [I'm omitting the accounts of natural and animal appetite in this passage.] Now some things are inclined toward what is good along with a cognition on the basis of which they cognize the essential nature of good—a condition proper to intellect—and these things are the ones most fully (*perfectissime*) inclined toward what is good. [It is,] of course, not as if they were directed toward what is good [for them] only by something other than themselves, like things that lack cognition, or [inclined] toward what is good only in some particular way, like things that have only sensory cognition. Instead, they are as if inclined toward *goodness itself*, considered *universally*. And *that* inclination is called *will*. (ST Ia.59.1c)[7]

Of course, Aquinas ascribes to one's will activities that have standardly been associated with it, such as making choices and, on that basis, directing one's other faculties. But in all the passages we've been considering so far, it is not will's activities that concern him, but rather its fundamental nature. And in Aquinas's view its nature is fundamentally not that of an independent, equipoised

---

[7] See also ST Ia.59.4c: '[T]he object of intellective appetite (which is called will) is what is good considered in connection with the universal essential nature of the good (nor can there be any appetite except for what is good). That is why appetite in the intellective part [of the soul] is not divided in accordance with a distinction of any particular goods, as the sensory appetite is divided [into the concupiscible and the irascible]. [The sensory appetite] is not oriented toward (*respicit*) good consid-ered in connection with [its] universal essential nature but rather toward some sort of particular good.' Perhaps Aquinas's fullest account of these species of appetite for the good is the one he provides in QDV 23.1c.

capacity for choice, but that of an innate inclination toward what is cognized as good by each individual intellect naturally associated with each individual will. Choosing, directing, and any other acts or states of will are manifestations of the appetite that is will's essence, manifestations that are variously but inevitably shaped by intellective cognition.

Although Aquinas mentions only creatures in these passages in which he is characterizing will quite generally, nothing he has to say about it there is incompatible with attributing will to God. Whatever Aquinas turns out to mean by identifying will *in human beings* with an inclination 'toward goodness itself, considered universally', it's an identification that seems (and is) made to order for an attribution of will to the being that, he has already argued, is 'goodness itself' (I.38) *and* a being that 'intellectively cognizes himself perfectly' (I.47).

4. Arguments from intellect

In SCG I Aquinas takes up the attribution of will to God just after he has argued at length for intellect as a divine attribute. He's likely to have adopted that ordering of topics partly because the essential connection between intellect and will strikes him as providing a basis for arguing that God must be characterized by will just because God is characterized by intellect. Naturally, he devotes the first of his seventeen chapters on will in God (72–88) to arguing simply that God must be characterized by will, and seven of the chapter's eight arguments do make some use of God's intellectivity to support that conclusion, the first of them more simply and directly than any of the others:

First argument from intellect

From the fact that God is intellective it follows that he is volitional (*sit volens*).[8] For since an intellectively cognized good is the proper object of

---

[8] Aquinas's use of a present participle here parallels his use of *intelligens* as the term with which to describe God as intellective. But the special force of the present participle, indicating presently occurrent activity of the sort signified by the verb, is more important in the case of willing than in the case of intellectively cognizing (or intellecting), just because will as *we* know it seems so markedly, characteristically an intermittently exercised power, which it could not be in God. For that reason (only)

volition (*voluntatis*),[9] an intellectively cognized good, considered just as such, must be what is willed. Now something is called intellectively cognized relative to what has intellective cognition. It is necessary, therefore, that what has intellective cognition of what is good be, considered just as such, volitional. But God does have intellective cognition of what is good; for, since he is perfectly intellective (as is clear from things said above [I.44–5]), he has intellective cognition of being (*ens*) together with the essential nature of good. He is, therefore, volitional. (72.618)

Aquinas seems to have thought well of this line of argument. In his earlier commentary on the *Sentences* he uses a longer version of it as his sole argument to show that there is will in God (In Sent. I.45.1.1c);[10] and in the slightly later *Compendium* he uses it again, in a shorter version, as the first of two arguments to the same effect (CT I.32.63).[11] His fondness for this reasoning is at least initially disconcerting because, in any of its versions, it looks invalid.

it's tempting to revive the obsolete English adjective 'volent' in this context. But I'm resisting the temptation, avoiding the oddness in the expectation that no one will find it difficult to remember that God's being volitional entails his being immutably, eternally, actively volent.

⁹ Aquinas uses *voluntas* for both the faculty and the faculty's generic activity. Accordingly, I translate *voluntas* either as 'will' or as 'volition', depending on context.

¹⁰ 'In every nature in which cognition is found, volition and delight are also found. The reason for this is that everything that has a cognitive power can discriminate what is suitable (*conveniens*) [for it] from what is unsuitable (*repugnans*), and whatever is apprehended as suitable must be what is willed or is an object of appetite [in some other way]. And so in us there are two appetitive [powers], in keeping with the two kinds of cognition, of sense and of intellect. One of those [appetitive powers] follows intellect's apprehending and is called will; the other follows the senses' apprehending and is divided into the irascible and the concupiscible. Thus, since there is intellective cognition in God (as was shown above [35.1]), there must also be volition and delight in him, inasmuch as God rejoices in activity that is one and simple (as the Philosopher says in *Ethics* VII [14, 1154b26]). For in connection with any cognitive nature an activity that is perfect and natural is delightful' (In Sent. I.45.1.1c). In the first sentence of this passage Aquinas appears to use *voluntas* more broadly than he does ordinarily, associating it with cognition generally. (See also ST IaIIae.6.2c, where some of the behaviour of non-rational animals is characterized as 'imperfectly' voluntary.) And although he attributes only two appetitive powers to human beings here, his doctrine of the universal appetite for good means that, as physical objects, human beings must also exhibit *natural* appetition, as in falling downstairs.

¹¹ 'Now it is clear, furthermore, that it is necessary that God be volitional. For he has intellective cognition of himself, and he is perfectly good (as is clear from things that have been said). But an intellectively cognized good is loved (*diligitur*) necessarily, and that is brought about through will. Therefore, it is necessary that God be volitional.'

As we saw in the passages in which Aquinas differentiates will from other kinds of appetite for good, his account of will associates it essentially with intellect. The first argument from intellect is plainly intended to build on that relationship. But the relationship delineated in his general account is will's essential dependence on intellect. Will is identified as the appetitive faculty whose proper object is a good cognized by intellect, and so being intellective is a necessary condition for being volitional. But in order to agree that '[f]rom the fact that God is intellective it follows that he is volitional', we would need to be shown that being intellective is also a sufficient condition for being volitional. That is just what this first argument purports to show us in its second sentence, which is where its apparent invalidity shows up: 'since an intellectively cognized good is the proper object of volition, an intellectively cognized good, considered just as such, must be what is willed.'[12] It looks as if this crucial sub-argument could be saved only by adding the question-begging proviso that associated with the intellect that cognizes that good *there is a will*. Perhaps I can bring out my worry with an analogy: since colour is the proper object of vision, colour, considered just as such, must be what is seen. Well, yes; but only provided that there is an eye to see it. And so, it seems, God's being intellective cannot serve as the basis for attributing will to him— not, at any rate, so directly and simply as on this line of argument.

But I think a closer look at part of Aquinas's general account of the nature of will suggests a way of seeing how being intellective might be construed as not just necessary but also sufficient for being volitional. The part I want to look at is just the part that has to do with sensory and intellective appetite—*cognitive* appetite: I'm going to omit any further consideration of appetite in inanimate things and plants. Any appetite for what is good typically has as its specific object the good of the being that has the appetite, a good which is for just that reason rightly construed as including (if not always identical with) self-preservation and self-fulfilment. In the case of a human being, which is sensory as well as intellective, animal appetite also plays an indispensable part in the being's achieving to any extent its preservation and fulfilment. But the preservation and fulfilment of the self considered just as intellec-

---

[12] *Cum enim bonum intellectum sit obiectum proprium voluntatis, oportet quod bonum intellectum, inquantum huiusmodi, sit volitum.*

tive—the preservation and fulfilment of what is distinctively human about us—depend on an appetite for such goods as only intellect can discern. Such preservation and fulfilment therefore require an appetitive faculty beyond animal appetite, one whose proper objects are goods of a sort the senses can't discern, including, above all, 'goodness itself, considered universally'. Viewed in this way, as the intellectively informed innate inclination, will is a condition necessary for the preservation and fulfilment of distinctively human being, considered just as such. And so, when intellective being is considered on the basis of the principle of developmental inertia, the presence of intellect may, after all, be recognized as a sufficent condition for the presence of will, considered as an intellective being's essential tendency to actualize its specifying potentialities.

Since a consideration of human intellect is the bridgehead from which Aquinas argues for will in God, perhaps this relationship between intellect and will influences the first argument from intellect, even though it's not a relationship that can obtain between perfect, atemporal intellect and will. Of the seven other arguments in SCG I.72 that set out to derive divine will from divine intellect, only one can be said to come close to making that line of thought explicit in a form that may be appropriate to arguing for will as a divine attribute.

Second argument from intellect

That which is entailed by (*consequitur*) every being is a concomitant of (*convenit*) being considered just as being. But whatever is of that sort must be found above all in that which is first being. Now it belongs (*competit*) to every being to have an appetite for its own fulfilment (*perfectionem*) and the preservation of its being, but to each in its own way—to intellective beings through will, to animals through sensory appetite, but to those that lack senses through natural appetite. Still, [an appetite for their own fulfilment and the preservation of their being belongs] differently [to those that have and [to] those that do not have [such preservation and fulfilment]. For those that do not have [it] tend by desire, with the appetitive power associated with their kind, to acquire what is lacking to them {*eis/ei*}, while those that have [it] are at rest in it. Therefore, this [latter aspect of appetite] cannot be lacking to first being, which is God. Since he is intellective, therefore, there is will in him, by which his being and his goodness is pleasing to him. (72.620)

The line discernible dimly in the first argument and more clearly in the second depends on recognizing that on Aquinas's interpretation the universal appetite for good is a fundamental, all-pervasive feature of reality, manifested differently depending on its occurring either in the perfect, atemporal being or in imperfect, temporal beings; and that among the latter it is manifested differently in non-living or living things, in non-cognitive or cognitive living things, in non-intellective or intellective cognitive living things. On the basis of that recognition, intellect can be seen to be not only necessary but also sufficient for will, when will is considered initially as simply the intellective form of the universal appetite.[13]

Besides the two arguments I've introduced here, there are five more from intellect in SCG I.72, the chapter in which Aquinas argues for will in God. In light of the essential connection between divine intellect and divine causation noted in Chapter Six, the most important of those other five is the one in which he argues that intellective *causation* entails volition: 'a form belonging to the divine intellect is a cause of movement and of being in other things, since [God] actualizes things through intellect . . . [but] a form considered through intellect does not move or cause anything except through will' (72.622). However, Aquinas treats this argument as only a foreshadowing of a fuller investigation of the nature of divine action,[14] and I will do the same, postponing a consideration of action to my projected book on SCG II.

---

[13] See also ST Ia.19.1c: 'There is will in God just as there is also intellect in him, for will is entailed by intellect (*intellectum consequitur*). For just as a natural thing has being in actuality through its form, so [is] intellect intellectively cognizant (*intelligens*) in actuality through its intelligible form. Now each thing has such a relationship to its natural form that when it does not have it, it tends toward it; and when it has it, it rests in it. And the same [is true] of each natural perfection, that it is what is good for [that] nature. (In things that lack cognition this relationship to what is good is called natural appetite.) That is why an intellective nature, too, has a similar relationship to a good apprehended through an intelligible form—viz. that when it has it, it rests in it; but when it does not have it, it seeks it. And both [of those states] pertain to will. And so in anything that has intellect there is will, just as in anything having sense perception there is animal appetite. And so there must be will in God since there is intellect in him. And just as his intellecting is his being, so is his willing.' See also SCG IV.19.3558.

[14] 'But a form belonging to the divine intellect is a cause of movement and of being in other things, for he actualizes (*agit*) things through intellect (as will be shown below [II.24]).'

5. Will, goodness, and freedom

Only one of the eight SCG arguments for will in God is entirely independent of considerations of intellect. Its simplicity and strength recommend it, and it has the further advantage of raising an important issue regarding Aquinas's account of volition generally and of God's will in particular.

Argument from freedom

What is free is what is by reason of itself (*Liberum est quod sui causa est*; *Metaphysics* I 2, 982b6[15]), and so what is free has the essential nature of what is *per se*. Now will is what primarily has freedom where acting is concerned, for a person is said to perform freely any action he performs to the extent to which he performs it voluntarily. Therefore, the first agent, with whom acting *per se* is associated most especially, is one to whom it is most especially suited to act through will. (72.624)[16]

This argument takes it for granted that what may be called the first agent's freedom of being—its metaphysical independence, or perseity—entails its freedom of action, and that its acting freely is its acting voluntarily. It serves Aquinas's purposes well in view of the centrality of considerations of metaphysical independence in the development of his conception of God (which we noted in Chapters Three and Four). But just because it identifies free action with voluntary action, it may seem ill suited to Aquinas's own account of the fundamental nature of will, in which will's essential relationship to intellectively cognized goodness is bound to raise questions about its freedom. If will is a faculty whose fundamental nature is that of an essential inclination toward a fixed ultimate end—goodness itself considered universally—and if its particular volitions for subordinate ends are informed by what intellect presents to will as good for progressing toward the ultimate end, then God's perseity, his absolute independence, may well seem to be an obstacle rather than a means to showing that will must be attributed to him. Understanding the nature of the freedom

---

[15] The medieval Latin version of this Aristotelian passage is ambiguous in a way that is clarified in a note supplied at this point by the Marietti editors: 'Quod scholastice «sui causā» dicitur, aristotelice αὐτοῦ ἕνεκα legitur, h.e., «suiipsius gratiā» nempe: «sibi causā agendi» (*infra*: **1243**).'

[16] See also e.g. QDV 23.1, sc 4; and SCG I.88.733 and 734, where this line is taken in support of attributing not merely will but free choice to God.

ascribed to the first agent here begins in understanding the analysis of necessity that Aquinas incorporates into his theory of will. (I'll *introduce* the relationships between volition and necessity in the context of *human* volition.)

The genus of what is necessary, as Aquinas sees it, is what cannot not be; he sorts out three species of it on the basis of the four Aristotelian causal principles. Two of those principles—matter and form—are *intrinsic* to what is necessitated by them. The necessity associated with either material or formal principles Aquinas calls 'natural' (or 'absolute'). This natural necessity is exemplified, he says, 'with respect to an intrinsic *material* principle when we say that it is necessary that everything with contrary components be perishable, or with respect to an intrinsic *formal* principle when we say that it is necessary that a triangle have three angles equal to two right angles' (ST Ia.82.1c).[17] Each of the two *extrinsic* Aristotelian causal principles, on the other hand, is associated with a further, distinct sort of necessity. The 'necessity of the *end*, sometimes called utility' is exemplified when something is recognized as necessary in that 'someone cannot attain, or cannot readily attain, some end without it—as food is necessary for life, and a horse for a journey' (ibid.). Finally, the necessity associated with *efficient* causation, 'the necessity of coercion', is exemplified 'whenever someone is compelled by some agent in such a way that he cannot do the contrary [of what he is compelled to do]' (ibid.).[18]

Now, since every will's inclination toward goodness is necessitated naturally by a formal principle, how can acting freely be equated with acting voluntarily? Will as an instance of the universal appetite for goodness certainly is naturally necessitated by a formal principle. But that sort of necessitation is not incompatible even with will's activity of choosing, the activity associated with freedom in the strongest sense of the word. As an act of will, choice is intellectively motivated, and some motives are intellectively subordinated to others. If there is a supreme motive—as in Aquinas's theory of volition there must be—then all other motives are of course subordinate to it. In the case of human beings he identifies the natural supreme motive or highest good as happiness. So, this (or any other) ultimate end is an intrinsic, formal, naturally (or

---

[17] See also the more elaborate presentation in SCG II.30.1069–75.
[18] See also the more elaborate presentation in SCG II.30.1076–9.

absolutely) necessitating principle of volition. As a pre-condition of choice, it lies outside the scope of choice. Objects available for choice can only be things that are *directed toward* that end (*ad finem*), things chosen because they are intellectively cognized as somehow making a contribution to the agent's relationship with the ultimate end. Such subordinate ends will typically be means, contributing more or less directly to achieving that naturally necessitated end, but they could also be enhancements, contributing to the enjoyment of the end when it is fully achieved.

Aquinas, following Aristotle, takes will's activity of choice to depend on its inclination toward the ultimate end as intellect's activity of demonstrative reasoning depends on its grasp of the first principles: 'just as principles are related to conclusions in connection with theoretical matters, so are ends related to things that are directed toward the ends in matters having to do with activities and appetite; for appetite and activity associated with things that are directed toward an end proceed from the end just as we cognize conclusions on the basis of principles' (76.650).[19] On this analogy, the predetermined ultimate end is a necessary but not a sufficient determinant of every volition for a subordinate end, so its being predetermined is not incompatible with freedom of choice regarding things that are directed toward the ultimate end.

Still, can there be genuine freedom of choice in these circumstances? Doesn't the (predetermined) end necessitate which things are to be directed toward it? No. Necessity of the end—utility—obviously poses no threat to freedom of choice in its weak, horse-for-journey form: you can, if you like, walk rather than ride. Aquinas takes it to be no more threatening in its strong, food-for-life form, because even when a subordinate end that is as rigidly oriented toward happiness as the continuation of one's life ordinar-

[19] See also e.g. ST Ia.82.1: '[I]n practical matters an end plays the role played by a principle in theoretical matters, as is said in *Physics* II [9, 200a15–34]'; also IaIIae.8.2c, where *Ethics* VII [9, 1151a16–17] is cited, and 9.3c. And see esp. SCG I.80.679: 'In connection with considerations of appetite and activity an end plays the role played by an indemonstrable principle in theoretical considerations. For just as conclusions are concluded from principles in theoretical considerations, so in connection with considerations of activity and appetite the reason for all the things to be done or to be sought (*appetendorum*) is drawn from the end. Now in theoretical considerations intellect assents to indemonstrable first principles necessarily and can in no way assent to their contraries. Will, therefore, clings (*inhaeret*) to the ultimate end necessarily, in such a way that it cannot will the contrary. And so if for the divine will there is no end other than himself, he necessarily wills that he be.'

ily is cannot be attained without a specific means such as food, one *can* choose to *reject* that subordinate end. The preservation of such an option is even clearer in another example he provides of this strong form of utility: 'from a volition to cross the sea comes the necessity in volition of wanting a ship' (ST Ia.82.1c). Of course, in the most directly relevant instance of utility, the ultimate end, happiness, is itself necessitated absolutely and hence impossible to reject; but the kind of necessity that is associated with human happiness as an ultimate end is the *weak* form of utility, allowing for choices among subordinate ends directed toward happiness.

But what about will's essential dependence on intellect? Can't that be construed as involving coercion, necessity of the sort associated with efficient causation, the one sort of necessitation Aquinas admits is incompatible with freedom of any sort? When intellect presents will with an object that intellect takes to be good, will can indeed be moved by intellect—not, however, as a ball is moved, willy-nilly, by someone who throws it. Will can be moved by intellect only in the way an agent can be moved by an end: 'an intellectively cognized good is will's object and moves it as an end' (ST Ia.82.4c). The only sort of necessitation, then, in intellect's presentation of goods to will is utility, necessity of the end, and we've already seen that such necessity does not preclude freedom of choice: will can will against any subordinate end presented to it by intellect as a contribution to achieving or enjoying the ultimate end. 'The only good that will cannot by its very nature will the non-existence of is the good whose non-existence totally abolishes the essential nature of good; but that [good] is nothing other than God. Therefore, will can, by its very nature, will the non-existence of any thing at all other than God' (81.684). (And, of course, even this restriction on volition will apply only in case the particular intellect associated with that will *recognizes* God as the good whose non-existence totally abolishes the essential nature of good.)

An even more telling consideration in certifying will's freedom in its relationship with intellect is the fact that the faculty of will also moves the faculty of intellect, and that will's moving of intellect *is* coercive, carried out 'in the way an agent moves something—as what alters moves what is altered and what pushes moves what is pushed. . . . The reason for this is that in connection with all active powers that are ordered [relative to one another] the power that is oriented toward a universal end moves the powers oriented toward the particular ends. . . . Now will's object is the good and the end in general, but every [other] power is related to some proper good suited to it—e.g. sight to the perception of colour, intellect to the cognition of what is true' (ST Ia.82.4c). So the only efficient, coercive causation in the relationship between intellect and will occurs in will's directing of intellect—a consideration that obviously enhances will's status as the locus of freedom and (relative) independence even in finite beings: 'an act is firmly in our power in so far as it belongs to will' (QDV 14.3c).[20] And, in fact, one of Aquinas's arguments in SCG I.72 uses just these distinct causal relationships between intellect and will as a basis for attributing will to God:

Among motive powers in beings that have intellect, will is found to be primary; for will applies every power to its activity. For we engage in intellection (*intelligimus*) because we will [to do so], and we employ our imagination (*imaginamur*) because we will [to do so], and so on as regards the others. And it has this role because its object is the end. [This is so] even though intellect does move will—not in the manner of an efficient and moving cause, but in the manner of a final cause—by presenting it with its object, which is an end. Having will, therefore, is associated above all with the *first* mover. (72.623)[21]

Everything we've seen in Aquinas's general conception of will, then, supports, or is at least compatible with, his arguing for will in God on the basis of God's intellectivity and on the basis of God's absolute independence.

[20] There is further relevant material in QDV 14.3c: 'Now an act is firmly (*consistit*) in our power in so far as it belongs to will, whether it belongs to will as elicited by it—e.g. loving, willing—or as commanded by it—e.g. walking, talking. . . . Now believing [an act of intellect] is characterized by (*habet*) assent only as a result of will's command.' (Acts *elicited* by will are acts of will itself; acts *commanded* by will also involve other powers of the agent.) See also QDV 14.3, ad 10: 'There is faith in intellect only in so far as it is commanded by will.'

[21] This argument, following the pattern of the arguments Aquinas develops in connection with his relational method, concludes to the presence of will in God on the basis of a consideration of will in creatures. And what it observes regarding human will as the initiator and director of the activities of other faculties in the agent seems clearly inapplicable to will in God. But the argument's only crucial observation regarding the indispensability of will is that 'its object is the end'; and God, conceived of as purposive, as a doer and not just a knower, must be characterized by direction, too.

6. Determinate, static, choiceless volition in God

Because will's act of choosing is what we ordinarily associate freedom with, I've been focusing on choice in showing how freedom is preserved in the thicket of necessities that characterize Aquinas's account of volition. So it's noteworthy that issues connected with freedom of choice are ignored in the opening stages of Aquinas's account of the divine will, even in what I'm calling the argument from freedom. There are good reasons for this, and for the fact that the series of seventeen chapters devoted to will in God exhibits a development in which the attribution of divine freedom of choice emerges unmistakably only at the very end of the series.[22] For Aquinas's initial concern is with divine will solely in the respect in which the Aristotelian principle of universal appetite entails an appetitive aspect in all being—and thus especially in first being—considered just as such.

Volition in us is typically directed toward the acquiring or achieving of something we don't already have—typically, but not always. You couldn't exist as a person without the sort of inner life that is essential to personhood. It isn't anything you could acquire or achieve; it isn't even clearly distinguishable from you. And yet, of course, it is something you *want*, as you can verify by imagining your reaction (in normal circumstances) to someone's offering to obliterate your thoughts and feelings. In willing your inner life in this way, even if only dispositionally, you might reasonably be described as willing your self. This static sort of appetite, the wanting of what one already has or even is, Aquinas identifies as appetitive *rest*, which is emphatically not to be confused with the

---

[22] The titles of the chapters provide a rough sketch of this development: 'God is volitional' (72); 'God's will is his essence' (73); 'What God principally wills is the divine essence' (74); 'In willing himself God also wills other things' (75); 'God wills himself and other things in a single act of will' (76); 'The great number of things willed [by God] is not incompatible with divine simplicity' (77); 'The divine will extends to individual goods' (78); 'God wills things that are not yet' (79); 'God wills his being and his goodness necessarily' (80); 'God does not will things other than himself necessarily' (81); 'Arguments leading to absurdity if God does not will things other than himself necessarily' (82); 'God wills something other than himself with conditional necessity' (83); 'God's volition is not for things that are impossible in themselves' (84); 'Divine volition neither removes contingency from things nor imposes absolute necessity on them' (85); 'A reason can be assigned for divine volition' (86); 'Nothing [other than God himself] can be a cause of divine volition' (87); 'There is free choice (*liberum arbitrium*) in God' (88).

cessation of appetite.[23] In our case, static appetite is standardly dispositional, especially when its object is an aspect of our essence. As for the occurrent, conscious phases of such ordinarily dispositional appetite informed by intellect, they will count as acts of (static) volition. And all of us lucky enough to possess something we want will know what Aquinas means by using 'joy, 'pleasure', and 'love' as his standard designations for the occurrent manifestations of static volition for something we intellectively cognize as good, especially when we have already achieved or acquired it, and even if it's part of our own nature.[24] (In Chapter Eight we'll be considering such acts of static volition.)

In any case, an object of static volition is something that can be recognized as at least *counterfactually* chosen—something the willer has or is and would choose to have or to be if an occasion for choosing it were to arise. But, with luck, such occasions don't arise very often, even for willers as vulnerable to threats and losses as we are. And, in any case, static volition itself involves no actual choosing, even when the currently possessed object of it was originally achieved as a result of choice. *Dynamic* volition, our willing to have what we recognize as good and *don't* yet have, is the sort of willing characterized by ordinary acts of choice and the sort we're bound to be far more often aware of. But static volition, too, is easy to recognize even in contingent, temporal, often disappointed beings like us.

It is in virtue of one and the same nature that something moves toward a goal (*terminum*) it has not yet attained and rests at a goal it has already attained. For that reason it pertains to one and the same power to tend toward a good when it is not yet possessed and to love it and take pleasure in it after it is possessed. Both these [activities or states] pertain to an appetitive power, even though [such a power] gets its name more from the activity in which it tends toward what it does not possess—which is why it is said that appetite belongs to what is imperfect. Will, on the other hand, is related to both [those activities or states] in just the same way (*indifferenter*). That is why, in a strict sense, will is attributable (*competit*) to God, but not appetite. (QDV 23.1, ad 8)

[23] See e.g. 72.620, the 'second argument from intellect' in sect. 4 above; also the passages quoted in n. 4 above.
[24] See e.g. In Sent. I.45.1.1c (n. 10 above) and QDV 23.1, ad 8, quoted on this page. See also Aquinas's detailed general discussions of love (ST IaIIae.26–8) and of pleasure (31–4).

One's inner life, my example of an object of *static* volition, also contributes to a paradigm of the *determinate* sort of volition that has as its object the willer's person or, more precisely, the willer's self-fulfilment. Self-fulfilment—individual human happiness in our case—typically involves self-preservation, too. But it's certainly a real possibility that a person—an imperfect person—should want something else even more than self-preservation, that such a person's intellect should, perhaps correctly, discern something else as better than the preservation of oneself, presenting it to one's will as nobly self-sacrificial, or perhaps even as self-fulfilling, as directed toward happiness, the ultimate end specific to human beings. Aquinas's Aristotelian account of human volition explains the *contingent* desirability of any *extrinsic* object of a person's volition in terms of its contributing more or less directly to the achieving of that formally necessitated end, self-fulfilment, the desirability of which is axiomatic, the volition for which is predetermined and not the outcome of choice. 'The fact that we will to be happy (*felices*) has to do not with free choice but with natural instinct' (ST Ia.19.10c).

In light of these considerations it's not surprising that almost all the arguments we've seen Aquinas using to support his attribution of will to God have to do with static, determinate volition whose object is in no way extrinsic to the willer—volition for what the willer fully possesses or, more precisely, simply is.[25] And since there cannot be unactualized potentialities or non-occurrent dispositions in absolutely perfect, atemporal God, this static, determinate divine volition that has as its proper object perfect goodness—God himself—must manifest itself in eternal love and pleasure, in ways we'll be investigating in Chapter Eight. If there is no being devoid of some sort of appetition in some appetitive state or other, eternal love and pleasure certainly seem to be at least the primarily appropriate aspects of absolute perfection. 'All things, in so far as they are, are assimilated to God, who is being, primarily and maximally. But all things, to the extent to which they are, naturally love their own being, each in its own way. Far more, therefore, does God naturally love his being. Now his nature is *per se necesse esse* (as

---

[25] The sole exception is the argument for divine will as entailed by divine intellective causation (72.622)—of things other than God, of course. See n. 14 above.

was proved above [I.22]).[26] God, therefore, necessarily wills that he be' (80.680), and, we might add, naturally and necessarily enjoys his being.

But eternal divine pleasure or joy is not to be identified as formally analogous to human happiness, as a divinely specific ultimate end for divine volition. Because of God's essence—perfect being and thus perfect goodness itself—and because of considerations of absolute simplicity, only God himself could qualify as the ultimate end for divine volition and, thereby, as the universally ultimate end for all creaturely appetition, even though not universally cognized as such.

In the case of any willer, what is principally willed is a cause of [the willer's] volition. For when we say 'I want to walk in order to be healthy', we consider ourselves to be indicating a cause; and if someone asks 'Why do you want to be healthy?', we will go on assigning causes until we arrive at the ultimate end, which is what is principally willed, which is [in turn] a cause of volition altogether on its own. Therefore, if God principally wills anything other than himself, it will follow that in his case something else is a cause of volition. But his willing is his being (*esse*) (as has been shown [I.73]). Therefore, something else will be a cause of being for him—which is contrary to the essential nature of first being. (74.635)

Besides, 'the ultimate end is God himself, since he is the highest good (as has been shown [I.41]); therefore, he himself is what is principally willed by his will' (74.636). 'The principal object of the divine will, therefore, is the divine essence. However, since the divine essence is God's intellective cognizing and everything else that is said to be in him, it is clear, further, that in that same way he principally wills his cognizing, his willing, his being one, and whatever else is of that sort' (74.637–8).

Here, then, at the core of divine volition, in what is principally willed by God, nothing could be left to choice.

God necessarily wills his being and his goodness, and he cannot will the contrary. For it was shown above [I.74, in the passages just quoted] that God wills his being and his goodness as the principal object, which is for him the reason for willing other things. Therefore, in connection with everything willed [by him] he wills his being and his goodness—just as sight

[26] The Marietti editors supply a reference to 15.124, where this formulation is introduced in argument G6 (see Ch. Three). However, the identification of God's nature with *per se* necessary being is argued for not in I.15 but in I.22, esp. 22.205 (see Ch. Four).

sees light in [seeing] any colour. Now, it is impossible that God not will anything actually, for [in that case] he would be volitional in potentiality only, which is impossible, since his willing is his being. Therefore, it is necessary that he will his being and his goodness. (80.676–7)

God's necessarily willing his own nature and existence is entirely in keeping with his perseity, or metaphysical independence. And, although this willing involves no choice, it doesn't exclude every sort of freedom: 'in respect of its principal object, which is God's own goodness, the divine will does have necessity—not, of course, the necessity of coercion but, rather, the necessity of natural order, which is not incompatible with freedom.[27] . . . For God cannot will that he not be good and, consequently, that he not be intellective, or powerful, or any of those things that the essential nature of his goodness includes' (QDV 23.4c). Although this freedom compatible with natural order rules out any real alternatives and is quite clearly and explicitly not freedom of choice, even an incompatibilist libertarian can, and should, acknowledge it as a species of freedom.[28] It can be characterized as *willingness* or, more positively, as *counterfactual choice*—the sort of volitional stance I described earlier as normally taken by a human being toward its naturally necessitated inner life of thought and feeling. If Richard's positive attitude toward his naturally necessitated susceptibility to emotion, say, is just what it would have been if he had freely chosen an inner life characterized by emotion from among relevant alternative possibilities and had found that it measured up to his expectations, then Richard may reasonably be described as having counterfactually chosen it, as willing his susceptibility to emotion freely, even though necessarily. And, of course, as a finite, imperfect being, he almost certainly will not have this positive volitional stance toward *every* aspect of his essential nature—I mean, toward those he recognizes as natural limitations.

7. God's willing of other things

I began this chapter with the claim that although ascribing intellect to first being was not enough to warrant identifying first being as

[27] At this point Aquinas cites Augustine, *De civitate Dei* V [x].
[28] On issues of freedom and necessity, particularly in connection with God's will, see Stump 1990.

personal God, the addition of will to intellect was all that was needed to fill out the warrant. And I characterized persons as entities that are typically (though of course not always) fully conscious, self-directed, responsible, free agents that are capable of certain personifying attitudes toward and relationships with other entities of this sort, relationships such as wronging or loving. But Aquinas's arguments for will in God and his account of divine will so far have not provided grounds for ascribing to God all those personifying characteristics. The two most important components of full-fledged personhood that have yet to make their appearance are choice and interpersonal relationships with creatures. In Aquinas's account, the second of those components is closely connected with the first.

The main reason why neither of those components has yet appeared is that choice has been expressly excluded from the account of God's willing of his essence, the principal object of divine volition: 'God *necessarily* wills his being and his goodness, and he *cannot* will the contrary' (80.676). Of course, there's nothing unexpected in that much of the account: it clearly does follow from all that's been developed in Aquinas's natural theology up to this point. But it leaves divine will looking not much like the will of a human person, and rather more like the earth's naturally necessitated, utterly non-personal, static appetite for remaining at the centre of the Aristotelian cosmos. If there's personifying choice anywhere in divine volition, then, it must be in God's willing of things other than himself—created things. But the way Aquinas introduces that sort of willing into his account seems unpromising in this regard.

To begin with, his own general theory of volition requires him to say that '*in* willing himself [God] also wills other things. For it belongs to anyone who principally wills an end to will things that are directed toward the end, [and to will them] because of the end. Now God himself is the ultimate end of things (as is clear to some extent from things said earlier [I.74]). Therefore, in virtue of the fact that he wills himself to be, he also wills other things, which are in an ordered relationship to him as to [their] end' (75.639–40). Imperfect willers can and sometimes do will an end without willing any things that are directed toward the end, but no such perverse dereliction of willing is thinkable in God's case; and so it does seem obvious that God could not engage in the necessary willing of himself without also willing whatever other things are appropriately directed toward that end.[29] Now, given the identification of that end with God himself, it is unthinkable that any things that may be directed toward that end could serve as *means* for attaining, sustaining, or enhancing it, even though in connection with human willing the things that are directed toward an end must most often be considered means. So it remains to be seen how, exactly, any things other than God could in any sense at all be willed by God because they are 'directed toward the end' that is God himself. But there's no doubt about *which* other things are being thought of here as willed by God for that reason. It's simply *all* of them; for 'in willing *himself* God wills all the things that are *in* him. But in a certain way *all* things pre-exist in him, through [their] own essential natures (as was shown above [I.54]). In willing himself, therefore, God also wills other things' (75.643).

At least two relevant problems emerge from this introductory account of God's willing things other than himself. First, since God's willing of other things is presented as occurring *in* his necessary, choiceless willing of himself, there's still no sign of divine choice even in God's willing of other things, the only other kind of divine willing there could be. And, second, attributing to God the willing of all the uncountably many other things there are certainly seems to threaten absolute simplicity. Aquinas, ever alert to apparent compromises of simplicity, deals promptly with that second problem. But the way he deals with it only makes the first problem harder, because he argues, as might be expected, that 'God wills himself and other things in *a single act* of will' (76.647).

His most effective argument for that conclusion proceeds by simply making the relevant aspects of his general theory of volition more precise:

What is cognized and desired perfectly is cognized and desired to the full extent of its power. Now the power of an end is measured not only in terms of its being desired in itself but also in terms of other things' becoming appetible on account of it. Whoever desires an end perfectly, therefore, desires it in both these respects. Now one must not posit any act of God's

---

[29] See also e.g. 83.705: 'Necessarily, anyone who wills anything wills the things that are necessarily required for it, unless there is some shortcoming in the willer, either because of ignorance or because some passion distracts him from correctly choosing what is directed toward the intended end—things that cannot be said of God.'

willing in which he wills himself and does not will himself perfectly, since there is nothing imperfect in him. Therefore, in any act in which God wills himself, he wills himself absolutely and other things on account of himself. But, as has been proved [I.75], he wills things other than himself only in so far as he wills himself. It remains, therefore, that he wills himself and other things not in separate acts of will but in one and the same act. (76.649)

This single act of will—God's sole, eternally occurrent, all-encompassing volition—has already expressly been shown to be necessary and choiceless as regards its principal object, even if it is free in an attenuated sense. How, then, could any act *identical* with that act count as an act of choice? As we go further into Aquinas's account of God's willing of creatures, it's becoming only harder to see how choice can enter into God's volition at all. Aquinas acknowledges the difficulty: 'Now, if divine volition is for the divine goodness and the divine being necessarily, it might seem to someone that it would be for other things necessarily as well, since (as was proved above [I.75]) [God] wills all other things in willing his goodness' (81.682).

8. Freedom of choice and motives for choosing

None the less, he says, 'to those who consider this *rightly* it is apparent that [God's volition] for other things is *not* necessitated' (ibid.). Aquinas's view of the right way to consider this can seem suspiciously simple, as when he uses a familiar thesis drawn from his general account of volition as the basis for an apparently unproblematic attribution of free choice to God: 'since God wills himself as the end but other things as things that are directed toward the end, it follows that in respect of himself he has *only* volition, but in respect of other things he has selection (*electionem*). Now selection is always accomplished by means of free choice (*liberum arbitrium*). Free choice, therefore, is attributable to God' (88.732). And the term 'free choice', he explains, 'is used in respect of things one wills *not* necessarily, but of one's own accord (*propria sponte*)' (88.730).[30]

The thesis he's relying on here is quite plausible in the setting of

---

[30] See also ST Ia.19.10c, which is even simpler: 'We have free choice in respect of things that we will not necessarily or by natural instinct.... Therefore, since God wills his goodness necessarily but other things not necessarily (as was shown above [19.3]), he has free choice in respect of those he wills not necessarily.'

his general account, where, as we've seen, it has to do with locating free choice in the selecting of means for achieving a predetermined end, and where will's choosing of any thing as a means is motivated by intellect's cognition of the thing as contributing to achieving that end. But since any and all other things are necessarily excluded from serving an omnipotent agent as *means*, it isn't immediately obvious how, if at all, that general thesis about ordinary ends and means applies to God's willing of things other than himself. In fact, it seems clear that nothing else could make any contribution to eternally absolute perfection in any respect. Utility, conceived of as widely as possible, seems entirely unavailable as the motivation for God's volition that there be things other than himself. In arguing against the view that other things, too, must be willed by God necessarily, Aquinas sometimes cites their very uselessness to God as a basis for establishing the total absence of necessity in God's willing of them: God's volition for anything other than himself 'is for other things as things that are in an ordered relationship to the end which is his goodness. Now will is not drawn necessarily to things that are directed toward an end if the end can be without them. . . . Therefore, since the divine goodness *can be without* other things and, of course, *gains nothing through* other things, in God's case there cannot be any necessity to will other things as a consequence of his willing his own goodness' (81.683). As I've just been suggesting, such a sweeping declaration of other things' uselessness to God isn't unexpected. But in the context of such a radical devaluing of all other things, what can it mean to say, as we've seen Aquinas saying, that God wills them '*on account of* himself (*propter se*)' (76.649), that God's 'being and his goodness . . . is for him *the reason for willing* (*ratio volendi*) other things' (80.677)? What can it mean even to describe them as 'directed toward the end' or 'in an ordered relationship to the end' that is God's perfect goodness or God himself? The existence of an absolutely perfect being and nothing else at all seems unquestionably the best of all possible worlds, so what could motivate God to choose to create anything at all?

All of Aquinas's replies to such questions, all his attempts to identify the motive for God's choosing to create, naturally involve considerations of God's goodness. But some of those considerations appear to get us no closer to a satisfactory answer. For instance, in the chapter devoted to arguing that 'God does not will things other than himself necessarily' he appears to be moving toward an explanation when he observes that 'since the proper object of volition is an intellectively cognized good, there *can* be a volition for *anything* in which the essential nature of good is preserved' (81.684), and then claims, plausibly enough, that 'in willing his own goodness God wills the being of things other than himself *in so far as they participate in* his goodness' (81.685). But in case anyone is tempted to suppose that the divine volition for perfect goodness itself might somehow *entail* a volition for other things just as participants in goodness itself, Aquinas goes on to issue the familiar disclaimer that 'the divine goodness does *not* necessarily require that there *be* other things that are in an ordered relationship toward it as toward their end' (81.688). The being of other things, he keeps saying, is not willed necessarily but is, instead, freely chosen by God.

Very well, then, what motivates God to choose not the world consisting solely of himself, the absolutely perfect being, but, instead, a world consisting of the absolutely perfect being accompanied by a universe swarming with countless other beings, none of which—not even any that is perfect of its kind—is or could be absolutely perfect? I find Aquinas's attempts to answer this question unconvincing. For instance, 'although the divine will is not *determined* to its effects, we need not say that it does not will *any* of them . . . For the divine intellect apprehends not only the divine being, which is his goodness, but also other goods (as was shown above [I.49]). Of course, it apprehends them as various sorts of likenesses of the divine goodness and essence, not as its principles. And in this way the divine will tends toward them *not* as *necessary* for his goodness but, rather, as *suitable* (*convenientia*) for his goodness' (82.699).[31] Even if we leave out of account the fact that creatures are frequently, lamentably *defective*, morally and otherwise, what could it be about finite, temporal beings, none of which at its best could itself be absolutely perfect, that might make them

---

[31] See also 82.700: 'Nor need one posit anything unnatural in God as a consequence of the foregoing considerations. For his will wills himself and other things in a single act, but his relationship (*habitudo*) to himself is necessary and natural. His relationship to other things, however, is in keeping with some sort of suitability (*secundum convenientiam quandam*)—not necessary and natural, of course, but also not violent or unnatural; instead, *voluntary*. For, necessarily, what is voluntary is neither natural nor necessary (*quod enim voluntarium est, neque naturale neque violentum necesse est esse*).'

suitable companions in existence for the absolutely perfect being? Again, Aquinas's reply strikes me as deeply unsatisfactory: 'God wills all other things *in so far as they have his likeness*' (84.708), which is why 'God wills the good of *the universe* of his effects more fundamentally (*principalius*) than any particular good, in that a *more complete* likeness of his goodness is found in it' (85.713).[32] From such passages I get the idea that it's supposed to be *suitable* to God's eternal, perfect pleasure in, and love of, perfect goodness that perfect goodness be surrounded by uncountably many variously incomplete *likenesses* of itself, and I find that idea repugnant. But I'm not much bothered by its repugnance, since it's also just plain unbelievable as an account of God's motivation for freely choosing to create, and since in Aquinas's own discussions of God's goodness and creation there are many expressions of a radically different, radically preferable explanation of God's willing of things other than himself.[33]

The libertarian explanation I've been presenting and criticizing is the one Aquinas explicitly endorses: 'one must hold, without any doubt, that God produced creatures in existence by a free choice of his will, without any natural necessity' (QDP 3.15c). But I believe that his conceptions of God, goodness, creation, and choice entail a necessitarian explanation to which he was clearly drawn and which gets expressed, perhaps inadvertently, even in the context of a thoroughgoing presentation of his official libertarian line, as in this passage from the chapters of SCG I on which I've been mainly drawing in this chapter: God's goodness 'is the cause of God's willing; and *it is also the very willing itself*' (87.724).

9. The Dionysian principle and the necessitarian explanation of creation

The claim that God's goodness is the very willing itself isn't merely the familiar sort of acknowledgement of the demands of simplicity. It is also, and much more importantly, an echo of a Neoplatonist principle Aquinas often appeals to, sometimes attributing it to

---

[32] See also e.g. 86.719: '[T]he good of the universe is the reason why God wills any one particular good in the universe'; 721: '[H]e wills that there be the good of the universe because it is fitting for (*decet*) his own goodness.'

[33] I've discussed some of these issues before. See Kretzmann 1983, 1991*a*, 1991*b*.

Dionysius: *Goodness is by its very nature diffusive of itself and (thereby) of being.*[34] I think this Dionysian principle expresses an important truth about goodness, most obviously about the goodness of agents, which is the only kind at issue here. There is no obvious inconsistency in the notion of knowledge that is unexpressed, never shared by the agent who possesses it even if that agent is omnipotent; but there *is* inconsistency in the notion of goodness that is unmanifested, never shared, even though united with omnipotence. The use Aquinas makes of the Dionysian principle on many occasions suggests that he, too, at least most of the time, considers it to be important and true.[35] He rejects it very rarely, but very emphatically, just when he is confronted with it as suggesting a necessitarian explanation of creation. For example, 'If God were to deny his goodness in such a way as to do something contrary to his goodness, or something in which his goodness was not expressed, it would follow that he would, *per impossibile*, deny himself. However, that would not follow even if he did not *share* his goodness *at all*, for it would be no loss at all to goodness if it were not shared' (QDP 3.15, ad 12).[36]

Despite Aquinas's explicit opposition to a necessitarian explanation of God's willing of other things, he sometimes writes in a way that indicates that he does see God's creating as an instance of the natural self-diffusion of goodness, as in this passage from SCG I, where he is discussing not creation itself but God's goodness: 'The sharing (*communicatio*) of being and goodness proceeds from goodness. This is of course evident, both from the nature of the good and from its definition (*ratione*) . . . It is for this reason that the good is said to be diffusive of itself and of being. Now this diffusion is attributable to God, for it was shown above [I.13] that he is the cause of being for other things' (37.307). God is perfect goodness itself, and goodness is *essentially*—from its nature and from its definition—diffusive of itself and of being. Doesn't it fol-

---

[34] 'Dionysius', or Pseudo-Dionysius, is the otherwise unidentified author of four Christian Neoplatonist treatises and ten letters dating from the sixth century. These works had special authority during the Middle Ages, when they were thought to have been written by the Athenian Dionysius mentioned in Acts 17: 34 as having been converted by St Paul's sermon on Mars Hill. On the history of this principle see esp. Peghaire 1932 and Kremer 1965.

[35] See the list in Peghaire 1932: 19* nn. 45 and 46, and scattered references in subsequent notes in that article.

[36] See also e.g. QDP 3.15, objs. 1, 5, 12, and 14 along with Aquinas's rejoinders.

low that the volition to create is a consequence not of God's free choice but of God's very nature?

As more pointed evidence that it does follow, consider, finally, this passage, in which Aquinas *is* discussing God's willing the existence of things other than himself: '[E]very agent, to the extent to which it is in actuality and perfect, produces something like itself. That is why this, too, pertains to the essential nature of will—that the good that anyone has he shares with others as much as possible. Moreover, it pertains above all to the divine will, from which every perfection is derived in virtue of a kind of likeness' (ST Ia.19.2c).

If I'm right about Aquinas's natural theology's committing him to a necessitarian explanation of God's willing of things other than himself, then we haven't yet found good grounds for attributing to God free choice and the full-fledged personhood that is to some extent dependent on free choice. But I think such grounds are available in his system, and that he sometimes comes very close to putting them forward in just the way I think would be appropriate: 'Speaking absolutely, God of course does not will things [other than himself] necessarily . . . because his goodness has no need of things that stand in an ordered relationship to it *except* for purposes of manifestation, which can be carried out appropriately in various ways.[37] *And so there remains for him a free choice for willing this one or that one*, just as in our own case' (QDV 24.3c). Goodness does require *something* other than itself as a manifestation of itself. God therefore necessarily (though with the freedom associated with *counterfactual* choice) wills the being of *something* other than himself. And the free choice in God's will is confined to the selection of which possibilities to actualize for purposes of manifestation. As I see it, then, God's will is necessitated as regards *whether* to create, but fully free as regards *what* to create.

[37] There is a textual difficulty at this point. See Kretzmann 1991a: 222 n. 48, where I (reluctantly) adopted a different reading.

EIGHT

JOY, LOVE, AND LIBERALITY

1. Passions and attitudes

In Book I of SCG, once Aquinas has justified attributing intellect and will to reality's ultimate explanatory principle, he does not go on immediately to consider creating, sustaining, and governing, the acts of intellect and will in terms of which his ultimate explanation has to be developed. In the investigations of creation and providence that make up Books II and III, he does, of course, undertake to show in detail how those activities are to be ascribed to God. But first, to fill out Book I's account of God considered in himself, Aquinas adds a few more chapters in which he tries to show, primarily, what reason enables us to say about virtue in God (89–96) and about God's existence considered as life (97–102).

Broadly speaking, it isn't hard to see why a mode of existence characterized essentially by intellective and volitional activity should be understood as life, even though not in the biological sense. For my present purposes, that broadly spoken observation is enough;[1] I won't have more to say now about attributing life to God. The consideration of what can be inferred about God's moral character is more challenging. It is also more obviously essential to natural theology's account of God's nature to take up moral character at this point in SCG, after the arguments for divine intellect and will, and before the thorough investigation of those acts of God's intellect and will that bring about and affect other beings.

We know by now that Aquinas's attributions of divine virtues will have to be developed as extrapolations from his understanding of their human counterparts, like all the other attributions justified

---

[1] Aquinas begins his consideration of the divine attribute of life by making just that observation: 'Now from things that have already been shown we have, necessarily, the result that God is living. For it has been shown that God is intellective and volitional [I.44 and 72], but intellective and volitional activity belongs only to what is living; therefore, God is living' (97.811–12).

by his relational method. Still, the first move he makes on his way toward considering virtue in God may seem to result from his paying too much attention to the human model. For although Aquinas's account of *human* virtues is, naturally, founded on his account of the passions which reason controls by means of those virtues,[2] even sympathetic readers are likely to think that he needn't have approached *divine* virtue by way of a full chapter (I.89) devoted to discussing in detail the possibility of passions in God, especially when the explicit outcome of the chapter is entirely negative, as we're sure it would have to be.

The general grounds on which he dismisses the possibility of divine passions are so obvious that he could have left it as an exercise for the reader to come up with them. There can be no passions of any sort in *God* because, for instance, passions are associated with the *sensory* part of the human soul (89.736), and they involve *bodily changes* (89.737). Of course, any one such consideration settles the matter. None the less, as if the five general grounds he offers might not have been enough, he goes on to examine various *specific* passions, because, he observes, 'some passions are denied of God *not only* on the basis of the genus of passions *but also* on the basis of their species' (89.742). Grief (*dolor*), for instance, must be denied of God not just generally, because it is a passion, but also specifically, because grief is specified as involving something bad's having happened to the one who has that passion (ibid.).

This is overkill; but overkill isn't all that his detailed treatment of the passions here achieves. Even though every explicit conclusion is negative and unsurprising, two other features of the chapter make important contributions to the positive portrayal of God, especially in connection with the person-specifying attitudes and relationships I discussed briefly at the beginning of Chapter Seven.

The first of those two features is only hinted at in I.89, but the hint is spelled out in the very next chapter, as we'll see. In setting the stage for specifically denying various passions to God, Aquinas claims that the defining character (*ratio*) of any passion gets specified on the basis of (O) its object—some thing, event, or state of affairs the passion's subject considers to be in some respect either

---

[2] See e.g. the account of the virtues in ST IaIIae.49–70, founded on and immediately preceded by the account of the passions in 22–48.

good or bad—and (R) (the subject's perception of) the relationship between the passion's subject and its object. So, for instance, the defining character of grief gets spelled out more precisely in terms of (O) some thing, event, or state of affairs the subject takes to be in some respect bad and (R) the subject's present possession of, awareness of, or involvement in (O).[3] It isn't hard to anticipate how, on this sort of basis, Aquinas rejects specifically the possibility of divine sadness, desire, fear, remorse, envy, and anger.[4]

But the most interesting development in his consideration of specific passions occurs in connection with his rejecting the possibility of divine hope (*spes*) (743). He specifies hope in terms of (O) some thing, event, or state of affairs which the subject takes to be in some respect good, and (R) the subject's not having already attained that good but conceiving of its attainment as desirable.[5] For Aquinas's purposes in this chapter the crucial aspect of hope is (R), 'which, of course, cannot be suited to God' because the subject's state as stipulated in (R) couldn't be the state of a perfect being. But it's *only* on the basis of (R) that hope can't specifically be attributed to God. There's nothing in (O), the description of hope's object, that's incompatible with God's nature as argued for so far. It's also only on the basis of (R) that hope differs from joy (*gaudium*), as Aquinas remarks (743); for in specifically dismissing the possibility of divine sadness or grief he contrasts them with joy, about which he says that its 'object is something good that is present and possessed' (742). In other words, joy is specified in terms of (O) some thing, event, or state of affairs the subject takes

---

[3] I'm distinguishing the components of this basis as (O) the object and (R) the perceived relationship because that seems to be what Aquinas intends, although his way of putting it in this chapter isn't quite so clear. In 89.742 he says that 'every passion gets its species from its object', and identifies the object of sadness (*tristia*) or of grief as 'something bad that is already closely associated' (*malum iam inhaerens*) with the subject, where 'something bad' picks out what I'm distinguishing as (O), and 'already closely associated' with the subject picks out (R). Then in the next section (743) he introduces (R) expressly, first describing it as an aspect of (O), stipulating that 'the defining character of a passion's object (*ratio obiecti alicuius passionis*) is drawn not only from what is good and what is bad, but also from someone's being related in some way toward the one or the other of them'. But he goes on almost at once to describe (R) as 'the very way in which one is related to *the object*'. So it's tempting to think that *obiecti* should be deleted from the phrase quoted just above, changing the claim to one that is simply about the defining character of *a passion*.

[4] As he does in 89.742–7, specifically rejecting one of those passions in each of those sections.

[5] The specification is a bit terse: *Spes autem, quamvis habeat obiectum bonum, non tamen bonum iam obtentum, sed obtinendum.*

to be in some respect good and (R) that good's being present to and possessed by the subject. So in the defining characteristic of the passion of joy there's nothing at all that provides a basis for specifically rejecting its attribution to God. Of all the passions considered in the chapter, only joy is rejected (tacitly) on general grounds alone. And that's the first of the two important features of this chapter I was alluding to.

The second of those features is an explicit claim rather than a hint, but the details of the claim aren't immediately clear. It occurs in the opening sentences of Aquinas's rejection of divine passions on general grounds, where we would expect him to be talking simply about passions (*passiones*), but where in fact he seems to be relying on some unexplained classifications: 'Now on the basis of things that have already been laid down one can know that in God there are no passions associated with *affectus* (*passiones affectuum*). For there is no passion in connection with an *intellective affectio*, but only in connection with a *sensory* one ... Now there can be no *affectio* of that *latter* sort in God. ... Therefore, ... there is no *affectiva* passion in God' (89.735–6). What interests me most here is the claim that 'there is no passion in connection with an intellective *affectio*' and the implication that there may, therefore, be no barrier to attributing an intellective *affectio* to God.

But what are we to make of *affectio* and the words related to it in this passage, and, for that matter, in the remainder of the sections on the general rejection of passions?[6] To simplify the issue, I think we can safely assume that the adjective *affectiva* is associated equally well with the two nouns *affectio* and *affectus*, and that there is no significant difference here between those nouns (the latter of which occurs only once in the chapter). So we can focus exclusively on *affectio*. In ST Aquinas considers all these terms and more that are relevant to the topic, concluding that 'the passions of the soul are the same as *affectiones*. But *affectiones* obviously pertain to the appetitive and not to the cognitive (*apprehensivam*) part of the soul. Therefore, the passions, too, occur in the appetitive rather than the cognitive part' (IaIIae.22.2, sc).[7] The SCG passage we're

---

[6] Only his presentation of the fifth and last general ground (in 740) involves no use of *affectio* or related terms. No such terminology occurs at all in the specific rejections (742–8).

[7] Here's the beginning of the passage: 'But opposed to this [the thesis that passion occurs in the cognitive rather than the appetitive part of the soul] is what Augustine

looking at can be illuminated by this ST conclusion if we read the conclusion as claiming only *generic* sameness between passions and *affectiones*, and we can read it that way without obliterating its point. In that case there are *affectiones* belonging to the *sensory* appetite, and they are the passions; but there are also *affectiones* belonging to the *intellective* appetite—that is, *affectiones* belonging to the will—and they could not be passions.[8]

But what are *affectiones*? Earlier in SCG, in discussing God's knowledge of human thoughts and volitions, Aquinas draws a relevant distinction: 'thought (*cogitatio*) belongs to the soul in virtue of the soul's taking in some sort of form, while an *affectio* is a kind of inclination (*inclinatio*) of the soul toward something; for we call even the very inclination of a natural thing natural appetite' (68.572).[9] Inclinations, then, occur in appetite at every level—natural, sensory, and intellective—and those associated with souls are called *affectiones*, either sensory or intellective. Still, 'inclination',

says in *De civitate Dei* IX [4], that "the movements of the soul that the Greeks call *pathē* some of our writers, such as Cicero, call *perturbationes*, while others call them *affectiones* or *affectus*, and still others call them—more precisely (and closer to the Greek)—*passiones*". On this basis it is clear that . . .' (What follows immediately is the passage I just quoted in the body of the text.)

[8] When he states this claim in the SCG passage, Aquinas describes it as having been 'proved in *Physics* VII'. The Marietti editors identify the reference further as 3, 247a3–248a9; 247 [*sic*; presumably 248]a23–248b28, which, as they point out, Aquinas discusses in his commentary at L6.921–7. On the basis of a first inspection it seems to me that the topics discussed in those places, whether by Aristotle or by Aquinas, are relevant to this claim too broadly to illuminate it. Things Aquinas says more simply elsewhere are at least as helpful—e.g. 'passion properly so-called is found where there is bodily change. Of course, bodily change is found in acts of the sensory appetite—and not just spiritual [bodily change], as there is in connection with sensory apprehension, but even natural. However, no bodily change is required in connection with an act of the intellective appetite, because that sort of appetite is not a power of any organ' (ST IaIIae.22.3c). Even if we set aside Aquinas's Aristotelian doctrine of the organlessness of the rational soul, everyone could agree that the kinds of bodily change associated with emotion—blushing, heavy breathing, tears, and the like—are quite different from any changes in brain states that may be associated with volition.

[9] Given Aquinas's theory of natural appetite (discussed briefly in Ch. Seven), I suppose that by 'even the very inclination of a natural thing (*et ipsam inclinationem rei naturalis*)' here he could be taken as bringing the notion of inclination down to the most primitive, literally interpreted kind of case—e.g. understanding that a stick's inclining against a wall exhibits the stick's natural appetite for a lower location. Cf. ST IaIIae.26.1c: '[T]he very naturalness of a heavy body for the centre of the earth (*ad locum medium*) is a consequence of weight (*gravitatem*) and can be called natural love'; also 26.2c: 'And weight itself, which is the source of [a body's] movement toward the location that is natural [for it] on account of [its] weight, can, in a certain sense, be called natural love.'

more especially 'inclination *toward* something', is too narrow for *affectio* where it must apply to fear as well as to hope, to grief as well as to joy. So I propose interpreting *affectiones* here as *attitudes*. Positive and negative attitudes are, of course, prominent features of our inner life, and we can readily recognize some of them as features of our lower appetite and others as characterizing our higher appetite—liking liquorice and hating hypocrisy.

The translation of the SCG passage in question can then be completed in this way: 'in God there are no *passions* associated with attitudes. For there is no passion in connection with an *intellective* attitude, but only in connection with a *sensory* one . . . Now there can be no attitude of that *latter* sort in God. . . . Therefore, . . . there is no attitudinal *passion* in God.' So, if we find in ourselves *intellective* attitudes corresponding to some or all of our passions, we have not been shown any *general* grounds that would prevent us from attributing such attitudes to God. And if there aren't any *special* grounds of that sort either, as there aren't in the case of joy, then we seem to have a prima-facie case for taking seriously the possibility that there is, for example, joy in God. And if the having of intellective attitudes is simply a corollary of the having of intellect and will, then Aquinas's relational method mandates attributing joy to God.

2. Intellective attitudes

Before looking directly at that possibility, I want to consider very briefly the general notion of intellective attitudes. If we consider just the examples Aquinas uses in I.89, we can in every case usefully and easily distinguish between an attitude of the sensory appetite— for example, an emotional reaction—and a rational attitude, *each* of which deserves and ordinarily gets the name 'fear', say, or 'anger'. Just imagine the difference between the fear of a house fire you'd feel if you woke up smelling smoke and the fear of a house fire that leads you to install a smoke alarm, or the difference between the anger you'd feel at being slapped in the face and the anger that leads you to vote against the party in power. I think all Aquinas's examples of passions have recognizable rational, un- emotional parallels, and I think he thinks so too: 'everything we long for by nature we can long for also in connection with the pleasure associated with reason, though not vice versa' (ST IaIIae.31.3c);[10] and 'just as a person avoids something bad in the future through the passion of fear, which occurs in the sensory appetite, so the intellective appetite performs the same operation without passion' (90.750). In some such cases, extending the use of the passion's name to the corresponding rational attitude sounds odd, as Aquinas acknowledges.[11] All the same, these extensions do succeed; and the reason they succeed is, I think, that his examples are *attitudinal* passions, the basic analyses of which are developed in terms of (O) an object taken by a subject to be good, or bad, and (R) certain specific perceived relationships between that subject and that object.[12] For such an analysis to be suited particularly to an attitudinal *passion* would require the addition of a third component, describing the associated bodily changes that mark the attitude as an emotional state. As long as we deal with only the first two components, as Aquinas typically does, we're employing an analysis that applies equally to attitudes of the sensory and the intellective appetites. Given Aquinas's general theory of appetite, he's bound to locate both sensory and intellective attitudes in appetitive faculties. Because the object is always described in *evaluative* terms and the subject–object relationship typically involves some *disposition* of the subject in relation to the object, it might be helpful to think of both the sensory and the intellective varieties as evaluative, motivational attitudes—or, perhaps, just *motives*, lower and higher. My present concern, however, is only with such intellective attitudes as can or must be attributed to God—person-specifying divine attitudes, the emotionless divine counterparts of emotions.

3. *God's pleasure and joy*

And, as I.89 hinted, one of those is joy, the attribution of which Aquinas argues for in I.90, where he discusses it along with delight,

[10] He's concerned with 'the *pleasure* associated with reason (*delectatione rationis*)' here, because the issue in 31.3 is 'whether pleasure differs from joy'; but the observation regarding rational and sub-rational wants seems quite general.

[11] See e.g. ST IaIIae 22.3, ad 3, where he quotes Augustine on this sort of extended application of the names of the passions; also QDV 26.7, ad 5.

[12] There are, of course, non-attitudinal passions for which rational parallels are non-existent or very rare, and for many of them, naturally, we have no good Anglo-Saxon names—e.g. *Weltschmerz*, ennui, *Angst*, malaise.

or pleasure (*delectatio*), drawing this acute distinction between them: 'pleasure stems from a good that is really conjoined [with the one who is pleased], while joy does not require that. Instead, just the will's resting (*quietatio*) in the object of its volition is enough for the defining characteristic of joy. That's why pleasure, in the strict sense of the word, has to do only with a good conjoined [with the one who is pleased], while joy has to do [also] with a good detached (*exteriori*) [from the one who is enjoying it]' (90.754). If both joy and pleasure are attributed to God, then, it will be 'clear that, strictly speaking, God is pleased by himself but enjoys both himself and other things' (ibid.).[13]

Aquinas introduces joy and pleasure as 'passions that are not suited to God in so far as they are *passions*, although the defining character of their *species* entails nothing incompatible with divine perfection' (90.749).[14] I've mentioned some of the general grounds on which we can rule out attributing any passion to God: a passion occurs in the sensory appetite and involves bodily changes, while God must be immutable, incorporeal, and without any aspect corresponding to the human sensory soul.[15] So, as we've seen, the first step in applying Aquinas's relational method to justify the analogical, non-metaphorical use of the name of a passion in talking about God must be to identify in human beings some corresponding attitude in the *intellective* appetite, or will; 'for cognized good and bad are an object of the intellective as they are of the sensory appetite' (90.750).[16]

Well, can we recognize in ourselves a state reasonably described as 'the will's resting in the object of its volition', a state that might plausibly be characterized as intellective joy? In keeping with my discussion of what I've been calling static volition—that is, our

---

[13] Aquinas's distinction between *gaudium* and *delectatio* seems not to be reflected precisely in our ordinary use of the words 'joy' and 'pleasure'; but if we were challenged to distinguish between them, I think we might very well do so along this same line.

[14] Later, in ST, Aquinas identifies joy as the species of pleasure 'that is consequent on reason', explaining that 'that is why not "joy" but only "pleasure" is applied to non-human animals' (IaIIae.31.3c), and identifying joy as 'the pleasure associated with the *intellective* appetite' (31.4c). If he were taking that line here, he would not be treating pleasure and joy as divine attributes on a par with each other.

[15] See 89.736, 737, and 738, where each of these three general grounds is presented.

[16] Aquinas of course recognizes that Scripture often uses names of passions in talking about God, and he discusses the metaphorical character of those ascriptions in 91.766–7.

willing (usually dispositionally) what we already have or even are—it seems to me that 'joy' is a perfectly appropriate designation for the set of one's will toward something intellectively cognized as good and as present to oneself, whether or not that object is 'really conjoined' with oneself. 'Intellective joy' is an appropriate (if unattractive) name for the attitude that is bound to characterize anyone lucky enough to be in those circumstances.

As for identifying that attitude in God, we can begin by observing that God is, of course, 'supremely at peace (*maxime contentatur*) with himself, the principal object of his will [I.74], as having every sort of sufficiency in himself. Therefore, through his will he enjoys and is pleased by himself supremely' (90.751).[17] We can add a little detail to this picture of necessitated divine self-satisfaction by considering the intellectively cognized goods with which a human being is most intimately associated, those that are *immediately* available to us as objects of pleasure and joy. Aquinas's paradigms of such goods are the very activities of the sensory and rational parts of the soul, all of which activities are themselves objects of intellective cognition. Some of those activities, he observes, are, considered just as such, 'actualizings (*actus*) or perfectings of the one whose activities they are: I mean intellective activity, sensing, willing, and the like. . . . In that way, then, those actions of the sensory and intellective soul are themselves a good for the one whose activities they are, and they are also cognized, through sense [some of them] or intellect [all of them]' (IaIIae.31.5c). And, of course, one also cognizes them especially clearly as a good that is 'really conjoined' with oneself. 'That's why pleasure arises also from those actions themselves and not only from their objects' (ibid.).[18] 'But God has the supremely perfect activity in [his] intellecting [I.45] . . . Therefore, if *our* intellective activity is pleasant because of the perfecting of *it*, the divine intel-

---

[17] See also SCG I.102.843.

[18] Aquinas's description here of one's intellective attitude toward aspects of one's inner life strikes me as providing a good picture of the state of appetitive rest I spoke of in Ch. Seven, where I observed that volition in us isn't always directed toward the acquiring or achieving of something we don't already have. You couldn't exist as a person without the sort of inner life that is essential to personhood. Nor is this anything you could acquire or achieve. And yet the inner life that is essential to you, that isn't even clearly distinguishable from you, is, of course, something you *want*. This static sort of appetite, the wanting of what one already has or is, is what Aquinas identifies as appetitive rest, which is not to be confused with the cessation of appetite.

lective activity will be supremely pleasurable to him' (90.752).[19] We can, then, most reliably reason to, and most readily appreciate, the nature of God's contentment, his being supremely pleased by or at peace with himself, if we focus on his supremely perfect intellective activity as the aspect of himself that is the proper object of his intellective pleasure.

But considering only the intellective attitudes corresponding to passions and identifying appropriate objects of those attitudes doesn't yet give us a full warrant for attributing pleasure or joy to God. Some of the general grounds for rejecting divine attributes of that sort are circumvented by making those moves, but no such ground is more fundamental than the simple observation that nothing properly describable as *passion*—or simply *passive*, as even an intellective attitude might conceivably be described—is compatible with the divine essence that has already been shown to be *actus purus* (I.16). God 'is, therefore, *active only* (*agens tantum*), and in *no* way does passion have any place in him' (89.740). If divine pleasure or joy is thinkable, then, it must be identified with not merely an intellective attitude or set of will but with some recognizable *act* of will essentially associated with that attitude. Is the name 'joy' properly attached to some human act of will that can serve as the bridgehead from which to extend the use of that name to an *activity* that must be associated with the will of God?

Aquinas certainly thinks so: 'in connection with the intellective appetite, which is will, we find activities that are like activities of the sensory appetite as regards the defining character of their species, [but] different [from them] in this, that in connection with the sensory appetite they are passions because they are conjoined with a bodily organ [that passively undergoes change], while in connection with the intellective appetite they are *simple activities*' (90.750). More precisely, 'the pleasure associated with the sensory appetite occurs along with a bodily change, while the pleasure associated with the intellective appetite is *nothing other than a simple movement of will*' (ST IaIIae.31.4c). In my view, the only simple act of will that fills the bill which Aquinas draws up here for intellective pleasure is what I've been calling static volition—actively willing the continued being and the continued presence of

[19] See also In EN VII: L14.1533: '[T]o each nature its own proper activity is pleasant, since it is the perfecting of that nature—which is why reason's activity is pleasant for a human being.'

the intellectively cognized good that is now conjoined with the willer. In human willers, as I've been saying, such static volition is of course often dispositional, but so close to the surface that it takes no more than a question to bring it into consciousness, to make it an occurrent simple act of will.[20] However, in God understood as *actus purus* such static volition would of course have to be eternally *occurrent*.[21]

But can we confidently identify as *pleasure* or *joy* the simple act of willing the continuing presence of a good state of affairs—even a *superlatively* good state of affairs? What about satiety? What about boredom? In dealing with worries of that sort, Aquinas would draw on Aristotle.

[F]or a human being, nothing [that remains] the same is pleasant *always*. And Aristotle says that the reason for this is that our nature is not simple but composite and, in so far as it is subject to corruption, changeable from one thing to another.... And he says that if the nature of any thing that takes pleasure were simple and immutable, one and the same activity would be most pleasant for it. For instance, if a human being were intellect *alone*, it *would* take pleasure in contemplation *always*. And it is because God is simple and immutable that he is characterized by joy (*gaudet*) with a single, simple pleasure *always*—the pleasure he has in contemplating himself.... And pleasure that is devoid of movement is greater than pleasure that occurs in connection with movement, for what is in motion is in a state of becoming, while what is at rest is in fully actualized being. (In EN VII: L14.1534–5)[22]

---

[20] Appropriate activating questions would, naturally, sound a bit stupid: e.g. 'Do you recognize your activities of perceiving and thinking as good to have?'; 'Are you pleased that you're a rational animal?'

[21] See also ST IaIIae.22.3, ad 3: '[W]hen love and joy and other [attitudes] of that sort are attributed to God and the angels, or to human beings in connection with intellective appetite, they signify a simple act of will together with a likeness of effect, without passion.' And see SCG II.1.854, where enjoying and loving are two of the four paradigms of God's immanent activity, along with acting intellectively and willing.

[22] See also In EN VII: L.14.1536. And see esp. ST IaIIae.31.5c, where part of Aquinas's basis for ranking intellective over sensory pleasures is the essential imperfection, or *incompleteness*, of the latter. An element of one's pleasure is one's being conjoined with what one cognizes as good, and in intellective pleasure that conjunction 'is more complete, because movement, which is an uncompleted actualization, is a feature of the conjoining of something sense-perceptible with one's senses. That's why sensory pleasures are not entirely present at once (*totae simul*). Instead, in connection with them something passes away and one anticipates something [else] for consummation, as is clear in connection with the pleasure of food and of

On this basis it seems clear how pleasure and joy are to be attributed to God in that 'God is pleased by himself' and 'enjoys . . . himself' (90.754). The attribution of such reflexive pleasure and joy really is a corollary of our consideration of will in God: the eternal act of static volition that is eternal pleasure and joy in oneself must belong to the appetitive aspect of absolutely perfect being. But Aquinas's chapter on pleasure and joy concludes by claiming that God 'enjoys *both* himself *and* other things' (90.754). In what way and to what extent are *other* things part of the object of God's joy?

Every being capable of joy 'naturally rejoices in what is *like* it, as in something that is *suited* to it (*quasi in convenienti*)—except *per accidens*, in so far as what is like it may interfere with its own advantage, as "potters quarrel among themselves" [*Nicomachean Ethics* VIII 2, 1155a35[23]] because one of them interferes with another's making money. But *every* good is a likeness of the divine goodness [I.40] . . ., and God loses nothing for himself as a consequence of *any* good. We are, therefore, left with the conclusion that God rejoices over *every* good' (90.753).[24] The *otherness* of other things, then, contributes nothing at all to their status as objects of God's joy. His enjoyment of creatures is, inevitably, his enjoyment in them of manifold, partial manifestations of the perfect goodness that is the more precisely described object of his enjoyment of himself. This account of divine joy could disappoint creatures hoping for a God who might enjoy them for themselves, just as they are. Still, it's only this sort of account that strikes me as having any claim on plausibility. It provides a picture of divine joy over creatures that resembles, I think, the joy the finest concert pianist might take in a beginner's getting something right—joy like a sparking arc of recognition, the joy that is your seeing in someone else even just a glimmer of the kind of goodness you know best in yourself, and your willing that that glimmering goodness continue to be, and that that likeness grow stronger.

sex. Intelligible things, on the other hand, are devoid of movement, which is why intelligible pleasures are entirely present at once.'

[23] The Leonine editors cite *Rhetoric* II 10, 1388a16. This correction is offered in Gauthier 1961: 51–2. Aquinas is conflating the two passages.

[24] See also SCG I.102.849: 'God has unsurpassable pleasure in himself and universal joy regarding all goods, without any taint of the contrary.'

4. God's love

Aquinas's natural theology succeeds only if its arguments for and investigations of the nature of first being turn up attributes that identify it as God. A crucial component of that identification is a set of attributes that establish personhood. In Chapters Six and Seven I claimed that the attributes of intellect and will are sufficient conditions of personhood. Still, their sufficiency is easier to appreciate when we're shown that certain personifying attitudes, such as pleasure and joy, are corollaries of perfect intellect and will. Personifying relationships would be more illuminating in that way than attitudes are, and so divine love would be more valuable than pleasure and joy for bringing out the personhood entailed by divine intellect and will. In fact, love for other persons is arguably the traditional divine attribute that is, even theoretically, most significant from a human point of view, because it would most fully reveal God as a person. And we needn't pretend that we have only a theoretical interest in seeking a rational basis for claiming that the ultimate principle of reality is not oblivious or indifferent to us, but knows us fully and loves us, even so.

We caught a glimpse of love as a corollary of will in Chapter Seven, where I claimed that since there can't be unactualized potentialities or non-occurrent dispositions in absolutely perfect, atemporal God, the divine static volition that has as its proper object perfect goodness, identical with God himself, must manifest itself in God's eternal love of himself and joy in himself. We've just seen Aquinas's derivation of joy as a corollary of God's nature. Earlier in SCG he offers this derivation of divine love: 'All things, in so far as they are, are assimilated to God, who is being, primarily and maximally. But all things, to the extent to which they are, naturally love their own being, each in its own way. Far more, therefore, does God naturally love his being. Now his nature is *per se necesse esse* (as was proved above [I.22]).[25] God, therefore, necessarily wills that he be' (80.680), and, we're now in a position to add, delights in the necessarily perfect fulfilment of that volition.

But the meagre, metaphysical self-love derived in that passage

---

[25] The Marietti editors supply a reference to 15.124, where this formulation is introduced in argument G6 (see Ch. Three). However, the identification of God's nature with *per se* necessary being is argued for not in I.15 but in I.22, esp. 22.205 (see Ch. Four).

does nothing even to enhance our understanding of divine personhood, let alone contribute to the concept of a loving God. In fact, since Aquinas here infers this divine self-love from the utterly universal ontological thesis that '*all* things, to the extent to which they are, naturally love their own being, each in its own way', the only love that's been attributed to God so far isn't even a personifying attitude, much less an interpersonal relationship of the sort that would illuminate the personhood established by the attribution of intellect and will and that would interest human beings most in connection with attributing personhood to first being. However, that short derivation is by no means all we have to go on. As soon as Aquinas has argued for pleasure and joy in God, he devotes a full chapter to God's love (I.91).

Now of course Aquinas recognizes the occurrence of love as a passion in human beings. He even argues for love's primacy among all the passions in one important respect.[26] But because his SCG chapter on God's love occurs just after he's developed his account of intellective counterparts of passions, he can and does avoid even mentioning love as a passion here. He begins by simply declaring that active divine love is a corollary of intellective appetite in God: 'in God there must likewise also be love, in accordance with the act of his will' (91.755)[27]—a declaration in which the words 'likewise also' smooth the way for the attribution of love by indicating that it's to be patterned on the immediately preceding attribution of pleasure and joy.

But the argument for divine love that is most like the arguments for pleasure and joy is also the least helpful one in the chapter, because its weak conclusion, that 'love is not incompatible with

[26] See e.g. ST Ia.20.1: 'Love, however, is oriented toward the good in general, whether it is possessed or not possessed, and so love is naturally the first act of will and of appetite [generally]. And for that reason all other appetitive movements presuppose love as their first root. For no one *desires* anything other than a loved good, nor does anyone *rejoice* over anything other than a loved good. *Hate*, too, is directed only toward that which is opposed to a loved good, and it is obvious that *sadness*, likewise, and others of that sort are traced back to love as to their first source. Thus in anything in which there is will or appetite [generally] there must be love; for if the first is removed, the others are removed.' Also ST IaIIae.25.2, 27.4; In DDN IV: L9.401; and SCG IV.19.3559.

[27] See also ST Ia.20.1, ad 1: '[L]ove, joy, and pleasure are passions in so far as they signify acts of the sensory appetite but not in so far as they signify acts of the intellective appetite. And it is in that way that they are posited in God. . . . [H]e loves without passion.'

divine perfection as regards the defining characteristic of its species' (91.759), is founded on oversimplified accounts of (R) the
relationship between love's object and the one who loves it and,
especially, of (O) love's object, which is identified in this argument
simply as what is good.[28] The argument's weak conclusion doesn't
really need more support than those oversimplifications provide,
but they leave out a formal feature of love that distinguishes it in
Aquinas's view from all other attitudes. Later in that same chapter
he points out that 'it is essential to know that although the soul's
other activities are concerned with only one object, love alone is
evidently directed (*ferri*) to *two* objects. For we must be related in
some way to some object in virtue of intellectively cognizing, or
enjoying[, for example]. Love, on the other hand, wills [O$_1$] something *for* [O$_2$] someone. For we are said [strictly speaking] to *love*
[O$_2$] that *for* which we will [O$_1$] some good . . . That's why, speaking
simply and strictly, we are said to *desire* (*desiderare*) the things we
long for (*concupiscimus*), but to *love* not them but rather ourselves,
for whose sake we long for those things. And for that reason those
things are said to be loved [by us] *per accidens* and not strictly
speaking' (91.763).[29] (Since this double-object analysis of human
love is carried out in terms of volitions, and since it's undertaken in
connection with attributing love to God, we may suppose that it's
intellective love that's being analysed, whether or not the analysis
is intended to apply as well to the love that is a passion.[30])

---

[28] 'Love considered in respect of its object does not entail anything incompatible
with God, since [love] is for what is good (*cum sit boni*). Nor [does it entail anything
incompatible with God] considered in respect of the way it is related to its object; for
the love of any thing when it is possessed is not less but more, since our affinity for
any good is enhanced when we possess it (*quia bonum aliquod fit nobis affinius cum
habetur*).' On this basis it's hard to see how divine love differs specifically from
divine pleasure or joy. (The part of the argument I'm omitting here doesn't help in
that respect.)

[29] Accounts of love's double object appear also before 759's oversimplified account—viz. in 756, 757, and 758—though they are less fully developed than the one
in 763. I think it's clear that the double-object analysis of love isn't meant to extend
all the way down to the sub-cognitive 'natural love' Aquinas sometimes recognizes;
see e.g. n. 9 above.

[30] Aquinas sometimes recognizes a technical distinction between *amor* and
dilectio, associating the latter specifically with *intellective* love—e.g. 'The supreme
appetite, however, is the one that occurs together with cognition and free choice
(*libera electione*), for that appetite [the will] somehow moves itself. And so the love
(*amor*) associated with it is also the most perfect and is called *dilectio*, in so far as
what is to be loved [with that love] is picked out by free choice' (In DDN IV:
L9.402). The etymological connection between *electio* and *dilectio* that Aquinas

The two objects of love are (O₁) *direct*—the good that is willed—and (O₂) *indirect*—the one for whom that good is willed. Only (O₂), love's indirect object, is ever loved strictly speaking, or *per se*, or for its own sake; (O₁), the direct object, is always loved only *per accidens*.[31] Furthermore, in any case of loving it's only what might be called the *terminating* (O₂) object that is loved for its own sake. Someone whose good a person wills is, considered just as such, an (O₂) object of that person's love, but he or she may not be its *only* (O₂) object: 'Someone whose good a person wills only in so far as it contributes to *another's* good is loved *per accidens*—just as a person who wills that wine be kept safe so that he may drink it, or that a human being be kept safe so that he or she may be of use or pleasure to him, loves the wine or the human being *per accidens* but himself *per se*' (91.757). And so '*true* love requires willing someone's good in so far as it is *that* person's good' (ibid.), in which case that person is the love's terminating (O₂) object.

As an analysis of intellective love of others, this is promising, but drastically incomplete. All that's been accomplished so far could stand as a full analysis only of *benevolence*, and of course benevolence isn't all there is to love, even to intellective love. Aquinas's terminology can occasionally suggest that he might think otherwise, as when he says that the love one has for another person whose good one wills 'is called by many the love that belongs to benevolence, or to friendship' (In DDN IV: L9.404). Friendship, however, involves more than benevolence as ordinarily understood, and the more it involves is *uni*volence. Aquinas of course recognizes this: 'friendship consists in sharing . . . But friends share themselves with each other most of all in intimacy (*convictu*), which is why living together seems especially appropriate and pleasurable in friendship' (In EN IX: L14.1946);[32] and 'to spend time together with (*simul conversari ad*) one's friend seems to be especially ap-

---

hints at isn't imaginary, though it's hard to believe it has much influence over the meaning of *dilectio*, which in this special sense seems close to the meaning of 'esteem'. In my discussion of the divine attribute I will use just the term 'love', as Aquinas uses just *amor*. For a fuller discussion of the technical differences among the four terms *amor*, *dilectio*, *amicitia*, and *caritas*, see ST IaIIae.26.3.

[31] Cf. ST IaIIae.26.4c: '[T]he love with which a thing is loved so that there may be what is good for it is love unconditionally (*simpliciter*), while the love with which something is loved so that it may be something else's good is love in a certain respect only.'

[32] Cf. *Nicomachean Ethics* IX 12, 1171b29–1172a1.

propriate to friendship' (SCG IV.22.3585).[33] These forms of togetherness that characterize friendship also occur among the *practicable* forms of the all-consuming union that passionate love may seem to demand, especially at its kindling, about which Aquinas had to learn from a pagan: ' "Aristophanes said that lovers would desire that one thing should be made of the two of them", but "since that would result in one or both of them being destroyed", they seek a union that is feasible and acceptable (*convenit et decet*)—living together, talking together, and being joined together in other such ways' (ST IaIIae.28.1, ad 2).[34]

So it's a recognition of love's essential *magnetism* that's still missing from the account of true intellective love as the willing of someone's good in so far as it is that person's good. What's still missing is an account of univolence, of the subject's willing some sort of *union* with the person who is loved for his or her own sake. No intellective personal relationship that does not entail a volition for somehow being together with a person can count as love for that person. How does this essential univolence fit into Aquinas's attribution of love to God?

As an ingredient in the divine self-love we've considered so far, univolence could seem to be utterly redundant. One might even object to attributing love to God at all simply *because* 'Love is a uniting and binding force (*vis unitiva et concretiva*), as Dionysius says in *De divinis nominibus* IV [§15.180]. But that can have no place in God, since he is simple' (ST Ia.20.1, obj. 3). Applied to God's loving himself, that's not a formidable objection—as Aquinas's rejoinder to it shows: 'in loving oneself one wills what is good for oneself and so seeks to unite that good with oneself as far as one can. To that extent love is called a *uniting* force, even in God: but [uniting] in the absence of any compositeness, because the good he wills for himself—he who is good through his essence . . .—is nothing other than himself' (ad 3). In keeping with absolute simplicity, of course, there are in God no real but only conceptual distinctions among all the elements into which love has been analysed so far: its subject, its two objects, the subject's volition of what is good for the one who is the principal object, and the subject's volition of union with that one. God's volition of union

---

[33] See also 3586–7.

[34] Aquinas read about Aristophanes' insights in Aristotle's *Politics* II 1, 1262b11–16.

with himself is necessarily, eternally fulfilled in a real union, supremely perfect in its utter seamlessness. (As you may know or suspect, Aquinas's account of God's love of himself becomes an account of divine interpersonal love in his exploration of the doctrine of the Trinity;[35] but that has no place in this development of *natural* theology, where only created things are available as possible objects of God's interpersonal love.)

We're looking at Aquinas's rejoinder to an objection that is concerned with an apparent difficulty in the notion of a simple God's loving himself, a difficulty we've seen him handle with dispatch. But in that same rejoinder he goes on to address the much more interesting, difficult question of the nature of univolence in God's love for *others*. The human terms in which he begins to develop his answer here depend heavily on his analysis of self-love, which he understandably treats as basic to his account of interpersonal love: 'In loving someone *else*, on the other hand, one wills what is good for *that* person. In doing so, one treats that person as oneself, directing good to that person as to oneself. To that extent love is called a *binding* force, because one attaches the other person to oneself, relating oneself to that person as to oneself' (ad 3). Having applied the first half of the Dionysian unifying-and-binding formula in showing how the volition of union is compatible with God's simplicity, Aquinas now takes up the second half—binding—in a way intended to deepen our understanding of what's involved in willing someone else's good when that willing is a component of loving. It can't be left at the level of one's broadly, blandly wishing 'May all be well with you!' It must be one's *willing*, one's *individuated* willing, that everything be good for that other person *in just the way one wills that for oneself.*

But notice that as Aquinas presents it here the *binding* aspect of love is tantamount to, and already fully realized in, that full-fledged willing of the other person's good, informed by one's understanding and willing of one's own good. Love's binding is completely achieved as soon as just that volition is in place. By that very volition of yours you have bound to yourself the other person whose good you will in this way, but unilaterally, in a manner that may leave him or her totally unaware of the bond, and even of you. If this 'binding' captures any of the associative aspect of love we're

[35] See e.g. ST Ia.37.2.

looking for, it does so only conceptually or attitudinally. It certainly entails no sort of real uniting of the beloved with the lover. It doesn't even involve on the lover's part a *volition* of real union in addition to the volition of the loved one's good.[36]

None the less, this attitudinal binding is all Aquinas offers here by way of accommodating God's love of others to the Dionysian formula (which he plainly accepts as providing part of the correct analysis of love): 'And in that way even divine love is a *binding force* . . . in so far as he wills good things for others' (ad 3). Whatever this consideration may add to our understanding of what God's love for others might come to, it is, after all, obviously *not* identifying, or not *fully* identifying, its *associative* aspect. To the extent to which anything of that sort has shown up so far in the analysis of God's love, it's been confined to self-love's volition of purely reflexive union, which Aquinas handled easily in dealing with the worry about 'a unifying and binding force' in the componentless context of divine simplicity.

But Aquinas approaches the associative aspect of God's love more encouragingly in the chapter of SCG he devotes to the topic, when he takes as *primary* what appears to be God's volition of union with other things, and then uses that as the *basis* for one of his arguments for the thesis that God loves himself and other things.

---

[36] Sometimes Aquinas calls binding and uniting two sorts of uniting. See e.g. ST IaIIae.25.2, ad 2: 'There are two sorts of uniting of what is loved to the one who loves it. One is indeed *real*—I mean the one that involves being conjoined with the thing itself. And it is that sort of uniting that pertains to joy or pleasure, which *follows* desire [and which may or may not be achieved]. But the other is *attitudinal* (*affectiva*) uniting, which occurs in accordance with suitability (*aptitudinem*) or appropriateness (*proportionem*)—I mean that to the extent to which one thing has a suitability for and an inclination toward another, it already shares something of it. And in this way love *implies* uniting—a uniting that indeed *precedes* the movement of desire.' Also IaIIae.28.1c: 'The uniting of the one who loves to what is loved is of two sorts. One is indeed *in reality*—e.g. when what is loved is now present to the one who loves it. But the other is *attitudinal* (*secundum affectum*), a uniting that must, of course, be considered on the basis of a preceding cognition, since appetitive movement follows cognition. . . . Therefore, love brings about the first [real] uniting in the manner of an *efficient* cause. For it moves [the one who loves] to desire and to seek the presence of what is loved as of that which suits him and pertains to him. But it brings about the second [attitudinal] uniting in the manner of a *formal* cause, since love itself *is* such a uniting or connecting. Thus Augustine says in *De trinitate* VIII [10] that love is, so to speak, "a kind of life linking, or seeking to link, two together". His phrase "linking together" refers to the *attitudinal* union, without which there is no love, but his "seeking to link together" pertains to *real* union.'

As Dionysius says [*De divinis nominibus* IV §15.180], moving toward union is a feature of love (*amoris est ad unionem movere*). For the attitude (*affectus*) of the one who loves is in a way united to what is loved because of a likeness or suitability between the one who loves and what is loved. And so his appetite tends toward the perfecting of   5 the union, so that a union that has already been founded in attitude may be completed in activity. (That is why it is appropriate even for friends that they enjoy each other's presence, and intimacy, and talking together.) But God moves all other things toward union [with himself]. For in so far as he gives them being and other perfections he   10 unites them to himself in the way in which that is possible. Therefore, God loves both himself and other things. (91.760)

I'm less interested in assessing this argument as an argument than in using it as a source of insight into Aquinas's understanding of the associative force in God's love for others. It begins with a version of the first half of the Dionysian formula, expressed here in words that bring out the uni*fying* force of love especially graphically: '*moving toward* union is a feature of love' (lines 1–2).[37] Love entails the lover's moving toward union with the beloved because it begins in the lover's recognition of 'likeness or suitability' in the beloved. On the basis of the recognition that that relationship is an inchoate, attitudinal union with something good, even if it should be only a one-sided relationship at this stage, the lover's appetite naturally 'tends toward the perfecting of the union, so that a union that has already been founded in attitude may be completed in activity' (lines 5–7). So the route of love's movement toward real union is mapped in lines 2–6, and, as we had some reason to expect, love's *unifying* force begins with and develops through the attitude Aquinas identifies as love's *binding* force. The real union of friends, described in standard terms parenthetically in lines 7–9, seems clearly to be offered as an image of the real union God wills that the creatures he loves have with him—and, naturally, as a *faint* image: 'it is appropriate *even* for friends'. And when the argument proper resumes with the premiss in lines 9–10, in the setting provided by that image of real union, it seems to be accepting this strong account of the uniting force of love as fully applicable

---

[37] The formula as Aquinas read it in the medieval Latin translation of Dionysius (who attributes it to Hierotheus, *nobilis noster sanctitatis perfector*), reads this way: *Amorem, sive divinum sive angelicum sive intellectualem sive animalem sive naturalem dicamus, unitivam quamdam et concretivam intelligimus virtutem.*

to God's love universally: 'God moves all other things toward union [with himself].'

But then in lines 10–12 we're given the terms in which Aquinas evidently thinks the strong account has to be accepted in God's case, and what a falling off is there! How is God supposed to move all creatures toward union with himself? Apparently only 'in so far as he gives them being and other perfections' (line 10). *That* is supposed to be God's uniting creatures 'to himself in the way in which that is possible' (line 11). But, as depicted here, the way that is possible seems clearly to fall far short of achieving love's real union. We have evidence of its failure. If we consider just human creatures, and if we suppose for the sake of the argument that our being and other perfections are indeed given us by God as goods willed by him for persons he loves, it hardly needs to be pointed out that many or most of us don't see it that way. Aquinas's analysis of loving strikes me as insightful in distinguishing (ideally) (1) an incipient stage of attitudinal binding, (2) a development characterizable as movement toward union, and (3) a culmination in some form of real union. On that analysis, God's binding even conscious, rational creatures to himself certainly can go unnoticed by the creatures, especially since the binding that is a component of *God's* love seems tantamount simply to his choosing which possible created things to actualize. But if God's moving creatures toward loving *union* with himself is of such a sort that those creatures can remain totally oblivious of that process, too, then how does uniting differ from binding in the case of God's love for others? Is divine love's moving toward union, like love's binding generally, simply an attitude of the lover's which the beloved can be, and often is, ignorant of?

As presented in this argument, moving toward union does differ sharply from binding, in being not merely a choice or a volitional attitude but the actual giving of actual gifts—the creature's nature and existence—the gifts of creation.[38] When a volition of some

---

[38] Because creation is *ex nihilo*, there is a formal difficulty about considering a creature's being and specifying perfections as gifts given to it: 'To that which gets made, the maker gives being. Therefore, if God makes something *ex nihilo*, God gives being to something. Therefore, either there is something receiving being, or nothing. If nothing, then through that action *nothing* is established in being, and in that case it is not true that something gets made. But if there is something receiving being, it will be other than that which is God, since what receives and what is received are not the same. Therefore, God makes [whatever he makes] out of

creature's good in the form of its being and its specifying perfections is *God's* volition, it is perfectly efficacious. And the chosen recipient, wittingly or unwittingly, and willy-nilly, is thereby indeed *united* to God, *ontologically*. With just a little embroidery at this point we can bring out that real ontological union as particularly lively. For, as we've seen, Aquinas's analysis of love includes the lover's willing the beloved's continued being—just what constitutes God's unremitting, eternal activity as universal first sustainer.

Still, real ontological union, which even the rational creature can remain utterly ignorant of, is a long way from love's culminating real union, of which both participants must be fully aware, since, as Aquinas often observes, it involves mutuality, sharing, intimacy, and enjoyment. Furthermore, ontological union is achieved by God unilaterally and all at once in creating and sustaining, and so could never be thought of as a union *toward* which God *moves* creatures. How, then, can Aquinas settle here for what I'm calling ontological union, where he's out to support the conclusion that 'God loves ... other things', and to support it *on the basis of* God's moving other things toward union with himself?

He can settle for it because he has to—*and* because settling for it doesn't mean settling for anything less than true love, as long as it's remembered that true love can be love unfulfilled by real union: 'love *is not* that very relationship of union; instead, union is a *consequence* of love. That's why Dionysius says that love is a *uniting force*' rather than an achieved union (ST IaIIae.26.2, ad 2).[39] Divine love, too, can be love unfulfilled. Not even omnipotence can compel the willing participation of the beloved, and without it love's culminating union can't be achieved.[40] That's why it's onto-

---

something pre-existent, and so not out of nothing (*ex nihilo*)' (QDP 3.1, obj. 17). Aquinas's rejoinder: 'Simultaneously with giving being, God produces that which receives being. And so [in giving being] he need not act on (*ex*) something pre-existent' (ad 17).

[39] Aquinas cites Aristotle as well to this same effect here: 'and the Philosopher says, in *Politics* II [1, 1262b10], that union is a *product* (*opus*) of love'.

[40] This possibility, which appears to be realized often, may seem to make God dependent on beings other than himself. The first thing to notice in this connection is that God's absolute independence could not rule out *logical* dependence. For instance, being omniscient depends on knowing that 2 + 2 = 4, and so God considered as omniscient is logically dependent on knowing that 2 + 2 = 4. But the claim at issue here is that God's nature entails a loving relationship with other persons, and that not even omnipotence can guarantee another person's love for him. This sort of dependence can't be described as merely logical. Still, God's nature

logical union alone in which God unites creatures 'to himself *in the way in which that is possible*'. But the real giving of real gifts that constitutes God's unilateral establishment of ontological union does constitute the first movement toward the sort of real union of creatures with him that could count as the culmination of love's uniting force; and, of course, gifts can be received by their chosen recipients without being acknowledged, without even being recognized as gifts. Since these gifts given to creatures are their being and the perfections that specify them, it's clear that the establishment of ontological union is an indispensable pre-condition of achieving love's union with creatures.

In at least one remarkable passage Aquinas clearly identifies God's love itself as the source of the indispensable pre-condition and of further steps in God's moving others toward loving union with himself:[41]

God, who is 'the cause of all things because of the outpouring of his goodness, loves all things' [quoting Dionysius], and out of love he 'makes' all things, giving them being, and 'perfects' all things, filling out individuals with their proper perfections, and 'contains' all things, sustaining them in being, and 'turns' all things—that is, directs them toward himself as toward their end . . . This divine love, I say, 'did not permit him to remain in himself, without offspring'—that is, without the production of creatures. Instead, love 'moved him to activity' in accord with the best possible mode of activity, in so far as he produced all things in being. For the fact that he willed to diffuse and to share his goodness with others as far as that was possible—that is, by way of likeness—and that his goodness did not remain

entails only his fully loving others, and his loving them couldn't be in any way dependent on their loving him. Even among human beings, X's love for Y would be recognized as weak or defective if it depended on Y's loving X. What does and must depend on other persons' love for God is what might be described as the best outcome of the divine–human loving relationship. The best outcome, real union with God, is not independent of the human being's free choices; but a human being's union with God could not be an aspect of God's nature. God's love for other persons, which must be an aspect of his nature, is in no way dependent on any will but God's.

[41] This identification could be viewed as a mere corollary of Aquinas's thesis that the role of intellective love among acts of will parallels the role of the passion of love among the passions (see n. 26 above): 'although evidently several acts pertain to will, . . . love is found to be the single source and common root of them all. . . . And since it was shown in the First Book [of SCG] that God's activity is his very essence [I.45] and that God's essence is his will [I.75], it follows that in God there is no volition as potentiality or as disposition, but [only] as act. But it has been shown that every act of will is rooted in love. Therefore, there must be love in God' (SCG IV.19.3559 and 3563).

in himself alone but flowed out to other things, was an outgrowth of the love associated with his goodness. (In DDN IV: L9.409)[42]

As detailed in that account, the ontological union prompted by love and effected in the gift-giving that is the creating, sustaining, and directing of creatures includes all that divine love can achieve on its own to begin the process of moving a creature toward real loving union with God.[43] The next move is up to the beloved, at least when the beloved creature is endowed with freedom of choice.

What might the next move be? It seems to me that a rational creature's merely coming to recognize and understand the fact of that ontological union can provide an altogether natural prompting of creaturely love for the creator, in very much the way a child progresses from instinctual attachment to its mother (presumably with no clear conception of any difference between the two of them initially) to a reflective, intellective love of her that begins in the child's dawning recognition of her gifts to him. *Some* sort of union between child and mother to *some* degree is essential to the child— the human analogue of what I'm calling 'ontological union'. And normal instances of that union incorporate from the very beginning

---

[42] See also the endorsement of this line of thought in 91.765: 'Even some philosophers have claimed that God's love is the source of things [cf. In Met. I: L5.101]. Dionysius's remark agrees with this when he says that the divine love did not permit him to be without offspring'; also SCG IV.20.3570.

[43] The new ingredient here, in addition to creating and sustaining, is divine directing, introduced in Aquinas's claim that God ' "turns" all things—that is, directs them toward himself as toward their end'. Such directing, however it is supposed to be manifested in the lives of creatures, is clearly a crucial further step in moving creatures toward union with God, but I'm leaving it out of account here because it plays no part in Aquinas's presentation of God's love in SCG I.91. (Does he omit it because he sees no way of arguing for it within natural theology?)

See also In DDN IV: L12.460. Here Dionysius 'again gathers together love's two forces, mentioned above, into one first love—viz. the divine, with which God loves: "a single, simple force", which *per se* moves all the things God loves toward a unifying binding, proceeding from the first good, which is God. And by way of a kind of detour (*derivationis*) it comes "all the way to" the lowest of the number "of existing things", and [then] through a kind of turning around (*conversionem*) toward the end, coming back "again from that"—viz. from the last of existing things— "next", going up (*ascendens*) "through all things", it returns to the first good by way of a kind of circular movement, "turning itself back, and always returning in the same way", by proceeding from that first force and "through it". For all the secondary forces derive from the first through a kind of likeness and return to it by the same cause. For the likeness of the first force is found not only through causes but also through effects. And in this way love remains in that force always and, further, always returns to it as to its end.'

the mother's love of the child and behaviour on the mother's part that should, normally, lead to the child's mature loving of her. But, of course, she can't get that just by willing it, or guarantee the development of it by doing all the things that should, normally, prompt the full return of love and the mutuality that goes with it. For all God's surpassing of even mothers in power and ingenuity, divine love, too, must finally leave some of the movement toward the culminating real union up to the beloved.[44]

5. God's liberality

In summarizing the results of his investigations of the personifying divine attributes analogous to human intellective attitudes, Aquinas observes that everything in SCG I.89–91 should show us that 'of our attitudes, *none* can be in God strictly speaking *except* joy and love, although [of course] even they are not in him considered as passion, as they are in us' (91.763). So, applying the relational method to the vast array of human feelings and their rational counterparts has provided us with just those two additional divine attributes. But those two play special roles among human attitudes, as Aquinas observes, expressing himself in a way that suggests he's at least contemplating such roles for their divine analogues as well: 'love and joy, which are in God strictly speaking, are the principles of *all* attitudes—love in the manner of a *moving* principle, obviously, but joy in the manner of an *end*' (91.766).

And now that these very few, very significant divine attitudes have been identified and examined, in an investigation that parallels the investigation of the passions in human beings, Aquinas is ready to proceed with the theological parallel to a treatise on the virtues, the regular sequel to a treatise on the passions.

It seemed obvious that the concept of a passion couldn't be applied to God, and the concept of a virtue may seem almost as obviously inapplicable. To begin with what's most obvious, at least some of the human virtues that Aquinas recognizes consist in reason's control of *passions*—for example, the virtues of sobriety and chastity in particular, of temperance or continence more gener-

---

[44] With different aims in view I discussed love as a relationship between God and human beings earlier in Kretzmann 1991b.

ally.[45] No such virtues could characterize God. Again, there are no conceivable circumstances in which an omnipotent, omniscient being could appropriately be called courageous.[46]

But we don't have to consider the virtues one by one in order to see that they can't be converted into divine attributes. A virtue is, by definition, a *habitus*, a disposition to act in a certain way in certain circumstances; and a *habitus*, as Aquinas points out near the beginning of the first of his five chapters on divine virtues, 'is an unperfected activity, midway between a potentiality and its actualization, one might say . . . In God, however, there is [only] supremely perfect activity. In him, therefore, there is no activity having the status of a *habitus*—for instance, [no *habitus*] such as *knowledge*—but, rather, [only its actualization,] such as *considering*, which is the final, complete activity' with which that *habitus*, knowledge, is associated (92.770). Aquinas offers plenty of other grounds, general and particular, on which to reject the attribution of virtues to God, but this sampling is enough, I think, to show what any attempt to make such an attribution is up against.

And yet, the principle at the heart of the relational method is itself enough to show that, despite all such obstacles, there must be some respect in which virtues can, after all, be attributed to God. 'For just as God's being is universally perfect, in some way or other containing within itself the perfections of all beings [I.28], so also must his goodness in some way or other contain within itself the goodnesses of all things. Now a virtue is a goodness belonging to a virtuous person, for "it is in accordance with it that one is called good, and what one does is called good" [*Nicomachean Ethics* II 6, 1106a22–4]. Therefore, *in its own way* the divine goodness must contain all virtues' (92.768).[47] And we know by now how absolute simplicity will shape the unique way in which they must be contained. 'For *being* good is not suited to God through something else added to him but rather [only] through his essence, since he is altogether simple. Moreover, God does not *act* through anything added to his essence, since his acting *is* his essence (as has been

---

[45] See 92.777, where all four of these are rejected; also ST Ia.21.1, ad 1: 'Some moral virtues have to do with passions—e.g. temperance with longings, courage with fear and rash attitudes, mildness with anger. And virtues of that sort cannot be attributed to God except metaphorically.'

[46] Courage (*fortitudo*) is rejected in 92.775 and 778.

[47] See also an earlier sketch of this account in 37.304.

shown [I.45 and 73]). Therefore, his virtue is not some *habitus*, but rather his own essence' (92.769).

These considerations remove some obstacles to attributing virtues to God, but only the general obstacles, those that seemed to crop up in the theoretical account of the nature of virtues and in the natural-theological account of God's nature as developed so far. However, a specific virtue's essential association with human passions constitutes an irremovable obstacle, at least as regards non-metaphorical, direct attribution to God, and in I.92 Aquinas explicitly blocks the attribution of seven different virtues on that basis, indicating that those are only a sampling of human virtues that can't be attributed to God.[48] Virtues such as those, he concludes, are in God not as characterizing his nature but only as divine ideas—'as is the case regarding other corporeal things' besides the passions with which those virtues are linked (93.790).

But since the general obstacles in the way of non-metaphorically attributing virtues to God have now been removed, some such attributions can (and must) be made if there are any human virtues that don't present the specific obstacle of being essentially associated with passions. The 'contemplative' virtues, such as knowledge and wisdom, are clearly free of any such association, and Aquinas devotes a chapter (I.94) to establishing them as divine attributes. But it's moral virtues we're interested in, and, Aquinas observes, 'there are some virtues directing the active life of a human being that have to do not with passions but with actions—e.g. truthfulness, justice, liberality, magnificence, prudence, and art' (93.779).[49] 'Virtues of this sort', he says, 'are perfectings of will and of intellect, which are the sources of activities devoid of passion. But in God there is will and intellect lacking no perfection. Therefore [virtues of this sort] cannot be absent from God' (93.781). Aquinas argues briefly for each of these as a divine attribute (except magnificence), but for present purposes I'm interested only in liberality, the one to which he gives the most attention here.

Liberality can be loveless, and worthless: 'though I bestow all my goods to feed the poor . . . and have not love, it profiteth me noth-

---

[48] Temperance and courage (775); sobriety, chastity, temperance, and continence (777); courage, magnanimity, mildness, 'and other virtues of that sort' (778).

[49] See also ST Ia.21.1, ad 1: 'However, other moral virtues have to do with activities, such as giving and spending—e.g. justice, liberality, and magnificence—which are also not in the sensory part but in the will. And so nothing prevents our positing attributes of that sort in God.'

ing.' But love can't be illiberal. Liberality is the virtue most pertinent to the rest of the subject-matter of this chapter because, of all
the virtues under consideration here, liberality's the one that's
indispensable to love.[50] All intellective, volitional loving, but especially divine loving, motivates freely giving of one's own what is not
owed, and liberality is the virtue that gets expressed in the act of
freely giving of one's own what is not owed.[51] God 'wills to share his
goodness with something not because he might thereby gain some
advantage for himself but because sharing himself is suited to him
as the spring of goodness; and to give, not for any benefit expected
from the giving but for goodness itself and for the appropriateness
of giving (*convenientiam dationis*), is the act of liberality ... God,
therefore, is characterized by liberality in the highest degree'
(93.785).[52] Viewed against the background of our discussion of
love, these descriptions show that to give in that way is also one of
the acts of love, an act that is a component of 'moving toward
union', especially when, as in this case, the giving of one's own is a
giving of oneself. On at least one occasion Aquinas argues that, for
just such reasons, the virtue expressed by God's giving might be
identified less precisely as liberality than as 'charity, which is the
greatest of the virtues', because 'divine giving stems from the fact
that he loves human beings' (ST IIaIIae.117.6, ad 1). But liberality
is the virtue standardly associated with God's giving, with God as
'the distributor of the totality of all goods' (93.790), and especially
with what I called earlier the gifts of creation: 'God ... brought
things into being out of no indebtedness, but out of sheer liberality'
(SCG II.44.1217).

In Chapter Seven I argued for a necessitarian explanation of the
creation of something or other, based on the Dionysian principle,
which Aquinas accepts: goodness is by its very nature diffusive of
itself and (thereby) of being. Is that explanation compatible with
this attribution of liberality? I think so, because, as I said at the end

[50] And at least once, albeit in an objection, liberality is picked out as the virtue
through which 'a human being is most of all assimilated to God, "who gives to all
abundantly and does not reproach", as is said in James 1[: 5]' (ST IIaIIae.117.6,
obj.1). Aquinas's rejoinder (excerpted later in this paragraph) doesn't really dispute
this claim.
[51] On the connection of liberality with love, see also SCG III.128.3007.
[52] See also ST Ia.44.4, ad 1: God 'alone is characterized by liberality in the highest
degree, since he does not [ever] act for some advantage (*utilitatem*) of his own, but
only for his own goodness'.

of Chapter Seven, God's will is necessitated as regards *whether* to create, but fully free as regards *what* to create. The created things that do actually exist are, then, the freely chosen recipients of divine liberality, of the freely given, unowed manifestations of goodness that constitute the pre-condition of love's real union and the first move toward it. As we've seen Aquinas putting it when the Dionysian spirit is on him, 'out of love God "makes" all things, giving them being, and "perfects" all things, filling out individuals with their proper perfections, and "contains" all things, sustaining them in being, and "turns" all things—that is, directs them toward himself as toward their end' (In DDN IV: L9.409).

Anyone who knows the whole story can't help being disappointed at the pale thinness of natural theology's best account of God's loving and giving. Still, this account is not to be disdained. On the contrary, it is part of what should be reason's master-work. The fullness of God's loving and giving emblazoned in John 3: 16 is out of natural theology's reach, though it needn't be out of the natural theologian's mind.

APPENDIX I

A Chronology of Aquinas's Life and Works

(based mainly on Torrell 1993 and Tugwell 1988)

1224/5	Born at Roccasecca
1231–9	Benedictine oblate at Monte Cassino
1239, spring–summer	Home at Roccasecca
1239, autumn, to 1244, spring	Student at University of Naples Joins Dominicans at Naples (1244)
1244	Sent by Dominicans to Paris Abducted by his family *en route* to Paris, taken to Roccasecca (1244)
1244–5	Kept at home by mother, Theodora Attempted seduction (1245) Allowed to return to Dominicans in Naples (1245)
1245–8	At University of Paris; studies with Albert the Great Offered abbacy of Monte Cassino by Innocent IV (1248)
1248–52	At University of Cologne; studies with Albert Ordained priest at Cologne (1250/1) *De principiis naturae, ad fratrem Sylvestrum* (On the Principles of Nature, for Brother Sylvester) (Cologne, 1248–52, or Paris, 1252–6?) *Expositio super Isaiam ad litteram* (Literal Commentary on Isaiah) (Cologne, 1251/2) *Postilla super Ieremiam* (Commentary on Jeremiah) (Cologne, 1251/2) *Postilla super Threnos* (Commentary on Lamentations) (Cologne, 1251/2)
1252–3	*Cursor biblicus* at Paris

	Postilla super Psalmos (Commentary on Psalms; incomplete: 1–54) (Paris, 1252–3? or Naples, 1273?)
	De ente et essentia, ad fratres et socios suos (On Being and Essence, for his Brothers and Companions) (Paris, 1252–6)
1253–6, spring	*Sententiarius* at Paris
	Scriptum super libros Sententiarum (Commentary on the Sentences) (Paris, 1253–6)
1256, spring	Inception as master in theology at Paris
	Principia: 'Hic est liber mandatorum Dei' et 'Rigans montes de superioribus suis' (Inaugural Lectures: 'This is the Book of God's Commandments' and 'Watering the Hills from his Places Above') (Paris, 1256)
1256–9	Regent master in theology at Paris, occupying the second Dominican chair ('for foreigners') at the university
	Contra impugnantes Dei cultum et religionem (Against those who Assail the Worship of God and Religion (a refutation of William of Saint-Amour's *De periculis novissimorum temporum*)) (Paris, 1256)
	Quaestiones disputatae de veritate (Disputed Questions on Truth) (Paris, 1256–9)
	Quaestiones quodlibetales [VII–XI] (Quodlibetal Questions; Quodlibets VII–XI) (Paris, 1256–9)
	Expositio super librum Boethii De trinitate (Commentary on Boethius's *De trinitate*; incomplete) (Paris, 1257/8–9)
	Expositio super librum Boethii De hebdomadibus (Commentary on Boethius's *De hebdomadibus*; incomplete) (Paris, 1259?)
	Summa contra gentiles [through I.53] (Synopsis (of Christian Doctrine) Directed Against Unbelievers) (Paris, 1259)
1259, end of academic year	Leaves Paris for Naples
1260–1	In Naples, at priory of San Domenico (?), writing SCG
	Designated a preacher general in his province (1260)

Summa contra gentiles [from I.54] (Naples, 1260–1)

1261/2–5

In Orvieto, as lector at the Dominican priory

Contra errores Graecorum, ad Urbanem IV Pontificem Maximum (Against Mistakes of the Greek (Fathers of the Church), for Pope Urban IV (on an anonymous treatise *De fide sanctae trinitatis contra errores Graecorum*)) (Orvieto, 1263/4)

Summa contra gentiles [through Bk. IV] (Orvieto, 1261/2–5)

De rationibus fidei contra Saracenos, Graecos, et Armenos, ad cantorem Antiochiae (On Arguments for the Faith Directed against Mohammedans, Greek Orthodox Christians, and Armenians, for the Cantor of Antioch) (Orvieto, 1264)

Expositio super Iob ad litteram (Literal Commentary on Job) (Orvieto, 1261–5)

Glossa continua super Evangelia (Catena aurea) (A Continuous Gloss on the Four Gospels (The Golden Chain)) (Orvieto, Rome, 1262/3–8)

Officium de festo Corporis Christi, ad mandatum Urbanae Papae IV (Liturgy for the Feast of Corpus Christi, at the Command of Pope Urban IV) (Orvieto, 1264)

De emptione et venditione ad tempus (A Letter on Buying and Selling on Credit) (Orvieto, c.1262)

Expositio super primum et secundum Decretalem, ad Archidiaconum Tudertinum (A Letter Explaining the First and Second Decretals, to the Archdeacon of Todi) (Orvieto, 1261–5?)

De articulis fidei et Ecclesiae sacramentis, ad archiepiscopum Panormitanum (A Letter on the Articles of Faith and the Church's Sacraments, to the Archbishop of Palermo) (Orvieto, 1261–5?)

1265–8

In Rome, appointed to establish a studium for Dominicans at Santa Sabina and to serve as regent master there

Expositio super librum Dionysii De divinis nominibus (Commentary on Dionysius's *De divinis nominibus*) (Orvieto, 1261–5, or Rome, 1265–8?)

Quaestiones disputatae de potentia (Disputed Questions on Power) (Rome, 1265–6)

Quaestio disputata de anima (Disputed Question on the Soul (21 articles)) (Rome, 1265–6)

Responsio ad fr. Ioannem Vercellensem de articulis 108 sumptis ex opere Petri de Tarentasia (Reply to Brother John of Vercelli Regarding 108 Articles Drawn from the Work of Peter of Tarentaise (on the *Sentences*)) (Rome, 1265–7)

Compendium theologiae, ad fratrem Reginaldum socium suum (A Compendium of Theology, for Brother Reginald, his Companion; incomplete) (Rome, 1265–7)

De regno (or *De regimine principum*), *ad regem Cypri* (On Kingship (or: On the Governance of Rulers), for the King of Cyprus (authentic only through Bk. II, ch. 4)) (Rome, 1267)

Summa theologiae Ia (Synopsis of Theology, First Part) (Rome, 1266–8)

Sententia super De anima (Commentary on Aristotle's *De anima*) (Rome, 1267–8)

Quaestio disputata de spiritualibus creaturis (Disputed Question on Spiritual Creatures (Angels) (11 articles)) (Rome, 1267–8)

1268	Leaves Rome for Paris, assigned to occupy the second Dominican chair at the university again
1268, Sept., to 1272, Apr.	Second regency at Paris

Quaestiones disputatae de malo (Disputed Questions on Evil) (Rome, Paris, 1266–72)

Sententia super De sensu et sensato (Commentary on Aristotle's *De sensu et sensato*) (Rome, Paris, 1268–70)

Sententia super Physicam (Commentary on Aristotle's *Physics*) (Paris, 1268–9)

Sententia super Meteora (Commentary on Aristotle's *Meteora*; incomplete) (Paris, 1268–9)

Summa theologiae IaIIae (Synopsis of Theology,

First Part of the Second Part) (Rome, Paris, 1268–71)

De forma absolutionis sacramentalis, ad generalem magistrum Ordinis (On the Form of Sacramental Absolution, for the Master General of the Order (John Vercelli)) (Paris, 1269)

De secreto (On Secret Testimony (a committee report in which Aquinas is the lone dissenter, supporting the right of a religious superior to compel a subject to reveal a secret even under the seal of confession)) (Paris, 1269)

Lectura super Matthaeum (Lectures on the Gospel of Matthew) (Paris, 1269–70)

De perfectione spiritualis vitae (On the Perfecting of the Spiritual Life (directed against Gérard d'Abbeville's *Contra adversarium perfectionis christianae*)) (Paris, 1269–70)

Sententia super De memoria et reminiscentia (Commentary on Aristotle's *De memoria et reminiscentia*) (Paris?, 1270?)

Tabula libri Ethicorum (An Analytical Table of Aristotle's *Ethics*; incomplete) (Paris, 1270)

De unitate intellectus, contra Averroistas (On the Unicity of Intellect, Against the Averroists) (Paris, 1270)

Sententia super Peri hermenias (Commentary on Aristotle's *De interpretatione*; incomplete) (Paris, 1270–1)

De aeternitate mundi, contra murmurantes (On the Eternity of the World, Against Grumblers) (Paris, 1271)

Responsio ad lectorem Venetum de articulis XXX (A Letter to the Lector at Venice on Thirty Articles) (Paris, 1271)

Responsio ad lectorem Venetum de articulis XXXVI (A Letter to the Lector at Venice on Thirty-Six Articles (this and the immediately preceding item are two preliminary versions of the next item)) (Paris, 1271)

Responsio ad magistrum Ioannem de Vercellis de articulis XLII (Reply to Master John Vercelli Regarding Forty-Two Articles (Aquinas's answers to doctrinal questions which Vercelli submitted also to Albert the Great and Robert Kilwardby)) (Paris, 1271)

Quaestiones quodlibetales [I–VI, XII] (Quodlibetal Questions; Quodlibets I–VI and XII) (Paris, 1268–72)

Sententia libri Politicorum (Commentary on Aristotle's *Politics*; incomplete) (prob. Paris, 1269–72)

Contra doctrinam retrahentium a religione (Against the Teaching of those who Dissuade (Boys) from Entering the Religious Life (opposing Gérard d'Abbeville)) (Paris, 1271/2)

Quaestio disputata de unione verbi incarnati (Disputed Question on the Unity of the Incarnate Word (5 articles)) (Paris, 1272)

Expositio super librum De causis (Commentary on the *Liber de causis*) (Paris, 1272)

Lectura super Ioannem (Lectures on the Gospel of John) (Paris, 1270–2)

Sententia libri Ethicorum (Commentary on Aristotle's *Nicomachean Ethics*) (Paris, 1271–2)

Sententia super Posteriora analytica (Commentary on Aristotle's *Posterior Analytics*) (Paris, 1271–2)

Quaestio disputata de virtutibus in communi (Disputed Question on the Virtues in General (13 articles)) (Paris, 1271–2)

Quaestio disputata de caritate (Disputed Question on Charity (13 articles)) (Paris, 1271–2)

Quaestio disputata de correctione fraterna (Disputed Question on Fraternal Correction (2 articles)) (Paris, 1271–2)

Quaestio disputata de spe (Disputed Question on Hope (4 articles)) (Paris, 1271–2)

Quaestio disputata de virtutibus cardinalibus (Disputed Question on the Cardinal Virtues (4 articles)) (Paris, 1271–2)

Summa theologiae IIaIIae (Synopsis of Theology, Second Part of the Second Part) (Paris, 1271–2)

De operationibus occultis naturae, ad quendam militem ultramontanum (A Letter on Natural Events that may seem to have no Natural Origin, to a Certain Italian Knight) (Paris, 1268–72?)

De iudiciis astrorum, ad quendam militem ultramontanum (A Letter on Astrology, to a Certain Italian Knight) (Paris, 1268–72?)

De mixtione elementorum, ad magistrum Philippum de Castro Caeli (A Letter on the Mixture of Elements (in Compounds), to Master Philip of Castrocaeli) (prob. Paris, 1270–1)

Epistola ad ducissam Brabantiae (A Letter to the Duchess of Brabant (on the treatment of the Jews)) (Paris, 1271)

De sortibus, ad Dominum Iacobum de Tonengo (A Letter on Deciding by Casting Lots, to Lord James of Tonengo) (Paris, 1270/1)

De motu cordis, ad magistrum Philippum de Castro Caeli (A Letter on the Motion of the Heart, to Master Philip of Castrocaeli) (Paris, 1270–1, or Naples, 1273?)

Responsio ad lectorem Bisuntinum de articulis VI (A Letter to the Lector at Besançon on Six Articles (Regarding Subjects Admissible in Sermons)) (Paris, 1271?)

1272, June   Leaves Paris for Naples

1272–3   In Naples, assigned to establish a studium generale for Dominicans and to serve as regent master there

Sententia super Metaphysicam (Commentary on Aristotle's *Metaphysics*) (Paris, 1270/1; and Naples, 1273?)

Expositio et lectura super Epistolas Pauli Apostoli (Commentary and Lectures on the Epistles of Paul the Apostle) (Paris, Naples, 1270–3)

De substantiis separatis, ad fratrem Reginaldum socium suum (On Separated Substances (Angels), for Brother Reginald, his Companion; incomplete) (Paris or Naples, 1271–3)

Sententia super libros De caelo et mundo (Commentary on Aristotle's *De caelo et mundo*; incomplete) (Naples, 1272–3)

Sententia super libros De generatione et

corruptione (Commentary on Aristotle's *De generatione et corruptione*; incomplete) (Naples, 1272–3)

Collationes in decem praecepta (Sermon Commentaries on the Ten Commandments) (Naples, 1273; or Orvieto, Rome, 1261–8?)

Collationes super Ave Maria (Sermon Commentaries on the Ave Maria) (Naples, 1273; or Paris, 1268–72?)

Collationes super Credo in Deum (Sermon Commentaries on the Apostles' Creed) (Naples, 1273)

Collationes super Pater Noster (Sermon Commentaries on the Our Father) (Naples, 1273)

Summa theologiae IIIa (Synopsis of Theology, Third Part; incomplete) (Paris, Naples, 1272–Dec. 1273)

1273, 6 Dec.	Religious experience; stops writing
1274, Feb.	Sets out for Council of Lyons
	Responsio ad Bernardum abbatem casinensem (A Letter to Bernard, Abbot of Monte Cassino (on Gregory the Great on Predestination)) (perhaps *en route* to Lyons, 1274)
1274, mid-Feb.	Injures head near Borgonuovo, *en route* to Lyons
1274, 7 Mar.	Dies at Fossanuova

APPENDIX II

A Table Indicating the Correspondence between Sections of Chapters of SCG I in the Pera (Marietti) Edition and the Pegis Translation

Edn.	Trans.	Edn.	Trans.	Edn.	Trans.
1.1	1.1	5.28	5.1	9.54	9.2
1.2	1.1	5.29	5.2	9.55	9.3
1.3	1.1	5.30	5.3	9.56	9.3
1.4	1.2	5.31	5.4	9.57	9.4
1.5	1.2	5.32	5.5	9.58	9.5
1.6	1.3	5.33	5.5		
1.7	1.4	5.34	5.6	10.59	10.1
				10.60	10.2
2.8	2.1	6.35	6.1	10.61	10.3
2.9	2.2	6.36	6.1	10.62	10.4
2.10	2.3	6.37	6.1	10.63	10.5
2.11	2.3	6.38	6.1	10.64	10.6
2.12	2.4	6.39	6.2	10.65	10.7
		6.40	6.3		
3.13	3.1	6.41	6.4	11.66	11.1&2
3.14	3.2			11.67	11.3
3.15	3.3	7.42	7.1	11.68	11.4
3.16	3.3	7.43	7.1	11.69	11.5
3.17	3.4	7.44	7.2	11.70	11.6
3.18	3.5	7.45	7.3	11.71	11.7
3.19	3.6&7	7.46	7.4		
3.20	3.8	7.47	7.5–7	12.72	12.1
				12.73	12.2
4.21	4.1	8.48	8.1	12.74	12.3
4.22	4.1&2	8.49	8.1	12.75	12.4
4.23	4.3	8.50	8.2	12.76	12.5
4.24	4.4			12.77	12.6
4.25	4.5	9.51	9.1	12.78	12.7
4.26	4.6	9.52	9.2	12.79	12.8
4.27	4.7	9.53	9.2	12.80	12.9

Edn.	Trans.	Edn.	Trans.	Edn.	Trans.
13.81	13.1	15.121	15.2	20.158	20.6
13.82	13.2	15.122	15.3	20.159	20.7
13.83	13.3	15.123	15.4	20.160	20.8
13.84	13.4	15.124	15.5	20.161	20.9
13.85	13.5	15.125	15.6	20.162	20.10
13.86	13.6	15.126	15.7	20.163	20.10
13.87	13.7			20.164	20.10
13.88	13.8	16.127	16.1	20.165	20.11
13.89	13.9	16.128	16.2	20.166	20.12
13.90	13.10	16.129	16.3	20.167	20.13
13.91	13.11	16.130	16.4	20.168	20.14
13.92	13.12	16.131	16.5	20.169	20.15
13.93	13.13	16.132	16.6	20.170	20.16
13.94	13.14	16.133	16.7	20.171	20.17
13.95	13.15			20.172	20.18
13.96	13.16	17.134	17.1	20.173	20.19
13.97	13.17	17.135	17.2	20.174	20.20
13.98	13.18	17.136	17.3	20.175	20.21
13.99	13.19	17.137	17.4	20.176	20.22
13.100	13.20	17.138	17.5&6	20.177	20.23
13.101	13.21	17.139	17.7	20.178	20.24
13.102	13.22&23	17.140	17.7	20.179	20.24
13.103	13.24			20.180	20.25
13.104	13.24	18.141	18.1&2	20.181	20.26
13.105	13.25	18.142	18.3	20.182	20.27
13.106	13.26	18.143	18.4	20.183	20.28
13.107	13.27	18.144	18.5	20.184	20.29
13.108	13.28	18.145	18.6	20.185	20.30
13.109	13.29	18.146	18.7	20.186	20.31
13.110	13.30	18.147	18.8	20.187	20.32
13.111	13.31			20.188	20.33
13.112	13.32	19.148	19.1	20.189	20.34
13.113	13.33	19.149	19.2	20.190	20.34
13.114	13.34	19.150	19.3	20.191	20.34
13.115	13.35	19.151	19.4	20.192	20.34
		19.152	19.5	20.193	20.35
14.116	14.1			20.194	20.36
14.117	14.2	20.153	20.1	20.195	20.37
14.118	14.3	20.154	20.2		
14.119	14.4	20.155	20.3	21.196	21.1
		20.156	20.4	21.197	21.2
15.120	15.1	20.157	20.5	21.198	21.3

Edn.	Trans.	Edn.	Trans.	Edn.	Trans.
21.199	21.4	26.237	26.1	30.276	30.2
21.200	21.5	26.238	26.2	30.277	30.3
21.201	21.6	26.239	26.3	30.278	30.4
		26.240	26.4		
22.202	22.1	26.241	26.5	31.279	31.1
22.203	22.2	26.242	26.6	31.280	31.2
22.204	22.3	26.243	26.7	31.281	31.3
22.205	22.4	26.244	26.8&9	31.282	31.4
22.206	22.5	26.245	26.10		
22.207	22.6	26.246	26.10	32.283	32.1
22.208	22.7	26.247	26.11	32.284	32.2
22.209	22.8	26.248	26.12	32.285	32.3
22.210	22.9	26.249	26.13	32.286	32.4
22.211	22.10			32.287	32.5
22.212	22.11	27.250	27.1	32.288	32.6
		27.251	27.2	32.289	32.7
23.213	23.1	27.252	27.3		
23.214	23.2	27.253	27.4	33.290	33.1
23.215	23.3	27.254	27.5	33.291	33.2
23.216	23.4	27.255	27.6	33.292	33.3
23.217	23.5	27.256	27.7	33.293	33.4
23.218	23.6	27.257	27.8	33.294	33.5
23.219	23.7	27.258	27.9	33.295	33.6
23.220	23.8			33.296	33.7
23.221	23.9	28.259	28.1		
		28.260	28.2	34.297	34.1–4
24.222	24.1	28.261	28.3	34.298	34.5&6
24.223	24.2	28.262	28.4		
24.224	24.3	28.263	28.5	35.299	35.1
24.225	24.4	28.264	28.6	35.300	35.2
24.226	24.5	28.265	28.7		
		28.266	28.8	36.301	36.1
25.227	25.1	28.267	28.9	36.302	36.2
25.228	25.2	28.268	28.10		
25.229	25.3	29.269	29.1	37.303	37.1
25.230	25.4	29.270	29.2	37.304	37.2
25.231	25.5	29.271	29.3	37.305	37.3
25.232	25.6	29.272	29.4	37.306	37.4
25.233	25.7	29.273	29.5	37.307	37.5
25.234	25.8	29.274	29.6	37.308	37.6
25.235	25.9				
25.236	25.10	30.275	30.1	38.309	38.1

Edn.	Trans.	Edn.	Trans.	Edn.	Trans.
38.310	38.2	42.348	42.17	45.387	45.6
38.311	38.3	42.349	42.18	45.388	45.7
38.312	38.4	42.350	42.19		
38.313	38.5	42.351	42.20	46.389	46.1
38.314	38.6	42.352	42.21	46.390	46.2
38.315	38.7	42.353	42.22	46.391	46.3
		42.354	42.23	46.392	46.4
39.316	39.1	42.355	42.24	46.393	46.5
39.317	39.2			46.394	46.6
39.318	39.3	43.356	43.1		
39.319	39.4	43.357	43.2	47.395	47.1
39.320	39.5	43.358	43.3	47.396	47.2
39.321	39.6	43.359	43.4	47.397	47.3
39.322	39.7	43.360	43.5	47.398	47.4
39.323	39.8	43.361	43.6	47.399	47.5
		43.362	43.7	47.400	47.6
40.324	40.1	43.363	43.8	47.401	47.7
40.325	40.2	43.364	43.9	47.402	47.8
40.326	40.3	43.365	43.10		
40.327	40.4	43.366	43.11	48.403	48.1
40.328	40.5	43.367	43.12	48.404	48.2
		43.368	43.13&14	48.405	48.3
41.329	41.1	43.369	43.15	48.406	48.4
41.330	41.2	43.370	43.16	48.407	48.5
41.331	41.3	43.371	43.17	48.408	48.6
41.332	41.4			48.409	48.7
41.333	41.5	44.372	44.1	48.410	48.8
41.334	41.6	44.373	44.2		
		44.374	44.3	49.411	49.1
42.335	42.1	44.375	44.4	49.412	49.2
42.336	42.2	44.376	44.5	49.413	49.3
42.337	42.3	44.377	44.6	49.414	49.4
42.338	42.4	44.378	44.7	49.415	49.5
42.339	42.5	44.379	44.8	49.416	49.6
42.340	42.6	44.380	44.9	49.417	49.7
42.341	42.7	44.381	44.10		
42.342	42.8			50.418	50.1
42.343	42.9–11	45.382	45.1	50.419	50.2
42.344	42.12	45.383	45.2	50.420	50.3
42.345	42.13&14	45.384	45.3	50.421	50.4
42.346	42.15	45.385	45.4	50.422	50.5
42.347	42.16	45.386	45.5	50.423	50.6

Edn.	Trans.	Edn.	Trans.	Edn.	Trans.
50.424	50.7	55.462	55.8	60.500	60.1
50.425	50.8	55.463	55.9	60.501	60.2
50.426	50.9	55.464	55.10	60.502	60.3
50.427	50.10			60.503	60.4
50.428	50.11	56.465	56.1	60.504	60.5
		56.466	56.2	60.505	60.6
51&52.429	51&52.1	56.467	56.3		
51&52.430	51&52.2	56.468	56.4	61.506	61.1
51&52.431	51&52.3	56.469	56.5	61.507	61.2
51&52.432	51&52.4	56.470	56.6	61.508	61.3
51&52.433	51&52.5	56.471	56.7	61.509	61.4
51&52.434	51&52.6	56.472	56.8	61.510	61.5
51&52.435	51&52.7			61.511	61.6
51&52.436	51&52.8	57.473	57.1	61.512	61.7
51&52.437	51&52.8	57.474	57.2	61.513	61.8
51&52.438	51&52.9	57.475	57.3	61.514	61.9
51&52.439	51&52.10	57.476	57.4		
51&52.440	51&52.11	57.477	57.5	62.515	62.1
		57.478	57.6	62.516	62.2
53.441	53.1	57.479	57.7	62.517	62.3
53.442	53.2	57.480	57.8	62.518	62.4
53.443	53.3	57.481	57.9	62.519	62.5
53.444	53.4	57.482	57.10		
53.445	53.5	57.483	57.11	63.520	63.1
		57.484	57.12	63.521	63.2
54.446	54.1			63.522	63.3
54.447	54.1	58.485	58.1	63.523	63.4
54.448	54.2	58.486	58.2	63.524	63.5
54.449	54.3	58.487	58.3	63.525	63.6
54.450	54.3	58.488	58.4	63.526	63.7
54.451	54.4	58.489	58.5	63.527	63.8
54.452	54.5	58.490	58.6		
54.453	54.5	58.491	58.7	64.528	64.1
54.454	54.5	58.492	58.8		
		58.493	58.9&10	65.529	65.1
55.455	55.1			65.530	65.2
55.456	55.2	59.494	59.1	65.531	65.3
55.457	55.3	59.495	59.2	65.532	65.4
55.458	55.4	59.496	59.3	65.533	65.5
55.459	55.5	59.497	59.4	65.534	65.6
55.460	55.6	59.498	59.5	65.535	65.7
55.461	55.7	59.499	59.6	65.536	65.8

Edn.	Trans.	Edn.	Trans.	Edn.	Trans.
65.537	65.9	69.575	69.1	71.614	71.14
65.538	65.10	69.576	69.2	71.615	71.15
65.539	65.11	69.577	69.3	71.616	71.16
65.540	65.12	69.578	69.4		
		69.579	69.5	72.617	72.1
66.541	66.1	69.580	69.6	72.618	72.2
66.542	66.2	69.581	69.7	72.619	72.3
66.543	66.3	69.582	69.8	72.620	72.4
66.544	66.4	69.583	69.9	72.621	72.5
66.545	66.5	69.584	69.10	72.622	72.6
66.546	66.6	69.585	69.11	72.623	72.7
66.547	66.7	69.586	69.12	72.624	72.8
66.548	66.7	69.587	69.13	72.625	72.9
66.549	66.8	69.588	69.14	72.626	72.10
66.550	66.8	69.589	69.15		
66.551	66.8	69.590	69.16	73.627	73.1
66.552	66.9	69.591	69.17	73.628	73.2
66.553	66.10			73.629	73.3
66.554	66.11	70.592	70.1	73.630	73.4
66.555	66.12	70.593	70.2	73.631	73.5
		70.594	70.3		
67.556	67.1	70.595	70.4	74.632	74.1
67.557	67.2	70.596	70.5	74.633	74.2
67.558	67.3	70.597	70.6	74.634	74.3
67.559	67.4	70.598	70.7	74.635	74.4
67.560	67.5	70.599	70.8	74.636	74.5
67.561	67.6	70.600	70.9	74.637	74.6
67.562	67.7			74.638	74.7
67.563	67.8	71.601	71.1		
67.564	67.9	71.602	71.2	75.639	75.1
67.565	67.10	71.603	71.3	75.640	75.2
67.566	67.11	71.604	71.4	75.641	75.3
		71.605	71.5	75.642	75.4
68.567	68.1	71.606	71.6	75.643	75.5
68.568	68.2	71.607	71.7	75.644	75.6
68.569	68.3	71.608	71.8	75.645	75.7
68.570	68.4	71.609	71.9	75.646	75.8
68.571	68.5	71.610	71.10		
68.572	68.6	71.611	71.11	76.647	76.1
68.573	68.7	71.612	71.12	76.648	76.2
68.574	68.8	71.613	71.13	76.649	76.3

Edn.	Trans.	Edn.	Trans.	Edn.	Trans.
76.650	76.4	81.685	81.4	86.721	86.5
76.651	76.5	81.686	81.5	86.722	86.6
76.652	76.6	81.687	81.6		
76.653	76.7	81.688	81.7	87.723	87.1
76.654	76.8			87.724	87.2
		82.689	82.1	87.725	87.3
77.655	77.1	82.690	82.2	87.726	87.4
77.656	77.2	82.691	82.3	87.727	87.5
77.657	77.3	82.692	82.4	87.728	87.6
77.658	77.4	82.693	82.5		
77.659	77.5	82.694	82.6	88.729	88.1
		82.695	82.6	88.730	88.2
		82.696	82.6	88.731	88.3
78.660	78.1	82.697	82.7	88.732	88.4
78.661	78.2	82.698	82.7	88.733	88.5
78.662	78.3	82.699	82.8	88.734	88.6
78.663	78.4	82.700	82.9		
78.664	78.5			89.735	89.1
78.665	78.6			89.736	89.2
78.666	78.7	83.701	83.1	89.737	89.3
		83.702	83.2	89.738	89.4
		83.703	83.3	89.739	89.5
79.667	79.1	83.704	83.4	89.740	89.6
79.668	79.2	83.705	83.5	89.741	89.7
79.669	79.3			89.742	89.8&9
79.670	79.4	84.706	84.1	89.743	89.10
79.671	79.5	84.707	84.2	89.744	89.11
79.672	79.6	84.708	84.3	89.745	89.12
79.673	79.7	84.709	84.4	89.746	89.13
79.674	79.8	84.710	84.5	89.747	89.14
79.675	79.9			89.748	89.15
		85.711	85.1		
80.676	80.1	85.712	85.2	90.749	90.1&2
80.677	80.2	85.713	85.3	90.750	90.3
80.678	80.3	85.714	85.4	90.751	90.4
80.679	80.4	85.715	85.5	90.752	90.5
80.680	80.5	85.716	85.6	90.753	90.6
80.681	80.6			90.754	90.7
		86.717	86.1		
81.682	81.1	86.718	86.2		
81.683	81.2	86.719	86.3	91.755	91.1
81.684	81.3	86.720	86.4	91.756	91.2

Edn.	Trans.	Edn.	Trans.	Edn.	Trans.
91.757	91.3	93.790	93.12	98.820	98.5
91.758	91.4			98.821	98.6
91.759	91.5	94.791	94.1		
91.760	91.6	94.792	94.2	99.822	99.1
91.761	91.7	94.793	94.3	99.823	99.2
91.762	91.8&9	94.794	94.4	99.824	99.3
91.763	91.10–12	94.795	94.5	99.825	99.4
91.764	91.13			99.826	99.5
91.765	91.14	95.796	95.1	99.827	99.6
91.766	91.15–17	95.797	95.2		
91.767	91.18	95.798	95.3	100.828	100.1
		95.799	95.4	100.829	100.2
92.768	92.1	95.800	95.5	100.830	100.3
92.769	92.2	95.801	95.6	100.831	100.3
92.770	92.3	95.802	95.7	100.832	100.4
92.771	92.4	95.803	95.8	100.833	100.5
92.772	92.5			100.834	100.6
92.773	92.6&7	96.804	96.1	100.835	100.7
92.774	92.8	96.805	96.2		
92.775	92.9	96.806	96.3	101.836	101.1
92.776	92.10	96.807	96.4	101.837	101.2
92.777	92.11	96.808	96.5	101.838	101.3
92.778	92.12	96.809	96.6	101.839	101.4
		96.810	96.7&8	101.840	101.5
93.779	93.1				
93.780	93.2	97.811	97.1	102.841	102.1
93.781	93.3	97.812	97.2	102.842	102.2
93.782	93.4	97.813	97.3	102.843	102.3
93.783	93.5	97.814	97.4	102.844	102.4
93.784	93.6	97.815	97.5	102.845	102.5
93.785	93.7			102.846	102.6
93.786	93.8	98.816	98.1	102.847	102.7
93.787	93.9	98.817	98.2	102.848	102.8
93.788	93.10	98.818	98.3	102.849	102.9
93.789	93.11	98.819	98.4	102.850	102.9

REFERENCES

(For references to ancient and medieval authors, see *Index locorum*)

Ackeren, Gerald F. van (1952), *Sacra Doctrina. The Subject of the First Question of the* Summa Theologica *of St. Thomas Aquinas* (Rome: Catholic Book Agency).

Adams, M. M., and Adams, R. M. (1991) (eds.), *The Problem of Evil* (Oxford: Oxford University Press).

Alston, William (1991), *Perceiving God: The Epistemology of Religious Experience* (Ithaca, NY, and London: Cornell University Press).

——(1993), 'Aquinas on Theological Predication: A Look Backward and a Look Forward', in Stump (1993), 145–78.

Ashworth, E. J. (1991), 'Signification and Modes of Signifying in Thirteenth-Century Logic: A Preface to Aquinas on Analogy', *Medieval Philosophy and Theology*, 1: 39–67.

——(1992), 'Analogy and Equivocation in Thirteenth-Century Logic: Aquinas in Context', *Mediaeval Studies*, 54: 94–135.

Baisnée, Jules A. (1952), 'St. Thomas Aquinas's Proofs of the Existence of God Presented in their Chronological Order', in J. K. Ryan (ed.), *Philosophical Studies in Honor of the Very Reverend Ignatius Smith, O.P.* (Westminster: Newman Press), 29–64.

Barnes, Jonathan (1975), 'Introduction', in *Aristotle's Posterior Analytics* (translated with notes), Clarendon Aristotle Series, ed. J. L. Ackrill (Oxford: Clarendon Press).

Blackwell, R. J., Spath, R. J., and Thirlkel, W. E. (1963) (trans.), *Commentary on Aristotle's* Physics *by St. Thomas Aquinas* (New Haven: Yale University Press).

Boyle, Leonard E. (1982), 'The Setting of the *Summa theologiae* of Saint Thomas', Etienne Gilson Series, 5 (Toronto: Pontifical Institute of Mediaeval Studies).

Braine, David (1988), *The Reality of Time and the Existence of God* (Oxford: Clarendon Press).

Brown, Patterson (1964), 'St. Thomas' Doctrine of Necessary Being', *Philosophical Review*, 73: 76–90.

Cahill, P. J. (1967), 'Apologetics', in *The New Catholic Encyclopedia* (Washington, DC: Catholic University Press).

Chenu, M.-D. (1950), *Introduction à l'étude de saint Thomas d'Aquin* (Paris: J. Vrin).

Craig, William Lane (1980), *The Cosmological Argument from Plato to Leibniz* (London: Macmillan).

Dales, Richard C. (1990), *Medieval Discussions of the Eternity of the World* (Leiden: E. J. Brill).

—— and Argerami, Omar (1991) (eds.), *Medieval Latin Texts on the Eternity of the World* (Leiden: E. J. Brill).

Davies, Brian (1992), *The Thought of Thomas Aquinas* (Oxford: Clarendon Press).

Davies, Paul (1983), *God and the New Physics* (New York: Simon and Schuster).

Flew, Antony (1976), *The Presumption of Atheism* (London: Pemberton).

Gauthier, René-Antoine (1961), 'Introduction', in *Saint Thomas d'Aquin: Contra Gentiles, Livre Premier*. Text of the Leonine edition; Introduction by A. Gauthier; Translation by R. Bernier and M. Corvez (Lyons: P. Lethielleux), 7–123.

—— (1993), *Saint Thomas d'Aquin: Somme contre les gentils. Introduction.* European Philosophy Series, ed. Henri Hude (Paris: Éditions Universitaires).

Geach, P. T. (1961), 'Aquinas', in G. E. M. Anscombe and P. T. Geach, *Three Philosophers* (Oxford: Basil Blackwell), 65–125.

Gerson, Lloyd P. (1990*a*), *God and Greek Philosophy. Studies in the Early History of Natural Theology* (London and New York: Routledge).

—— (1990*b*), 'Aristotle's God of Motion', in Gerson (1990*a*), 82–141.

Griffiths, Paul J. (1993), 'Stump, Kretzmann, and Historical Blindness', *Faith and Philosophy*, 10: 79–85.

Hibbs, Thomas S. (1995), *Dialectic and Narrative in Aquinas: An Interpretation of the Summa Contra Gentiles* (Notre Dame, Ind.: University of Notre Dame Press).

Howard-Snyder, D. (1995) (ed.), *The Evidential Argument from Evil* (Bloomington, Ind.: Indiana University Press).

Hughes, Christopher (1989), *On a Complex Theory of a Simple God: An Investigation in Aquinas' Philosophical Theology* (Ithaca, NY: Cornell University Press).

Jordan, Mark D. (1986*a*), *Ordering Wisdom. The Hierarchy of Philosophical Discourses in Aquinas* (Notre Dame, Ind.: University of Notre Dame Press).

—— (1986*b*), 'The Protreptic Structure of the "*Summa contra gentiles*"', *Thomist*, 50: 173–209.

—— (1993), 'Theology and Philosophy', in Kretzmann and Stump (1993), 232–51.

Kaufman, Gordon D. (1989), ' "Evidentialism": A Theologian's Response', *Faith and Philosophy*, 6: 35–46.

Kenny, Anthony (1969) (ed.), *Aquinas: A Collection of Critical Essays* (Garden City, NY: Doubleday, Anchor Books).

—— (1992*a*), *What Is Faith?* (Oxford and New York: Oxford University Press).

——(1992*b*), 'Is Natural Theology Possible?', in Kenny (1992*a*), 63–74.

——(1993), *Aquinas on Mind* (London and New York: Routledge).

Kremer, Klaus (1965), 'Das "Warum" der Schöpfung: "quia bonus" vel/et "quia voluit"? Ein Beitrag zum Verhältnis von Neuplatonismus und Christentum an Hand des Prinzips "bonum est diffusivum sui"', in K. Flasch (ed.), *Parusia: Studien zur Philosophie Platons und zur Problemsgeschichte des Platonismus* (Frankfurt am Main: Minerva), 241–54.

Kretzmann, Norman (1983), 'Goodness, Knowledge, and Indeterminacy in the Philosophy of Thomas Aquinas', *Journal of Philosophy*, 80: 631–49.

——(1985), 'Ockham and the Creation of the Beginningless World', *Franciscan Studies*, 45: 1–31.

——(1990), 'Faith Seeks, Understanding Finds: Augustine's Charter for Christian Philosophy', in T. Flint (ed.), *Christian Philosophy* (Notre Dame, Ind.: University of Notre Dame Press), 1–36.

——(1991*a*), 'A General Problem of Creation: Why Would God Create Anything at All?', in MacDonald (1991), 208–28.

——(1991*b*) 'A Particular Problem of Creation: Why Would God Create This World?', in MacDonald (1991*b*), 229–49.

——(1991*c*), 'Infallibility, Error, and Ignorance', in R. Bosley and M. Tweedale (eds.), *Aristotle and His Medieval Interpreters*, Canadian Journal of Philosophy suppl. vol. 17: 159–94.

——(1992), 'Evidence Against Anti-Evidentialism', in K. J. Clark (ed.), *Our Knowledge of God: Essays on Natural and Philosophical Theology* (Dordrecht/Boston/London: Kluwer Academic Publishers), 17–38.

——(1993), 'Philosophy of Mind', in Kretzmann and Stump (1993), 128–59.

——(1994), 'Mystical Perception: St Theresa, William Alston, and the Broadminded Atheist', in A. G. Padgett (ed.), *Reason and the Christian Religion: Essays in Honour of Richard Swinburne* (Oxford: Clarendon Press), 65–90.

——(1995), 'St. Theresa, William Alston, and the Broadminded Atheist', *Journal of Philosophical Research*, 20: 45–67.

——and O'Connor, T. (1992), Review of Hughes (1989), *Faith and Philosophy*, 9: 526–35.

——and Stump, E. (1993) (eds.), *The Cambridge Companion to Aquinas* (Cambridge: Cambridge University Press).

Lobkowicz, N. (1968), '*Quidquid Movetur ab Alio Movetur*', *New Scholasticism*, 42: 401–21.

McCabe, Herbert (1964), 'Causes', Appendix 2 in the Blackfriars translation of ST, vol. 3 (London: Eyre & Spottiswoode; New York: McGraw-Hill), 101–3.

MacDonald, Scott (1991*a*), 'Aquinas's Parasitic Cosmological Argument', *Medieval Philosophy and Theology*, 1: 119–55.

MacDonald, Scott (1991*b*) (ed.), *Being and Goodness* (Ithaca, NY: Cornell University Press).

—— (1993), 'Theory of Knowledge', in Kretzmann and Stump (1993), 160–95.

—— (forthcoming), 'What is Philosophical Theology?'

McInerny, Ralph M. (1961*a*), *The Logic of Analogy* (The Hague: Martinus Nijhoff).

—— (1961*b*), 'The Analogical Cause', in McInerny (1961*a*), 126–35.

Mackie, J. L. (1982), *The Miracle of Theism* (Oxford: Clarendon Press).

Maitzen, Stephen (1995), 'God and Other Theoretical Entities', *Topoi*, 14: 123–34.

Martin, Christopher (1988), *The Philosophy of Thomas Aquinas. Introductory Readings* (London and New York: Routledge).

Matthews, Gareth B. (1963), 'Aquinas on Saying that God Doesn't Exist', *Monist*, 47: 472–7.

Pasnau, Robert (1993), 'Justified Until Proven Guilty: William Alston's New Epistemology', *Philosophical Studies*, 72: 1–33.

Peghaire, Julien (1932), 'L'Axiome "Bonum est diffusivum sui" dans le néo-platonisme et le thomisme', *Revue de l'Université d'Ottawa* (Special Section), 1: 5*–30*.

Pegis, Anton C. (1975) (trans.), *Saint Thomas Aquinas. Summa Contra Gentiles. Book One: God*, with an introduction and notes (Notre Dame, Ind.: University of Notre Dame Press; repr. of 1955 edn.).

Pera, C. (1961), 'Introductio' to vol. 1 of the Marietti edition of SCG.

Peterson, M. L. (1992) (ed.), *The Problem of Evil* (Notre Dame, Ind.: University of Notre Dame Press).

Plantinga, Alvin (1967), *God and Other Minds* (Ithaca, NY: Cornell University Press).

—— (1974), *The Nature of Necessity* (Oxford: Clarendon Press).

—— (1982), 'The Reformed Objection to Natural Theology', *Christian Scholar's Review*, 11: 187–92.

—— (1983), 'Reason and Belief in God', in Plantinga and Wolterstorff (1983), 16–93.

—— (1985), 'Self-Profile', in J. Tomberlin and P. van Inwagen (eds.), *Alvin Plantinga* (Dordrecht: Reidel), 3–97.

—— (1986*a*), 'Coherentism and the Evidentialist Objection to Belief in God', in R. Audi and W. J. Wainwright (eds.), *Rationality, Religious Belief and Moral Commitment* (Ithaca, NY: Cornell University Press), 109–38.

—— (1986*b*), 'The Foundations of Theism: A Reply', *Faith and Philosophy*, 3: 298–313.

—— (1987), 'Justification and Theism', *Faith and Philosophy*, 4: 403–26.

—— (1992), 'The Reformed Objection to Natural Theology', in B. Brody (ed.), *Readings in the Philosophy of Religion: An Analytic Approach*, 2nd edn. (Englewood Cliffs, NJ: Prentice-Hall), 74–86.

——and Wolterstorff, N. (1983) (eds.), *Faith and Rationality* (Notre Dame, Ind.: University of Notre Dame Press).

Ross, James F. (1969), *Philosophical Theology* (Indianapolis: Bobbs-Merrill).

Rowe, William L. (1975*a*), *The Cosmological Argument* (Princeton: Princeton University Press).

——(1975*b*), 'The Cosmological Argument and the Principle of Sufficient Reason', in Rowe (1975*a*), 60–114.

——(1975*c*), 'Two Criticisms of the Cosmological Argument', in Rowe (1975*a*), 115–67.

Salamucha, Jan (1958), 'The Proof *Ex Motu* for the Existence of God: Logical Analysis of St. Thomas's Arguments', *New Scholasticism*, 32: 334–72; repr. in Kenny (1969), 175–213.

Steenberghen, Fernand van (1966), *Hidden God: How Do We Know that God Exists?* (Louvain: Publications Universitaires de Louvain).

——(1971), 'Le Problème de l'existence de Dieu dans le *Commentaire* de Saint Thomas sur la *Physique* d'Aristote', *Sapientia*, 26: 163–72.

——(1974), 'The Problem of the Existence of God in Saint Thomas' *Commentary on the Metaphysics* of Aristotle', trans. J. F. Wippel, *Review of Metaphysics*, 27: 554–68.

——(1980), *Le Problème de l'existence de Dieu dans les écrits de S. Thomas d'Aquin* (Louvain-la-Neuve: Institut Supérieur de Philosophie).

Stump, Eleonore (1985), 'The Problem of Evil', *Faith and Philosophy*, 2: 392–423.

——(1990), 'Intellect, Will, and the Principle of Alternate Possibilities', in Michael Beaty (ed.), *Christian Theism and the Problems of Philosophy* (Notre Dame, Ind.: University of Notre Dame Press), 254–85.

——(1993) (ed.), *Reasoned Faith* (Ithaca, NY, and London: Cornell University Press).

——(forthcoming), 'Wisdom: Will, Belief, and Moral Goodness'.

——and Kretzmann, Norman (1981), 'Eternity', *Journal of Philosophy*, 78: 429–58.

————(1982), 'Absolute Simplicity', *Faith and Philosophy*, 2: 353–82.

————(1987), 'Atemporal Duration: A Reply to Fitzgerald', *Journal of Philosophy*, 84: 214–19.

————(1988), 'Being and Goodness', in T. V. Morris (ed.), *Divine and Human Action: Essays in the Metaphysics of Theism* (Ithaca, NY: Cornell University Press), 281–312; repr. in MacDonald (1991), 98–128.

————(1990), 'Theologically Unfashionable Philosophy' (a reply to Kaufman 1989), *Faith and Philosophy*, 7: 329–39.

————(1991), 'Prophecy, Past Truth, and Eternity', in J. W. Tomberlin (ed.), *Philosophical Perspectives*, 5, Philosophy of Religion, 395–424.

Stump, Eleonore, and Kretzmann, Norman (1992), 'Eternity, Awareness, and Action', *Faith and Philosophy*, 9: 463–82.

——— (1994), 'Blindingly Obvious Christian Anti-Semitism' (a reply to Griffiths 1993), *Faith and Philosophy*, 11: 279–85.

——— (1995), 'God's Knowledge and its Causal Efficacy', in T. D. Senor (ed.), *The Rationality of Belief and the Plurality of Faith* (Ithaca, NY: Cornell University Press), 94–124.

Swinburne, Richard (1977), *The Coherence of Theism* (Oxford: Clarendon Press).

——— (1979), *The Existence of God* (Oxford: Clarendon Press).

——— (1981), *Faith and Reason* (Oxford: Clarendon Press).

——— (1992), *Revelation: From Metaphor to Analogy* (Oxford: Clarendon Press).

——— (1994), *The Christian God* (Oxford: Clarendon Press).

Tomberlin, J., and van Inwagen, P. (1985) (eds.), *Alvin Plantinga* (Dordrecht: Reidel).

Torrell, J.-P. (1993), *Initiation à Saint Thomas d'Aquin: sa personne et son œuvre* (Fribourg and Paris: Éditions Universitaires and Cerf).

Tugwell, Simon (1988), *Albert and Thomas: Selected Writings* (Mahwah, NJ: Paulist Press).

Webb, Clement C. J. (1915), *Studies in the History of Natural Theology* (Oxford: Clarendon Press).

Weisheipl, James A. (1965), 'The Principle *Omne quod movetur ab alio movetur* in Medieval Physics', *Isis*, 56: 26–45.

——— (1968), '*Quidquid Movetur ab Alio Movetur*: A Reply [to Lobkowicz 1968]', *New Scholasticism*, 42: 422–31.

——— (1974), *Friar Thomas d'Aquino. His Life, Thought, and Work* (Garden City, NY: Doubleday).

Wippel, John F. (1984*a*), *Metaphysical Themes in Thomas Aquinas* (Washington, DC: Catholic University of America Press).

——— (1984*b*), 'Thomas Aquinas on the Possibility of Eternal Creation', in Wippel (1984*a*), 191–214.

——— (1992), 'Thomas Aquinas on What Philosophers Can Know About God', *American Catholic Philosophical Quarterly*, 66: 279–97.

——— (1993*a*), 'Metaphysics', in Kretzmann and Stump (1993), 85–127.

——— (1993*b*), *Thomas Aquinas on the Divine Ideas*, Etienne Gilson Series, 16 (Toronto: Pontifical Institute of Mediaeval Studies).

Wissink, J. B. M. (1990) (ed.), *The Eternity of the World in the Thought of Thomas Aquinas and his Contemporaries* (Leiden: E. J. Brill).

Wolterstorff, Nicholas (1983), 'Can Belief in God Be Rational If It Has No Foundations?', in Plantinga and Wolterstorff (1983), 135–86.

INDEX LOCORUM

GENERAL INDEX

226, 234–5, 248 n. (simple 235–6);
and assent 212 n.; and choice 217;
and faith 212 n.; and goodness
202–3, 206, 208–9; and inclination
208–9; and independence 212;
and intellect 198–9, 202–8,
211–12, 215; and love 204 n.,
212 n., 238–50; and necessity 209–
13; and other powers 212; and
affectiones 230; as rational or
intellective appetite 233, 235;
distinguished from appetite 214;
freedom of 146 n., 208, 212, 217,
219; essential nature of 202–3,
208, 225; object of 201 n., 203–5,
211–12; perfecting of 252; set
of 235; simple movement of 235;
virtues in 252 n.; *see also* God's
will; human will
willingness 217
Wippel, John F. 41 n., 68 n., 140 n.,
172 n., 180 n.
wisdom 44–5, 48, 52–3, 85, 133, 134–5,
156, 177–9, 252; and knowledge
178; *see also* God's wisdom;
human wisdom
Wissink, J. B. M. 68 n.
Wolterstorff, Nicholas 21–2
world: as mereological sum 103 n.;
belief in external 16–17;
beginningless 64, 68 n., 79–80,
99–101, 102 n., 109 n., 167; cause
of 64, 96, 156–7, 167, 172 n.;
considered diachronically 79, 101;
considered synchronically 104;
explanation of 94, 96, 107, 119;
governance of 88; observable 96,
114, 119; soul of 130; -stuff 130;
the good of the 223
worlds, best of all possible 221–2
wronging 197–8, 218